from

The Japan Foundation

Lessons from Japanese Development

Lessons from Japanese Development

An Analytical Economic History

Allen C. Kelley
Jeffrey G. Williamson

The University of Chicago Press
Chicago and London

Allen C. Kelley is professor and chairman of the Department of Economics at Duke University. Jeffrey G. Williamson is professor of economics at the University of Wisconsin and the author of *American Growth and the Balance of Payments, 1820–1913.* Professors Kelley and Williamson also coauthored, with R. J. Cheetham, *Dualistic Economic Development: Theory and History* (University of Chicago Press, 1972).
[1974]

The University of Chicago Press, Chicago 60637
The University of Chicago Press, Ltd., London

Published 1974
Printed in the United States of America
International Standard Book Number: 0–226–42981–4 (clothbound)
Library of Congress Catalog Card Number: 73–90945

To Moses Abramovitz, our friend and teacher.

Contents

PART THREE THE LESSONS OF MEIJI ECONOMIC DEVELOPMENT

Preface

This book attempts to explain Japanese economic development during a critical phase in her history—from the 1880s to the beginning of World War I. It could not have been written without the impressive data body which has been carefully reconstructed by the Hitotsubashi group led by Professor Kazushi Ohkawa. We owe a great debt to Professor Ohkawa, not only for his unselfish willingness to share this data with us, but also for his encouragement and constructive criticism. On this side of the Pacific, Professor Henry Rosovsky has been equally helpful. Professor Rosovsky spent much of his valuable time educating us in Japanese economic history, and in supplying substantive suggestions at several points in our research project.

We were fortunate in having the opportunity to air provisional versions of our research to the specialists who attended the Second Conference on Economic Growth: A Case Study of Japanese Experience (Tokyo, 1972). In particular, we take special pleasure in acknowledging the help supplied by Colin Clark, Yujiro Hayami, Ryoshin Minami, Gustav Ranis, Saburo Yamada, and Yasukichi Yasuba.

In addition to the numerous writings cited throughout this book, we have also benefited from the comments of Martin Bronfenbrenner, Russell Cheetham, Vernon Ruttan, Joseph Swanson, Kozo Yamamura, and our colleagues at the University of Wisconsin. The participants at the Cliometrics Conference (Madison, 1972) also lent a helping hand.

Mr. Leo de Bever supplied research assistance of unusual quality and often beyond the call of duty. The assistance of Nina Davis and Tat-wai Tan should also be conspicuously acknowledged.

Finally, we owe a special debt to Professor Moses Abramovitz. He has never seen this manuscript. Nevertheless, his influence on these two of his students has been enormous. The book is dedicated to Professor Abramovitz with fondness and respect.

Allen C. Kelley
Jeffrey G. Williamson

PART ONE

The Problem of Economic Development

1

Meiji Japan and Modern Economic Growth

1.1. Japan and Modern Economic Growth Lessons from History

The antecedents and the causes of economic growth have constituted a pervasive theme in political economy from the times of Adam Smith to the present, though in the mid-1940s interest in growth was on the wane. From the 1950s to the 70s, three fields of economics—growth, development and economic history—have simultaneously enjoyed a resurgence. Reasons for this renewed interest are not difficult to find. Widening income disparities between rich and poor lands have become sufficiently conspicuous that, unless the sources of these trends are better understood and remedial action is taken, major economic and social crises may be expected. Equally important, population pressures, arising largely from precipitous reductions in mortality rates in low-income countries, have dramatically increased the need for techniques to insure that output growth will outstrip advances in population. Gloomy Malthusian accounts are reappearing in abundance. Major and competing strategies have been implemented to confront these development problems, ranging from the Chinese and Cuban experiments, to the austere socialist regimes of Russia and Eastern Europe, to the more market-oriented approaches of much of Asia, Latin America, and Africa. However, the successes and failures are too diffuse and short-lived to be evaluated adequately.

The history of currently advanced economies must, as a result, still constitute the primary means for understanding development problems. Unfortunately, case studies of successful economic development are often considered to be largely irrelevant to development problems in the present low-income countries. Europe, North America, and Australasia developed in a relatively resource-abundant and land-rich environment, their cultural, institutional, and social attributes in striking contrast to those of the Third World. It has been argued that attention must be shifted elsewhere if useful scenarios of the development process are to be uncovered. Japan has been the prime recipient of such attention; the present study adds to an already sizable and growing literature.

Our objectives in this book are several: (i) to provide a "new economic history" of Japan during its formative years of Modern Economic Growth; (ii) to employ modern theoretical and quantitative techniques in the process; (iii) to utilize the most current macroeconomic estimates of Japanese performance; and (iv) to confront several of the leading development issues which appear particularly relevant to today's developing nations. Can or should Japan be taken as a "model" for other countries to follow, and, if so, how? If not, why? What were the sources of Japanese economic development? Were there factors "unique" in the Japanese case which make its experience atypical of the development process?

1.2. The Sources of Meiji Japanese Growth: Theory, History, and the Quantitative Record

It would be helpful at this point to place in perspective the specific objectives of the present study in relation to the existing literature on Japanese economic growth. In so doing, both the strengths and limitations of our book will become apparent. We take a somewhat novel approach to economic growth problems in general, and to Japan in particular. Our approach involves several steps: formal model building, the application of a general equilibrium model to economic history, quantitative analysis and testing, and an extensive use of the "counterfactual." These elements, in conjunction or separately, have been the primary tools of the new economic history. Yet their combined utilization in the Japanese case has been rare. We are prepared to defend our approach as appropriate, and possibly even essential, to confronting the leading issues of Japanese economic development (see chapter 5). On the other hand, the successful application of these tools is predicated upon, and greatly enriched by, the wealth of institutional and descriptive studies in the Japanese historical literature. We attempt to strike a balance between the application of the new economic history methodology and the use of the more traditional and voluminous descriptive accounts of Japanese economic development. Clearly the usefulness of any methodological approach can best be judged by the insights it renders. Those rendered by our own are summarized in chapter 2, and we believe they constitute a somewhat far-reaching reinterpretation of Meiji Japanese growth and structural change.

1.2.1. General Equilibrium Models and Historical Analysis[1]

Growth theory, general equilibrium analysis, and quantitative economic history have a natural intersection, which has been exploited only recently. Analytical economic historians have become increasingly sensitive to the limitations of partial equilibrium analysis and the potential of growth theory to many issues in economic history. At the same time, growth theorists in their analysis of neoclassical models appear to be encountering diminishing returns, and only a confrontation with historical evidence can alleviate the situation. A great deal could be gained by more serious dialogue between these two subdisciplines in economics. This book provides a modest illustration of how the gap might be bridged.

The first requisite step of our methodology, model formulation, must be treated with care, since "good specification is vital for good economic model-building" (Brown 1970, p. 50), whether the issues are historical or not. An effort will be made in chapter 3 to establish the plausibility of each component of our model of the early Japanese economy.

It is the second step, estimation, that distinguishes historical from contemporary econometric research. How do we estimate macroeconomic parameters when time series data are, in many cases, nonexistent? When detailed macrodata are available, the conventional technique is to estimate the parameters of the system simultaneously. We have no such option. Instead, the parameter values presented in Appendix B are derived independently from diverse data bodies including demographic studies, census information, budget surveys, national accounts, and other data fragments. We have derived parameter values from the best quantitative and qualitative information on the Meiji Japanese economy available to us. Even though the model has been developed with an eye to minimizing data requirements for parameter estimation, our efforts have often been frustrated by missing data and notable inconsistencies.

Having established parameter values for our modeled economy, its empirical plausibility is evaluated by comparing a simulated history with "fact." The initial conditions are established in Appendix B; Appendix A provides an inventory of the quantitative historical record which the model was constructed to replicate. The initial conditions are made to correspond to the 1887 Japanese economy in several key dimensions: employment distribution by sector, output distribution by sector, the overall capital-output ratio, the economy-wide savings rate, the share of capital consumption requirements in total gross savings, relative sectoral capital-labor ratios, and so forth. Establishing initial conditions which employ a *consistent* macro-accounting framework places enormous demands on even the carefully revised Japanese series. Some of these problems are serious; they are discussed in section 6.1, and in Appendixes A and B.

Given these initial conditions and the estimated parameters, the model is capable of simulating a precise quantitative history from the late 1880s to the beginning of World War I. Is the simulated history fact or fiction (see chapter 4)? The answer is obviously crucial. While the resulting simulated history in one sense is "fiction," the critical issue is whether the model is a sufficiently close representation of history to merit extensive analysis. Summary measures which permit comparisons of simulated and actual economic performance are numerous, but they all share the same weakness: What do we accept as "good" performance? The ultimate test, of course, is to compare our model's descriptive accuracy with a competing economic model of the Meiji period. Unfortunately, few such competitors currently exist. We hope this book may goad other researchers into supplying them. Only then can we expect to edge closer toward the truth.

If the model produces a fairly accurate empirical representation of the Meiji economy up to 1915, we can then undertake a detailed analysis of several leading issues of Japanese economic development (see chapters 6–11). The technique employed throughout is the historical counterfactual. The counterfactual has been utilized extensively in recent American historiography, but seldom applied elsewhere. The procedure is to ask relevant hypothetical questions of the historical environment which the model is designed to describe, and to compare the model's predictions corresponding to these counterfactuals with the model's predictions where actual historical conditions are taken to prevail. The difference represents the impact of the counterfactual. For example, one might ask: What would have been the impact of rapid population growth on early Japanese development? What proportion of Japanese economic success can be attributed to "unique" and favorable demographic conditions? By varying the model's population growth parameter to represent a case of rapid demographic change, the impact of demographic variables can be isolated.

In summary, the present book attempts to make a contribution to Japanese economic history by examining several leading development issues in the context of the new economic history. It employs the counterfactual, a technique which is ideally suited to confront the types of issues normally asked of history. Moreover, our approach to Japanese economic development highlights interactions between sectors. Viewing economic development as a general equilibrium process, and examining critical facets of this process in an integrated framework, yield, we believe, sizable returns.

1.2.2. The Quantitative Record of Meiji Japanese Economic Development

While the quantitative economic historian is fortunate to have available a wide range of historical time series for Japan, the estimates themselves have been under continuous revision for almost two decades (see chap. 6, sec. 6.1). The result has been a frustrating attempt by economic historians to revise their interpretations of Japanese development to conform with the most recent quantitative descriptions of the Meiji economy. The first major quantitative history of modern Japan appeared in 1957 with Professor Kazushi Ohkawa's *The Growth Rate of the Japanese Economy since 1878*. Economists found various aspects of Ohkawa's early national income estimates to be deficient. The most notable challenge, relating to the agricultural estimates, appeared in Professor James Nakamura's book *Agricultural Production and the Economic Development of Japan, 1873–1922*. Ohkawa and his associates responded to the challenge, and continuous revisions have appeared since 1957. These have been accompanied by reinterpretations of Japanese economic history.

The year 1972 marks yet another decisive point in the development of the Japanese historical statistics. Under the leadership of Professor Ohkawa, Japanese scholars concluded and made available in that year the last portions of a complete set of revised historical estimates of the Japanese economy. These series, found in *Estimates of Long Term Economic Statistics of Japan since 1868* (Ohkawa, Shinohara, and Umemura 1966–72; hereafter *LTES*), are employed in the present study. Some of the key *LTES* series are yet to be published, but they were made available in several working papers presented at the Second Conference on Economic Growth held in Tokyo, July 1972. Appendix A provides a complete inventory of the estimates we have employed, including, for the convenience of the nonspecialist, those figures which are yet unavailable in published form. Our study is the first to utilize these most recent quantitative estimates of the Japanese historical record. If we are willing ourselves to take advantage of the "lessons from history"—that is, if the past is any guide to the future, we too must be prepared to modify our analysis and conclusions in the face of future revisions of the Japanese data base. In our judgment, however, the present "state of the art" of Japanese historical national income accounting is such that major changes in the data are not likely to be forthcoming, given known basic data sources and estimation procedures. Moreover, those estimates which we feel are still too tentative—estimates of tertiary activities—have been disregarded in our analysis. Our focus will be exclusively on commodity production, where the empirical record is on firmer ground.

1.2.3. Previous Attempts at Modeling Meiji Japanese Development

This book had its beginnings in our study *Dualistic Economic Development: Theory and History* (Kelley, Williamson, and Cheetham 1972*b*), which attempted to construct a model of economic dualism broadly applicable to the low-income countries currently enjoying successful economic growth. Our primary interest was the growth-theoretical aspects of the model. Its static general equilibrium properties—existence, stability, uniqueness—were identified, and feasible growth paths were ascertained. Even with a relatively simple dualistic framework, however, mathematical techniques did not yield unambiguous results for all the issues of interest to a study of growth and structural change. As a result, we examined a numerical representation of the modeled dualistic economy, employing parameters representative of the developing countries. The quantitative experience of the Philippines was most extensively utilized, although estimates taken from other Asian economies were also employed. None of the initial conditions or parameters used in the simulations were taken directly from, or based on, Japanese experience.

While we were able to show that the resulting simulated development patterns were in rough conformity with the development experience of a wide range of low-income economies, it seemed useful to explore the ability of the modeled economy to reproduce a single country's growth experience. Japan was taken as the case study. Two difficulties plagued these comparisons. First, the *LTES* estimates were still under revision and, at that time, unavailable. Second, there were major differences between Japanese initial conditions and parameter values and those of the simulated model. However, by employing rough adjustments, we were able to satisfy ourselves and, we trust, our readers that the model was a useful first approximation of Japanese development during the Meiji period. Our early research on Meiji Japan, then, used the Japanese experience with Modern Economic Growth as one test of the general development model's veracity.

In a subsequent study, "Writing History Backwards: Meiji Japan Revisited" (Kelley and Williamson 1971), the results of this test were substantially expanded. Using the same model, we attempted to reinterpret the growth of Meiji Japan. This excursion into Japanese economic history proved successful in two respects. First, although the model used parameters and initial conditions applicable to contemporary developing countries (and not necessarily Japan)—in this sense we were writing history backwards—the model appeared to yield reasonable predictions of Japanese development. Second, we were able to successfully employ "sensitivity analysis" to gauge the relative importance of several factors underlying Japanese economic growth. Sensitivity analysis involves varying a specific parameter by 1 percent and then computing the impact on selected economic variables.

"Structural elasticities," or the sensitivity of the model to marginal changes in savings rates, population growth rates, rates of technical change, and other key economic parameters, were identified and interpreted within the context of Meiji economic development. While we were cautiously optimistic that the insights afforded by this approach to economic history were useful, a notable deficiency remained. Some of the parameters and initial conditions, which were drawn from Southeast Asia, differed considerably from the Japanese case, so that our adjustments to take the differences into account could only be considered as rough first approximations, given the historian's natural propensity to write history "forwards."

Writing history "forwards" was initiated in our 1972 study, "Simple Parables of Japanese Economic Progress: Report on Early Findings," which was read at the Second Conference on Economic Growth in Tokyo. An attempt was made in that paper to estimate, with the then available data, parameters and initial conditions specifically applicable to the Japanese case. Judged by a comparison of the model's predictions with the historical series, an improved rendering of the Japanese historical record was obtained. Yet the study fell short of our aspirations in three respects. First, the data still did not take advantage of the most recent unpublished quantitative estimates of Meiji economic development. Second, the model was seriously lacking in one particular specification: land was not treated as an explicit factor of production, and, as a result, the impact of land-resource constraints on development was not captured. Third, given these known deficiencies, we elected to employ a somewhat more efficient methodology—structural elasticities—rather than the more interesting method of the historical counterfactual. The counterfactual requires greater attention to the qualitative evidence in justifying the experiment under examination. The results of this first attempt at writing Meiji economic history forwards were encouraging. A basis was laid for modifying the analytical framework to make it more applicable to Meiji Japan.

In contrast to previous studies, the present book utilizes the most recent quantitative estimates of Meiji Japanese economic progress. The underlying dualistic model has also been revised to incorporate a more realistic specification of Meiji agriculture. It provides a modified version of the agricultural production process in general, and the land-resource constraint in particular. Finally, wishing to use Japanese history to provide insight into the development process applicable to the Third World, we adopted historical counterfactuals as our primary expositional device. These historical counterfactuals are typically formulated with reference to the experience of currently developing countries. We have attempted to interpret the results in this context throughout.

The revisions to the basic analytical model permit a somewhat different orientation of the present study from those which preceded it. Most notably, we are able to examine in greater depth several leading issues of Japanese development. The increased confidence we have in the present framework, and the substantial literature which has now accumulated to support it, justify our devoting additional attention to the qualitative-institutional settings surrounding the theoretical model and the quantitative experiments under consideration. Moreover, in the light of our previous extensive mathematical analysis of the dualistic economy, we have elected to employ mathematics as an expositional device in the present book only where it is clearly appropriate. While some rigor may appear to have been lost along the way, the benefits from expanded communication with the economic historian outweigh any significant costs. Indeed, our attempt to provide an integrated *historical* interpretation of complex development problems, imbedded in a growth-theoretic general equilibrium framework, may represent one of the book's more notable features.

1.3 Survey of the Terrain

Part 1 provides an overview of the scope, objectives, and main findings of this study. Chapter 2 summarizes several key results relating to the leading issues in Meiji Japanese development. Each of these issues is examined in greater detail in part 3.

A framework for analyzing the economic development of Meiji Japan is presented in part 2. Chapter 3 begins with a detailed exposition of the model. A dualistic theoretical framework is presented which highlights rural-urban differences in production and demand. An attempt is made to justify the model not only by reference to modern economic theory but, more important, by attention to the descriptive accounts of Japanese economic growth and structural change. In a real sense, the model represents an extension of a vast literature on the conditions surrounding Japanese economic progress. We are not only aware of the richness of this literature, but have attempted to draw widely upon it in our modeling effort. Our limited success is in no small part the result of the extensive work by many scholars of Japanese economic history.

Having established the a priori plausibility of the formal model, we ask in chapter 4: "Does it work?" To answer this question, we assign to the model initial conditions and parameters which are representative of the Meiji economy and then compare the "predicted" model performance with "actual" economic history. While considerable judgment must be exercised in making an appraisal of our success in identifying a plausible model, we hope that our efforts have uncovered at least one useful paradigm of Meiji Japan.

Chapter 5 considers some methodological issues raised by this study. The counterfactual is defended as an essential analytical device for isolating the lessons of history. Since the present study represents perhaps the most extensive application of this methodology yet available in the literature, detailed attention is directed to a comparison of this technique with alternatives. We describe how and why the counterfactual has evolved as one of the most powerful tools available to the economic historian. The chapter concludes with a discussion of the role of general equilibrium models in historical analysis, and the specific types of formal analysis which appear most relevant given the interests of the development economist and economic historian.

The proof of the pudding lies in its eating, and it is to this final test that part 3 is addressed. Selected key issues which are important in the development process in general, and in Japan in particular, are confronted. An attempt is made to relate each issue both to the development and to the historical literature. The issue is then examined quantitatively with reference to the modeled economy of Meiji Japan, and the results of selected counterfactuals are presented. Implications for the development process are provided.

Chapter 6 considers the factors which give rise to acceleration and deceleration in long-term growth rates in Japan. While much of the growth and development theory would predict a retardation in aggregate growth rates over the process of long-run development, Japan experienced marked acceleration. Why? Does the underlying model predict such experience? If so, why? If not, why not? Investment spurts, military expenditures, and Meiji fiscal policy are examined in chapter 7. Even though Japanese economic history has been used by historians to document "phases" and "stages" of economic development—for example, the studies of Rostow and the Fei-Ranis-Lewis labor surplus models—a key issue remains. Are these apparent discontinuities exogenous to Japanese economic development? Or, on the other hand, are they explained by endogenous forces inherent in the long-term development process? Investment "spurts" are examined in some detail. We find that the magnitude and timing of fiscal policy and military expenditures explains much of the instability in Meiji economic growth. The role of demographic factors is examined in chapter 8. What would have been the impact on Meiji economic development had Japan sustained the high population growth rates common to the current developing low-income economies?

Japan has become a battleground for competing theories of economic development. Most prominent in this controversy has been the "testing" of the labor-surplus and the neoclassical models. It is therefore appropriate that the framework underlying the present inquiry—a neoclassical model—be analyzed in the context of this literature. This is accomplished in chapter 9, where a partial reconciliation of both the apparent discrepancies in the competing models, and the confusion in the model testing debates, is provided. Chapter 10 confronts one of the most important issues in the development literature: the relative impact of demand and supply as a source of industrialization and structural change. Does demand really constitute an important force explaining the shift of production from rural to urban-industrial activities? Or, alternatively, can demand be considered as passively accommodating changes occurring elsewhere in the system?

Possibly no other issue has occupied more attention in the development literature than the role of agriculture. Hypotheses vary from those stressing agriculture as a "leading" sector to those characterising its role as "lagging." In Japanese economic history, these debates have focused on the "prerequisite" and "concurrent" hypotheses of agricultural growth. These issues are resolved in chapter 11, where we identify the sources of Meiji Japanese agricultural development. We then pose several counterfactuals to assess with greater precision the alternative forces influencing agricultural development: the land-resource constraint, capital formation, and technological change. A synthesis of much of the current literature and debate surrounding Meiji agriculture is provided.

In the concluding chapter, one possible extension of the model framework is outlined. Attention is focused on the possible role of foreign trade in Meiji economic development, together with speculation on ways in which trade might be examined in a neoclassical dualistic model. We offer no concrete judgment on "trade as an engine of growth," but rather raise issues which future Japanese economic historians must confront. And that is how it should be, since there are no absolute lessons of history, only alternative interpretations of history. We eagerly await fresh revisionist positions, which we hope will follow in the wake of our own modest effort to reinterpret Meiji economic development.

2

The Lessons of History

2.1. Meiji Japanese Growth as a Case Study of Economic Development

Historical generalizations based on the experience of one nation can be dangerous, but it is equally hazardous to rely on the predictions of theoretical models which have not been critically subjected to empirical analysis. Our own bias should be readily apparent, but perhaps a flat statement will make our position even more explicit: in future efforts to understand the development process, highest returns are likely to accrue to studies which ferret out the "lessons of history" by exploiting well-specified analytical frameworks. Our primary objective in this book is to explore Japanese economic development during the Meiji period using modern theoretical and quantitative techniques. If our more general interest is in analyzing the economic development process generally, why select Japan for study, and why the period 1887–1915?

2.1.1. Why Japan?

In terms of the pace of economic growth and structural change (including industrialization and urbanization), Japan provides a record of success which is widely envied by the developing countries. The transformation of the Japanese economy has been so pronounced that it has frequently been called the "Japanese miracle." From late in the nineteenth century to the present, Japan has emerged from a largely feudalistic, low-income, agrarian society to a modern, high-income, industrial economy vigorously and successfully competing with the advanced nations of the world. Japan represents the most conspicuous success of Modern Economic Growth in the non-Western world. On these grounds alone, Japanese economic development merits extensive attention.

Japan is one of the few for which there is a quantitative record of sufficient quality to allow the analysis of almost the entire course of modern growth and structural change. Thanks largely to the pioneering efforts of Professor Kuzashi Ohkawa and his associates, data are available from virtually the beginning of Japanese Modern Economic Growth to the present (Ohkawa et al. 1957). They include data by sector (agriculture, secondary, tertiary), a wide breakdown of economic outputs and inputs (labor force, capital stock, land), and a wealth of information on commodity prices and factor input prices (wages, interest rates). While theoretical and descriptive accounts of the development process are important and useful, in the final analysis the key issues will be formulated in quantitative terms. Given the relative abundance of the Japanese economic data, a detailed quantitative investigation of Japan's historical performance is fully possible.

Finally, Japan offers the economist a superb laboratory within which to examine many leading development issues. Included among these are the role of agriculture in the development process, the nature and significance of "dualism," the impact of the government sector, the relevant factor pricing scheme at low income levels, and so forth. Even though the literature abounds with studies confronting these and other issues, unanimity is rare. Controversy is typically based on the use of quite different analytical models and approaches, or on wide variations in the quantitative record used to confront development issues.

What is true of the development literature is amplified in Japanese economic history. Japan has been described by some as the classic example of labor-surplus development; she has been considered by others to provide a useful representation of the neoclassical full employment model. Japan has been cited by some as an example of "concurrent" development, exhibiting a balanced expansion between agriculture and industry; others have viewed Japan as illustrating "prerequisite" agricultural growth, where the development of agriculture preceded and was necessary to that of other sectors. Furthermore, the factors cited as "critical" to Japanese success are equally varied: rapid technological progress, "unique" demographic conditions, imported

Western technology, the heritage of the Tokugawa period, government enterprise, and many others. The time is ripe to confront these and other development problems in an integrated theoretical framework, one which can confront the current set of quantitative macroeconomic estimates, and one which employs a methodology—the historical counterfactual—appropriate for analyzing the leading issues of economic development. Before examining our approach to historical analysis, however, we shall attempt to provide a justification for the particular period of Japanese development selected for study.

2.1.2. Why 1887–1915?[1]

The development phase we wish to examine is one which has been denoted by Simon Kuznets as "Modern Economic Growth." This stage of development possesses four conditions: (1) the application of modern scientific thought and technology to industry; (2) a sustained and rapid increase in real product per capita, usually (but not always) accompanied by high rates of population growth; (3) a rapid rate of transformation of the industrial structure (changing sectoral output, labor force, and capital stock distribution); and (4) an expansion in international contacts. (Kuznets 1959, lecture 1). While several attributes of Modern Economic Growth were present at the Meiji Restoration of 1868—namely, rapid economic, political, and social change—it was not until somewhat later that Kuznets's criteria became a verifiable fact. Indeed, Henry Rosovsky describes the period 1868–85 as one in which Japan entered a "transition" to Modern Economic Growth (Rosovsky 1966, pp. 91–139; Ohkawa and Rosovsky 1965, pp. 47–66). This transition saw the social barriers to progress attenuated, political power in government consolidated, the development of a modern banking system, fiscal and monetary reform, and the emergence of a significant international participation. The year 1885, which Rosovsky takes as the beginning of Japanese Modern Economic Growth, ends a period when the joint priorities of industrialization and growth were elevated to national objectives. The Matsukata Deflation in 1885 marks a phase when currency reform, banking development, and government political and economic structure were all consolidated toward the ends of Modern Economic Growth. We begin our comparisons of the model structure with the Japanese economy in 1887, the first year for which the recently revised quantitative estimates for several critical economic magnitudes become available.

Our analysis concludes with World War I, a logical terminal point in Japanese historiography. The war created an unusually strong exogenous shock to the Japanese economy. More important, this period is considered by several Japanese scholars to represent a sharp dividing line when the labor-augmenting bias in Japanese technical change may have been greatly attenuated or eliminated. Furthermore, sectoral productivity and wage differentials increased sharply during the war years suggesting an epochal change in the efficiency of factor market behavior. In more general terms, Ohkawa and Rosovsky have highlighted the importance of the World War I demarcation: "In spite of the sustained character of growth in Japan, the relative position of major sectors in the economy changed considerably. . . . World War I marked a distinct structural change especially pronounced in the relationship between agriculture and industry" (Ohkawa and Rosovsky 1960, p. 43). The war was also a strong impetus to further opening the economy to international trade, and thus the applicability of the closed, two-sector framework may become increasingly tenuous.

2.2. The Lessons of Japanese Economic History

2.2.1. Aggregate Growth Performance: Trend Acceleration, Miracles, and the Take-off

The apparently unique rapidity of Japanese growth had not been seriously questioned until very recently by scholars of economic development, and as a result terms like "miraculous" progress and the "Japanese model" are commonplace in the literature. It is therefore notable that recent studies have begun to arrive at very different conclusions. Indeed, when we use the most current estimates of Japanese historical progress in chapter 6, Japan's GNP per capita and per worker growth rates turn out to be roughly comparable with those achieved by the North American and Western European nations. Furthermore, they fall short of the rates documented for the noncommunist, less developed economies between 1955 and 1965, including the countries in contemporary underdeveloped Asia.

This shifting characterization of early Japanese development followed in the wake of substantial revisions in the historical statistics made over the past few years. This reinterpretation of the dimensions of Japanese growth makes an appropriate point of departure for the present study. Rather than seeking an explanation for the "unusual"—an understandable preoccupation for much of the literature on early Japanese economic development —we shall instead undertake a systematic review of a wide range of potential factors accounting for the impressive, but not unusual, early Japanese growth.

The first factor is an acceleration in the long-run growth rate in Meiji Japan. Trend rate deceleration, not acceleration, would be predicted in a conventional neoclassical model if the economy were viewed as adjusting to an initial positive shock centered on the Restoration period. What, then, explains the Japanese record of growth rate acceleration? The historical explanations focus almost exclusively on exogenously determined investment "spurts." In contrast, our analysis assigns a notable portion of the Japanese trend rate acceleration to endogenous forces. Indeed, our model of Meiji Japan also traces out trend rate acceleration, and this model is *not* subjected to periodic exogenous stimuli in the form of increased savings rates. Thus, our analysis does not confirm a widely accepted "lesson from history" that significant changes in the savings effort constitute a necessary condition for successful economic growth. Rostow's "take-off," and Lewis's famous dictum that the central problem of development theory is to explain an increase in net savings rates from 5 to 12 percent, are both prominent examples of the conventional wisdom (Lewis 1954; Rostow 1960). While these hypotheses appear plausible and command limited empirical support, increasing savings shares do *not* appear to have been the primary vehicle by which rapid and accelerating rates of capital accumulation were achieved in early Japan. Having said as much, it is important to note that the magnitude of the trend-rate acceleration in Japan is substantially greater than in the model; other factors must be identified to fully account for the observed long-run growth acceleration.

2.2.2. Investment Spurts and Long Swings in Japanese History

While the long-run trend in Japanese output growth has been continuously upward, this pace has not been without significant interruption. As in many other countries, Japanese long swings have been identified which describe periodic surges and lapses in the pace of development, lasting approximately twenty years. One such episode in the Meiji period has attracted special attention. There is a marked rise in output growth after 1905. This surge has been interpreted by most scholars as a recovery from the depressed long-swing conditions of the previous decade. This recovery is widely attributed to an "investment spurt," a dramatic shift in the demand for investment goods. Attention by Japanese economic historians has therefore focused on demand-oriented explanations for long swings, both for the Meiji era and for subsequent periods.

Evidence is not sufficient to support this interpretation. Indeed, chapter 7 argues that long swings may have been supply-oriented. That is, long swings may have been largely the result of movements in the availability of savings for capital formation, as distinct from variations in the induced demand for capital goods themselves. Since Japanese savings rates did indeed vary significantly over this period conforming to the long-swing chronology, an interesting counterfactual suggests itself. What would have been the effect on output growth and capital formation in our model of Meiji Japan had the depressed savings conditions (a "savings constraint") in the late 1890s and early twentieth century been replaced by savings rates consistent with the prosperous conditions of the surrounding periods? The results are notable. In the counterfactual regime, long swings appear which possess characteristics broadly similar to those in the Japanese historical record. These results, coupled with the meager evidence of secular variations in Japanese long-run labor force utilization rates, lead us to conclude that a supply-oriented, as distinct from a demand-oriented, interpretation of long swings in Japan merits close scrutiny. Moreover, "surges" or "spurts" in investment demand may offer an entirely inappropriate framework to interpret this—and possibly even subsequent—periods. Rather, the lackluster performance in the late 1890s and early twentieth century may instead reflect the appearance of an exogenously imposed savings constraint; the subsequent "spurt" may reflect largely "normal" long-run conditions, made dramatic primarily by reference to the previous depressed period. Could a comparable interpretation be applied to the amazing "investment spurt" in the period after 1954?

A critical issue in assessing this revisionist interpretation of Japanese development is, of course, our explanation of variations in savings performance and, in particular, the apparent savings constraint over such considerable periods of time.

2.2.3. Meiji Fiscal Policy and Military Adventurism

A key may lie in Japan's aversion to military adventurism and a fiscal policy which facilitated this activity. Wars demanded massive amounts of Japanese productive resources and drew heavily on potential savings through government financing operations. The period of relatively low private capital formation between 1894 and 1905 may have been largely the result of the two international conflicts in which Japan was engaged (chapter 7). War financing tended to bid resources away from private investment. The counterfactual reappears as a useful device in sorting out the impact of these military activities. What would have been the course of Meiji development had the resource costs of Japanese military adventurism—foregone private investment due to the impact of government war financing—been removed as a constraint on development? Much of the long swing disappears in the counterfactual regime; moreover, the post-1905 performance can no longer be interpreted as a dramatic "spurt" in activity. These results pose an additional, equally intriguing question: Could the "surge" in post-World War II performance also represent less a dramatic structural shift in the Japanese economic conditions than a recovery to the long-run growth path of this dynamic economy? Can the unusually high savings rates after 1954 be attributed in large part to a similar mechanism?

2.2.4. Demographic Change and Meiji Economic Development

While population pressure constitutes a major concern in analyses of the growth prospects for currently low-income countries, the role of population growth in Japanese historical experience has seldom been assessed. This is surprising since, on the eve of the Restoration, Japan was supporting population growth rates even lower than those in contemporary *advanced* countries. Using contemporary quantitative estimates on the relation between aggregate population growth and the rate of economic progress, we might conclude that Japanese development success was explained in large part—if not totally—by the unique demographic conditions inherited from the past. If this were the case, the ability to generalize from the Japanese experience would be limited indeed. Put differently, it would be futile to search for the sources of Japanese progress in terms of agricultural expansion, capital formation rates, fiscal policy, technical change, and trade patterns when, in fact, the rate of Meiji progress was largely demographically determined. Do demographic factors largely account for the "Japanese miracle"?

This question is confronted in chapter 8 with a historical counterfactual: What would have been the nature of Japanese economic growth had Japan sustained the high population growth rates prevailing in the contemporary developing world? The results of this counterfactual are surprising. Contemporary population pressure would have exerted a small effect on Meiji economic development. While the direction of the impact was anticipated, the relatively small magnitude was not. Contrary to the usual economic analyses where high population growth exerts unequivocal negative effects on per capita output growth, some important offsetting influences are revealed in our analysis of Japan.

We conclude that the unusual demographic conditions inherited from Tokugawa Japan do not appear to explain the notable rate of Meiji economic progress. Possibly the Japanese economic historian's preoccupation with nondemographic factors has been based on forces little understood.

2.2.5. Standards of Living and Real Wages

An apparent contradiction frequently arises in historical accounts of Japanese development. On the one hand, the economy is characterized as dynamic and growing at rates which, while not unique, are still impressive by most standards. On the other hand, the model most often employed to analyze early Japan is one where labor-surplus conditions prevail. The labor-surplus model predicts wage stability for workers in the large premodern or traditional sector of the economy. Indeed, wage stability is a crucial vehicle whereby the surplus available for capital formation is increased, making trend acceleration possible. The labor-surplus model implies that none of the benefits of modernization accrue to workers in the small "modern" sector. What is the historical evidence? Was extreme austerity the vehicle by which peasants and laborers in the "traditional" sector contributed to Japanese progress? The analysis in chapter 9 leads both to a reconciliation of the apparent contradiction and to an alternative interpretation of the fate of the Japanese worker during the process of development. True, wage rates were relatively stable over the Meiji period. But this does *not* imply that living standards were lagging. Indeed, because Japanese laborers tended to work longer and harder, and became increasingly skilled over time, this "augmented" laborer enjoyed substantial advances in material standards during early periods of growth and structural change.

A critical question arises. How is it possible to reconcile *stable* wages with rising living standards, given the typical predictions of the neoclassical dualistic model? The solution is simple. Our special form of the neoclassical model is fully capable of generating a prediction of stable wages *and* rising living standards. Moreover, our paradigm of early Japan, when assigned initial conditions and parameters thought characteristic of the Meiji period, yields precisely such a forecast. The key lies in our specification of technical change, widely supported by the research of Japanese economic historians. The economy is characterized by a general labor-augmenting bias in the way in which technology is applied to production. As a result, arbitrary factor pricing schemes found in the labor-surplus formulations are not necessary to confront the Japanese experience with stable wages and rising living standards. A neoclassical model, modified to conform to the special character of Meiji Japan's technical change, does the trick.

2.2.6. Imported Technology and Labor Saving

Presumably it was the magnitude of the general labor-augmenting bias in technical change which explained both the apparent paradox of stable wages and rising living standards, and which simultaneously held down the share of aggregate income accruing to labor in this period. But current analysis of Japan suggests that the character of technology changed dramatically over time, especially with the importation of modern machinery and techniques from the West after World War I. By the post-World War II period, Japan is described by some as characterized by capital-augmenting technical change. It would be interesting to assess what this "epochal" change would imply in terms of Meiji economic development. Consider the following counterfactual (chapter 9): What would have been the impact on Japanese wages and living standards during the Meiji period had technical change not been labor-augmenting but comparable to that in the post–World War II period, where a strong capital-augmenting bias was the rule? The direction of the results were fully predictable; the quantitative magnitude was not. Our analysis of this counterfactual leads us to conclude that it was not so much labor-surplus conditions as the nature of technical change in the Meiji period which kept laborers' living standards, although rising, in tow. This facilitated the relatively rapid rates of capital accumulation and led the way for the subsequent growth and structural change in the interwar period. Could technical change of this form also play a significant role in the developing countries of today?

2.2.7. The Impact of Demand on Industrialization

While high rates of aggregate per capita growth represent the manifest objective of policy makers in the current low-income countries, it is equally true that most consider rapid industrialization the way to achieve this goal. Indeed, a shift in the center of gravity from rural-agricultural to urban-industrial pursuits is an overriding concern of development planners and economists. Understandably, the identification of the sources of industrialization has occupied the attention of Japanese economic historians for some time. Some scholars consider supply conditions—changing comparative advantage and technology—to be the key; others place emphasis on demand conditions and, in particular, the impact of Engel effects. In fact, both the traditional historian and the modern cliometrician share a common concern with the "uniqueness" of Japanese demand conditions. Emphasis on the "simple tastes" of the Japanese people appears frequently in the qualitative literature; and this hypothesis is confirmed to a certain extent by econometric analyses.

The impact of Engel effects in encouraging a shift out of agriculture into industry as development takes place is clear. What is most relevant is an assessment of the quantitative importance of the possible unique Japanese demand conditions on structural change. Our analysis in chapter 10 leads to a guarded conclusion. If we accept the recent estimates of Japanese food elasticities during the Meiji period, then counterfactual analysis leads us to conclude that demand played a powerful role in the rapid rates of structural change in Meiji Japan. But these demand studies are deficient in several ways; we must await for confirming evidence before strong confidence can be placed in the specific counterfactual results. Although it is apparent that demand could have exerted a strong and pervasive impact on Japanese growth, opposite influences may be at play in accounting for the somewhat slower rates of structural change in the developing low-income countries of today.

2.2.8. A Revisionist View of Japanese Agricultural Progress

Early and rapid progress in the agricultural sector is viewed by most economists as strategic to development. Agriculture supplies food, labor, savings, and export revenues to feed the engine of industrialization. A lagging rural sector may seriously inhibit growth and structural change. It comes as no surprise that the notable Japanese success in agricultural development has attracted the extensive attention of development economists and economic historians. What makes the Japanese case particularly fascinating is that land supply increased only slowly during the Meiji period, fixed capital stock growth was lagging, and the labor force *declined* in absolute numbers. Moreover, Japan developed in an institutional setting where the small farm prevailed, apparently foregoing the benefits of large-scale production considered so important by many development planners. What explains the success Meiji Japan encountered in agriculture?

Most two-sector development models are totally deficient in confronting the Japanese experience—or, for that matter, the agricultural experience of most other countries as well. These models utilize technical change specifications which are largely at variance with the empirical record; most important, they identify no role for capital inputs purchased from the modern sector. In contrast, our revisionist interpretation of the dualistic model highlights capital formation and technical change in agriculture (chapter 11). This specification appears to yield high returns to understanding Meiji agricultural growth. Not only did Japanese agriculture benefit from a diffusion of technology and knowledge unleashed by the Restoration, but the success of this technology was critically influenced by purchased inputs from the modern sector. While these factors largely account for Japan's progress in agriculture, the impressive rate of output growth still needs an explanation. Why the dramatic break in agricultural labor productivity growth between the earlier Tokugawa and the later Meiji periods? Why have not the current low-income countries, which have also had available impressive new technologies, encountered the same degree of success experienced by Meiji Japan? Could it be that the apparently stagnant conditions of the Tokugawa times masked the real contributions of this period to subsequent development? This may indeed be the case. The success in applying new technology to agriculture relied significantly on the availability of a disciplined and energetic labor force: literacy rates and health standards inherited from Tokugawa were high. More importantly, a sophisticated irrigation system had been developed in pre-Meiji Japan. The returns on this social overhead capital were only fully realized when it was combined with new seed varieties, fertilizers, and technology. A careful analysis of the Tokugawa heritage, coupled with the role of intermediate capital inputs and the nature of technological change, goes far in explaining what for so long has intrigued economists about the "Japanese model" of agricultural growth. That is, how was it possible for Japanese agriculture to advance so impressively in an institutional setting of small farm holdings? This is in contrast to many other countries where economies of scale, collectivization, and large holdings were stressed. Is it possible to generalize from the Japanese model, especially to the rice culture of much of the developing world? Is it the dearth of proper initial infrastructure conditions which explains some of the difficulties in India and other countries which are currently attempting to improve agriculture in the face of enormous population pressures?

2.2.9. Technical Change and the Dynamics of Agricultural Expansion

One of the lessons of early Japanese history relates to the role of technical change, a dynamic force which is taken by some to represent the most critical ingredient in Japanese agricultural expansion. The pace of technical change in Meiji agriculture was very rapid, even more so given its notable decline in the interwar period. In assessing the role of technical change, an interesting counterfactual suggests itself: How would the pre-1915 Meiji economy have been influenced had the rate of total factor productivity growth been that prevailing during the 1920s and 1930s rather than the much higher rates achieved in the earlier decades? Several fascinating results are forthcoming from this exercise (chapter 11). Consider just two. First, it is apparent that the unusual pace of technical change accounts for a substantial portion of the success of Meiji agriculture, perhaps even more than would have been identified using the typical sources-of-growth accounting. Second, and more significant, it was *not* the high rate of technical change that caused rapid rates of Japanese urbanization and industrialization. Just the opposite was the case. In a regime of more moderate agricultural expansion and lower rates of technical progress, the pace of industrialization would have been higher. Moreover, the acceleration in industrialization following the 1910s may in part be explained by the *retardation* in agriculture's technological performance. These findings are in striking contrast to the predictions of the labor-surplus models, where the transformation of the economy is highly sensitive to agriculture's total factor productivity growth, a critical determinant of the "turning point" and the disappearance of labor slack.

2.2.10. Resource and Land Constraints as a Barrier to Development

Japan faced severe land and resource constraints in agriculture; the stock of cultivated land increased only slowly over the entire Meiji period. Augmented land, which includes the effects of increased cropping frequency and rising rates of complementary inputs, rose somewhat more rapidly. Still, it is notable that Japanese agricultural expansion was so very rapid in the face of apparently severe land constraints. To assess the role of this widely recognized constraint on development, consider the following counterfactual (chapter 11): What would have been Meiji Japan's agricultural performance had she been blessed with the land expansion rates typical of, say, the contemporary Philippines—a rate roughly three times that of early Japanese development? The results are surprising. While labor productivity would have increased, the magnitude of this increase is substantially less than the measured impact of technical change, more important ingredient in Meiji agriculture's more interesting is the impact of land expansion ructural change—especially on the rate of urbani- i, one would expect that land constraints would ul effect in pushing workers off the farm, and that relaxing land constraints would ease these pressures. Just the opposite prevails. Countervailing dynamic forces (discussed in chapter 11) more than offset the simple comparative static effects on labor force redistribution, and a regime of more elastic land supply results in greater, not less, urbanization. These results underscore once again the critical importance of examining the sources of growth and structural change in a dynamic, general equilibrium framework, where critical feedbacks are highlighted.

The lessons from Japanese economic history will be reexamined in detail in part 3. It will become clear in that reexamination, however, that history renders its insights only grudgingly. A legacy of records describing the historical process of economic change has been left for both the historian and the economist to mine. The key to a successful harvest of this information lies in the provision of a set of tools which permit selective, yet reliable, pruning from the extensive information available. Such a tool is an analytical framework within which the historical record may be interpreted. This is the task of part 2.

PART TWO

A Framework of Economic Development

3

A Model of Meiji Japanese Growth

3.1. Introduction: An Overview of Economic Dualism

While economic systems are admittedly complex, the analysis of Japanese economic development and structural change must begin by constructing a model which incorporates only the most basic elements of the historical growth process. In contrast with a model possessing extreme detail, a simpler framework has an incontestable advantage: it is capable of empirical implementation in spite of the current limitations on Meiji historical data. The model developed in this chapter is able to generate empirical predictions which can then be compared with the historical record. If historical experience is successfully reproduced, then at least one useful paradigm of development from low income levels has been uncovered. Our paradigm of Meiji economic development incorporates several key features prominent in Japanese historiography. This chapter will attempt to convince the reader that our model, although simple, is indeed relevant for historical analysis. Not only are the critical assumptions made explicit, but the chapter also provides a detailed defense of these assumptions based on the quantitative and qualitative studies in the growth, development, and Japanese historical literature. The paradigm will take on additional support in chapter 4, where consistency with the historical record is taken as more evidence for judging the model's usefulness.

Following the lead of Lewis (1954), Fei and Ranis (1964), and Jorgenson (1961), the economy is divided into two sectors. This permits an examination of the relation that disproportional growth and structural change—industrialization and urbanization—bears to aggregate economic performance. The dichotomy is justified by the extensive historical literature on industrial revolutions and by the critical role assigned to agriculture in early Japanese development. In contrast to the growth-theory literature, which only distinguishes between capital and consumption goods' sectors, our model is in the historical-development tradition where rural-agricultural and urban-industrial activities are highlighted. This sectoral breakdown is closely related to the Ohkawa-Rosovsky framework which emphasizes modern and traditional activities. Like Ohkawa and Rosovsky (1968, p. 4), we agree that there are "many blurred areas where traditional and modern facets intermingle," but we conclude that dualism is a theoretically useful notion nevertheless.

Our historical conception of dualism is multidimensional. In the Lewis, Fei and Ranis, and Jorgenson models, dualism is exclusively captured by an asymmetry in production conditions where it is postulated that different combinations of factors are employed in each sector: labor and land in the "traditional" sector, labor and capital in the "modern" sector. Yet the Japanese historical record suggests that sectors differed not only in the exclusion or inclusion of particular factors in the production process but also in the relative intensity of their use, in the nature of the specific technology employed as reflected in production parameters, and in the rate and bias of technological change. Japanese history also points to other elements of economic dualism; in particular, consumer demand. It appears that the preferences of the Meiji urban household tended to favor urban goods while farmers favored rural goods even when income levels were the same. Our paradigm must therefore expand and modify previous conceptions of economic dualism.

There are several ways of incorporating production dualism in formal analysis: (i) sectoral parameter differences (elasticities of substitution), (ii) sectoral differences in production arguments (capital and labor in industry, labor and land in agriculture), (iii) sectoral differences in the rate and bias of technological change, and (iv) sectoral differences in observed ratio variables (capital intensity and labor productivity) The latter form of dualism is pervasive. Early Japanese agriculture is well known to have been more labor-intensive than industry, even in early stages of Meiji development before the advent of large-scale capital-intensive industry around 1905–10. In the absence of technical change and with no factor reversal, it can be easily shown that average labor productivities in industry may exceed those of agriculture even under conditions of sectoral wage equalization. The "productivity gap"—a notable feature of Japanese historical development after 1880—should be produced by any serious model of the Meiji economy, even when equalization of marginal value products across sectors is assumed.

The framework presented here also emphasizes two of the three remaining forms of production dualism. These are crucial in understanding the early phases of Japan's Modern Economic Growth. First, labor-saving biases in industrial technology constitutes a widely documented and important feature of the Meiji Japanese economy. Most dualistic models abstract from these historical biases in technological progress. Second, we postulate differing sectoral production parameters. The industrial sector is assumed to be one which takes greater advantage of techniques imported from the West, implying a somewhat more limited range of factor substitution. In translating this notion into the formal analysis, the elasticity of substitution is taken to be considerably lower in industry than in agriculture.

Land is incorporated in the agricultural production process to capture the classical natural resource constraints on Japanese growth. If the long-term evolution of agriculture is a point of focus, then it is also imperative to include capital explicitly in the agricultural process. This we do in our model. Considerable historical evidence is available on the relatively early application of purchased inputs such as fertilizers, insecticides, and machinery in Japanese agriculture. This sector became "commercialized" over time and increasingly took advantage of large amounts of capital purchased from the industrial sector; it also accumulated farm-formed capital contributing to land improvement. A model structure which abstracts from this historical evolution may be inapplicable to the Japanese economy even before World War I. Our framework departs, therefore, from the conventional dualistic models which rely heavily on exogenous determinants of agricultural labor productivity[1] (for example, fixed land endowment and exogenously determined efficiency levels), and which minimize or exclude the role of investment in agriculture. Since our framework highlights the accumulation of capital inputs in agriculture, labor productivity is endogenously determined. Furthermore, in contrast to industry, agricultural technological progress is assumed to be labor-using (land-saving). This duality in bias is consistent with the Japanese economic historian's characterization.

Our paradigm of early Japanese development incorporates an explicit spatial dimension. The empirical literature supports the existence of rural-urban differences in consumer behavior and production technologies. While neither of these sectors is homogeneous in character, their combined dualistic attributes provide a basis for an explicit rural-urban dichotomy. This spatial dimension contrasts with the Fei and Ranis and Jorgenson approaches which highlight "traditional" production utilizing land and labor alone, and "modern" production employing capital and labor. The traditional enterprise in their models may be either in agriculture or in industry, depending on whether any purchased capital inputs are used in production.

The remainder of this chapter translates this broad characterization of the dualistic Meiji economy into a formal general equilibrium model which can be used for quantitative historical analysis.

3.2. A Model of Dualistic Development: A Verbal Statement[2]

3.2.1. Production Conditions

We shall consider the case of a simplified economy consisting of an agricultural and an industrial sector, each of which produces a single homogeneous commodity. Except for the transportation and communications sectors ("facilitating" industries in *LTES* terminology), services are excluded from our analysis and thus only commodity-producing sectors are considered. The exclusion of services is dictated by limitations of the historical data (Appendix A). The output of the agricultural sector can be used only for consumption. In contrast, industrial output may be consumed (e.g., textiles) or invested (e.g., producer durables), or both. The latter assumption distinguishes our model from those developed by Uzawa and others (Uzawa 1961, 1963), where it is conventionally assumed that one sector produces capital goods and the other produces consumption goods. The Uzawa dichotomy, common in formal growth analysis, is rarely maintained in the development theory literature. Both Fei and Ranis and Jorgenson, for example, admit the possibility of industrial output being used both for consumption and for investment purposes. Two further assumptions must be made explicit. First, there are no intermediate goods in our dualistic economy: all production satisfies final demand requirements. Second, the dualistic economy is closed to international trade. Commodity prices are determined endogenously as a result. This assumption will be critically evaluated in chapter 12.

There are three types of production agents in our two-sector economy: workers who supply only labor services for employment in each sector, and capitalists and landlords who supply no labor services, but who are the owners of capital and land, respectively. Capitalists and landlords provide the entrepreneurial services required for the operation of the production units and they determine the optimal method of producing firm outputs. In agriculture, these assumptions imply that farm units behave *as if* the peasant owner-operator status played an insignificant role in Meiji agriculture.

We assume the usual neoclassical description of the production process to hold in both sectors. In particular, entrepreneurs compensate the factors of production according to the value of their marginal products. Moreover, factor returns are permitted to vary such that labor, capital and land are, on average, fully employed. This class of model is consistent with the dualistic framework of Jorgenson, and in contrast to the ones of Lewis and Fei and Ranis, where in early stages of development labor is paid more than its value marginal product in the "traditional" sector. A defense of our approach to the factor pricing issue, as it applies to Japanese history is essential and is provided in section 2.3; an empirical confrontation of this aspect of our framework with the Japanese historical record is taken up in chapters 4 and 9.

Output in each sector is produced by two homogeneous and mobile factors, labor and capital, while agriculture utilizes in addition a specific and immobile factor, land. Production in each sector is subject to constant returns to scale and diminishing marginal rates of substitution are assumed to prevail. Factor-augmenting technical change applies to both capital and labor, but not to land. Given the low rate of growth of arable land in upland and paddy during the Meiji period (Appendix A), our characterization of agriculture introduces the possibility of classic restrictions on output expansion in that sector. Historically, these restrictions have been overcome largely by the discovery of new technologies which allowed for the more intensive utilization of land.

The production functions are written as:

$$Q_1(t) = A_1 \{\xi[x(t)K_1(t)]^{\frac{\sigma_1-1}{\sigma_1}} + (1-\xi)[y(t)L_1(t)]^{\frac{\sigma_1-1}{\sigma_1}}\}^{\frac{\sigma_1}{\sigma_1-1}}, \quad [3.1]$$

$$0 < \sigma_1 < 1,$$

$$Q_2(t) = A_2 \{[x(t)K_2(t)]^{\alpha_K}[y(t)L_2(t)]^{\alpha_L}R(t)^{\alpha_R}\}, \quad [3.2]$$

$$0 < \alpha_K, \alpha_L, \alpha_R < 1, \alpha_K + \alpha_L + \alpha_R = 1;$$

we label the industrial sector as "sector 1" and the agricultural sector as "sector 2"; Q_i is the quantity of the ith good currently produced; $K_i(t)$ and $L_i(t)$ are, respectively, the amounts of capital and labor currently employed in the ith sector; $R(t)$ is the arable land under cultivation; ξ is a distribution parameter in the constant elasticity of substitution (CES) production function; and $x(t)$ and $y(t)$ are the respective technical progress variables which augment physical capital and labor. We shall refer to $x(t)K_i(t)$ as "efficiency capital" and $y(t)L_i(t)$ as "efficiency labor," although a more meaningful historical interpretation will be attached to these concepts in the chapters which follow. In any case, it shall become evident that the distinction between physical and efficiency units of capital and labor is crucial to understanding contemporary Asian development as well as Meiji growth experience.

In our model production in the industrial sector is assumed to be more capital-intensive (compared to labor) than in agriculture. The importance of this assumption was first stressed in the development literature by Eckaus (1955) and it is well established with Meiji Japanese data as well (see Appendix A). Eckaus argued that in underdeveloped economies industrial production is more capital-intensive than in agriculture, which, together with sharp differences in elasticities of factor substitution, gives rise to the phenomenon of "technological dualism." These notions have also been embedded in Gerschenkron's "imitative thesis," which enjoys wide currency in Japanese historiography.[3] Economic historians continue to emphasize the importance of Western technology on Japanese development. Since industry takes greater advantage of imported Western technology, the sector is "likely to be capital-intensive compared with prevailing techniques in Japan . . . [implying] a limited range of factor substitution" (Watanabe 1968, p. 114). Watanabe's view is seconded by Odaka and Ishiwata:

> In the process of Japanese economic development, the introduction of borrowed technology has played a very important role. The usage of such foreign-born technology, adopted in conformity to foreign endowment ratios, implies that there has been comparatively little room for substitution between capital and labor. In other words, there was little choice of technology for the Japanese entrepreneurs who were launching into the new area of industrial development. [Odaka and Ishiwata 1972, p. 25]

The production specifications in our model are consistent with this view of Meiji Japan. The elasticity of substitution in industry, σ_1, is not only assumed lower than that of "traditional" agriculture, but further it is assumed to be less than unity. A hypothesis of relatively low substitution elasticities in industry is not, of course, unique to Meiji Japanese historiography. The successful application of the CES production function to manufacturing in advanced economies is reviewed by Nerlove (1967), where substitution elasticities are also found to be less than unity. More recent support for the hypothesis of less than unitary elasticity of substitution in industry can be found in Ferguson and Moroney (1969), utilizing a factor-augmentation model such as equation 3.1. The Ferguson and Moroney result has been supported by data drawn from contemporary developing economies. For example, in an analysis of Philippine manufacturing the elasticity of substitution was found to be less than unity, and technical progress biased against labor: similar results have been identified for Latin America (Williamson 1971*a*; Clague 1969). It should be pointed out that in no case was the estimated elasticity zero. Thus, although the estimated substitution elasticity is less than unity, the limiting fixed coefficient case does not appear to be an appropriate characterization of the developing Asian economy even when imported Western technologies dominate: this seems especially true for a model as highly aggregative as the one developed here.

In most of the development literature, agricultural output is solely a function of labor and land (Lewis 1954; Fei and Ranis 1961, 1963, 1964 chap. 2; Jorgenson 1961, 1967). In these theories the essential distinction is between a "commercialized" agricultural sector which uses capital produced in the "modern" sector and a peasant agricultural sector which uses only traditional forms of capital. Jorgenson, for example, argues that commercialized agriculture should be included in the modern sector of the economy (1967, pp. 291–92). For Jorgenson, the relevant dualistic asymmetry in sectoral production conditions is that the modern sector uses capital while the traditional sector uses land. Given our interest in an explicit treatment of the impact of demand as well as supply conditions on the Meiji Japanese economy, and given that consumers clearly viewed agricultural output as being different from industrial output, the distinction emphasized by Jorgenson and others is inappropriate for our purposes. Indeed, we have already argued that the "commercialization" of agriculture is a notable characteristic of Meiji Japanese development and that this characteristic must be explicitly captured by the model. Inclusion of purchased capital in agricultural production is based on considerable historical evidence that suggests the relatively early application of nonfarm-formed capital (such as fertilizer, insecticides, machinery and modern irrigation) in Meiji Japan. This was certainly a key aspect of agriculture's commercialization. The most detailed studies establishing this interpretation can be found in the excellent research of Hayami, Ruttan, Yamada, and Akino.[4] The extent to which purchased capital inputs are substituted for traditional inputs depends on the relative prices of these inputs given technical parameters. Apparently, the relative prices of "modern" capital inputs declined during the Meiji period and the scope for their introduction into Japanese agriculture was extensive—indeed, the evidence suggests that "traditional" capital (irrigation, etc.) and "modern" capital are complements rather than substitutes. More will be said on this below and in chapter 12. In summary, modern purchased capital inputs tended to allow for the more extensive utilization of both unimproved land and traditional agricultural capital (embodied in paddy improvements) in Meiji Japan. It remains for us to describe the new agricultural technologies which made that process possible.

We turn now to a defense of the specific functional form used to describe agricultural production. The Cobb-Douglas specification is commonly used in econometric research on Japanese agriculture (Akino and Hayami 1972; Hayami and Yamada 1968). Furthermore, there have been attempts to estimate CES production functions from farm and time series data drawn from the interwar period. The findings of these econometric studies are fully consistent with the Cobb-Douglas specification. Using a time series on value added in Japanese agriculture for the period 1917–37, Sawada (1970) estimates the elasticity of substitution between gainfully employed workers and the area of paddy and upland fields to be 0.930. Similarly, Akino's (forthcoming) estimates of CES production functions in agriculture across prefectures for the 1930s yield comparable results. Akino and Hayami have reviewed the extensive evidence and argue that "the constant production elasticities in the Cobb-Douglas production function is not a critical limitation for the short to the medium range analysis."[5] Akino and Hayami therefore regard agricultural output elasticities as remarkably stable within epochs of Japanese history. Although these output elasticities underwent pronounced shifts between the pre–World War I and the interwar period, and between the interwar and the post–World War II period, they are stable within each of these epochs. Since our focus is on one such "epoch," 1885–1915, the assumption of stable output elasticities in equation 3.2 appears reasonable.

This specification also implies two other aspects of Meiji Japanese agriculture which we shall define and defend below: (i) a land-saving bias in technical change, and (ii) competitive input pricing conditions in Japanese agriculture.

3.2.2. The Nature of Technological Progress

Given the assumption of factor-augmenting technical progress, we must now interpret more precisely the nature of this characterization of the Meiji economy. Needless to say, theoretically acceptable endogenous treatments of technical change are still in their primitive stages of development. As a result, we have employed the standard practice which takes the rates of factor-augmenting technical change as exogenously given and stable.

The two characteristics of technical progress that are important for our purposes are: (i) the current rate or *intensity* of technical progress *(total-factor productivity growth)* in the ith sector, $R_i(t)$, which measures the output-raising effect of technical change, holding inputs constant; and (ii) the *factor-saving bias* or direction of progress in the ith sector, $B_i(t)$, which traces the output-raising effect to the specific inputs.

The determinants of total-factor productivity growth in our model can be most easily seen by some formal manipulation of one of the sectoral production functions. Consider, for example, industry (Amano 1964; Fei and Ranis 1964, chap. 3). Based on the above definition of total-factor productivity growth—output growth holding factor stocks constant—we differentiate equation [3.1] with respect to t, for fixed $K_1(t)$ and $L_1(t)$, and divide through $Q_1(t)$, yielding

$$T_1(t) = F'_K \frac{x(t)K_1(t)}{Q_1(t)} \frac{\dot{x}(t)}{x(t)} + F'_L \frac{y(t)L_1(t)}{Q_1(t)} \frac{\dot{y}(t)}{y(t)}.$$

This expression has a simple interpretation. Total-factor productivity growth is simply a weighted average of the rates of factor efficiency augmentation; that is, a weighted average of the growth in $x(t)$ and $y(t)$. The weights themselves also have a straightforward interpretation. The marginal products of efficiency capital and labor are, respectively. F'_K and F'_L. The weights are then the marginal products of efficiency factors times the total input of the efficiency factors divided by output. But these factor shares are also output elasticities with respect to the inputs: the current output elasticities are denoted as $\alpha_{1K}(t)$ and $\alpha_{1L}(t)$ for capital and labor, respectively. Note that these α's are *variable* in the CES case. Thus, total-factor productivity growth in manufacturing is not constant over time even though the growth in $x(t)$ and $y(t)$ may be assumed fixed. Since agricultural production is taken to be Cobb-Douglas, then the α's *are* constant and so too must be the rate of agricultural total-factor productivity growth.

We assume that $x(t)$ and $y(t)$ grow at exogenously given rates, λ_K and λ_L, respectively, and are the same in both sectors. As we shall see, this latter assumption does *not* imply similar biases or rates of total-factor productivity growth in agriculture and industry. We have

$$x(t) = x(0)e^{\lambda_K t}, \tag{3.17}$$

$$y(t) = y(0)e^{\lambda_L t}. \tag{3.18}$$

From the discussion above, sectoral rates of total-factor productivity growth can therefore be rewritten as

$$T_1(t) = \lambda_K \alpha_{1K}(t) + \lambda_L \alpha_{1L}(t),$$
$$T_2 = \lambda_K \alpha_{2K} + \lambda_L \alpha_{2L},$$

where the α's, once again, are the current elasticity of output with respect to a given input. The rates of total-factor productivity growth in each sector are a weighted average of the rates of factor efficiency augmentation. In manufacturing, $T_1(t)$ has variable weights although $\alpha_{1K}(t) + \alpha_{1L}(t) = 1$. Thus, $T_1(t)$ is itself variable. In agriculture, T_2 has constant weights; so T_2 is constant.

Note that in computing total-factor productivity growth in agriculture, the sum of the output elasticities does not exhaust the total factor inputs' role, since this sector additionally uses land.[6] Formally, $\alpha_{2K} + \alpha_{2L} < 1$. Moreover, the historical evidence presented in Appendix B confirms that in Meiji Japan $\alpha_{2L} < [1 - \alpha_{1K}(t)]$; that is, although labor intensity was lower, labor's share was higher in industry than in agriculture because of the presence of rents in the latter sector. Given that our model assumes λ_K and λ_L to be the same regardless of the sector in which capital and labor is utilized, and given the arguments below that $\lambda_L > \lambda_K$, it follows that $T_2(t) < T_1(t)$: in short, our model of Meiji growth implies that rates of total-factor productivity growth are higher in industry than in agriculture. Although Meiji Japan's success in raising agricultural productivity has attracted the most attention in the literature (Hayami and Yamada 1970; Ohkawa and Rosovsky 1960; Johnston 1951), the empirical evidence nevertheless supports our specification of relative sectoral productivity growth (Yuize 1964; Sawada 1960; Economic Planning Agency 1965, pp. 11–19; Ueno and Kinoshita 1968, pp. 14–48; Yamada and Hayami 1972).

The nature of the bias in technical progress can be analyzed in terms of the Hicksian concept of neutrality. According to this definition, technological progress is neutral if it leaves the capital-labor ratio unaltered at a constant ratio of factor prices.

The Hicksian factor-saving bias is defined to be the proportionate rate of change in the marginal rate of factor substitution in that sector. Given the expressions for the proportionate rates of change over time in the marginal products of capital and labor, then (Fei and Ranis 1964, chap. 3; Williamson 1971*a*, pp. 42–46)

$$B_i(t) = \frac{[\lambda_L - \lambda_K][1 - \sigma_i]}{\sigma_i}.$$

Thus, the nature of the bias depends on the difference between the rates of factor augmentation and on the magnitude of the elasticity of substitution. If we accept the standard interpretations of biased technical progress during the Meiji period, then industry should be characterized as labor-saving ($B_1(t) > 0$). It follows that $\lambda_L - \lambda_K > 0$. In words, Meiji Japanese technical progress should be interpreted as strongly labor-augmenting. To the extent that industrial technologies in the Meiji period were imported from abroad (with considerable *adaptation,* we might add), an empirical basis for our technological bias specification is readily forthcoming (Odaka and Ishiwata 1972, p. 25; Ohkawa and Rosovsky 1961, pp. 476–501). Econometric studies confirm this labor-saving characterization of Meiji Japanese technological change. For example, Watanabe (1968, pp. 121–22) has found that

> The process of industrialization in Japan can be termed an imitative development with a special emphasis on the absorption of imported technology. In other words, advantages as a latecomer have been to a considerable extent realized, resulting in faster industrialization. . . . This imitative process of technological change is a labor-saving type of improvement in the early stage of industrialization. This hypothesis is confirmed quantitatively for the prewar period. . . . [D]uring the postwar period [however] a labor-saving bias . . . has been disappearing.

But the development economist has argued that positive labor-saving has emanated from *two* sources: (i) the appearance of labor-saving innovation imported from abroad, *and* (ii) the increasing importance of capital intensive sectors as modern economic growth takes place. The latter source has been termed the "compositional effect," and it has been found to have been strongly labor-saving in Asia in general, and in the Meiji period in particular.[7]

This labor-saving characterization is specific to industry and is not applicable to agriculture. Even though $\lambda_L > \lambda_K$, in the Hicksian sense technical progress is neutral in agriculture since $\sigma = 1$. Thus our model embodies a relevant historical duality in the nature of sectoral technical progress. At first glance, our assumption of Hicksian neutrality in agricultural technical progress may appear to be inconsistent with the historical literature. Land-saving (labor-using) biases in agricultural technology, embodied in new biological discoveries and their adoption, constitute a widely documented feature of the Meiji Japanese economy. The most recent research on this issue can be found in the writings of Hayami and Ruttan. Hayami and Ruttan (1971, chaps. 6–10; 1970*a*) test the induced innovation hypothesis utilizing Japanese agricultural experience since 1880 and find abundant evidence confirming the thesis. That is, high and rising land prices in Japan from the earliest period, coupled with stable real wages and falling relative fertilizer prices, induced the discovery and introduction of biological seed improvements in Meiji agriculture which were highly land-saving. How do we reconcile these empirical results with our assumption of neutrality? The apparent conflict is only one of semantics. The agricultural economic historian is *not* describing a land-saving bias in the Hicksian sense. "In agriculture in prewar Japan, in that land was relatively scarce and labor was relatively abundant, efforts for technical improvements were concentrated on saving land *or increasing output per unit of limited land area,* primarily through the development of fertilizer-responsive high-yielding varieties and related cultural practices" (Akino and Hayami 1972, p. 4; italics ours). The agricultural historian classifies observed increases in land productivity as land-saving technical progress. Under this alternate definition of bias, our specification of agricultural production in [3.2] is also land-saving. If labor and capital are augmented through technical progress over time while land is a relatively stable input, then it follows from our model too that land productivity increases and thus "land-saving" will be observed.

3.2.3. Factor Markets

$K(t)$ and $L(t)$ are defined as the total stocks of capital and labor available for employment in the economy at a given point in time. When these two mobile factors are fully employed,

$$K(t) = K_1(t) + K_2(t), \qquad [3.13]$$

$$L(t) = L_1(t) + L_2(t). \qquad [3.14]$$

The total stock of capital currently available in the economy is determined by the past levels of net investment undertaken by capitalists. Thus,

$$K(t) = K(0) + \int_0^t [I(\tau) - \delta K(\tau)]d\tau, \qquad [3.19a]$$

where $I(\tau)$ is the gross investment in period τ and δ is the fixed rate of replacement of the capital stock. Labor force growth is determined exogenously.

The controversy over interpretations of Meiji Japanese growth centers on the behavior of factor markets. Two fundamental issues are being debated. First, what is the relevant characterization of historical factor mobility? Second, what is the appropriate description of factor pricing within sectors during the Meiji period? We adopt a conventional neoclassical position on each of these two issues. Full factor mobility and marginal product pricing is assumed throughout. This section defends our position.

A fundamental proposition of the theory of general equilibrium and competitive markets is that discrepancies in factor payments lead to appropriate reallocations of productive factors until equilibrium is restored. Interindustry or interregional factor mobility is a force which tends to equalize prices for homogeneous factors between markets. We assume that capital and labor adjust instantaneously to any price differentials between sectors and that there are no costs associated with the transfer. Such conditions, of course, never prevailed in Meiji Japan, nor have they been satisfied by any other developing economy. Yet how much violence do these assumptions do to historical fact? The usefulness of these factor mobility assumptions depends on the observation that the time required for factor markets to adjust to discrepancies in factor payments is short relative to the time implicit in the study of growth. Justification for the assumption that no resources are used in effecting the transfer of factors between sectors must rest on a belief that, relative to the resources available in the economy, the costs associated with the transfer are small and therefore can be ignored for the purposes of the analysis. How do we reconcile these convenient theoretical assumptions with the historical reality of "wage gaps"? Let us explore this proposition in terms of Meiji Japanese experience with labor migration.

Much is made of the wage gap and duality in the wage structure in Japanese historiography (Watanabe 1968; Ohkawa and Rosovsky 1968; Taira 1970, chaps. 1–3). In fact "The term 'dual structure' is usually used [in Japanese economic history] to describe merely *the existence of large differences in wages,* capital intensities, and labor productivities among sectors" (Minami and Ono 1968; p. 2; italics ours). We have already discussed our production function specifications. Among the aspects of production dualism captured in our model is a higher capital intensity in industry. Furthermore, the model embodies the historical reality of more rapid rates of total-factor productivity growth in industry. Given those conditions, and in the absence of factor reversal, it inevitably follows that average labor productivities in industry will always exceed those of agriculture even under a regime of sectoral wage equalization. As we noted above, the "productivity gap" highlighted in the Japanese historical literature is faithfully reproduced by our neoclassical model, even with the absence of duality in the wage structure. But what is the evidence on *wage* duality in the Meiji period? Is our assumption of instantaneous and costless labor mobility—and thus wage equalization—an inappropriate characterization of labor markets during the period? Granted that an initial wage differential will always exist because of cost of living differentials and quality differences in sectoral labor forces, a relevant issue is whether the differential in sectoral wage rates *rise* markedly up to World War I, suggesting a denial of our mobility specifications. Since there were indeed increases in sectoral labor productivity differentials over this period, then a widening gap in wages would be consistent with the proposition that factors were not moving sufficiently fast to "clear the market." Were factor immobilities sufficiently important to vitiate the factor price equalization properties of our model?

The most recent historical evidence supports our view of labor mobility. The wage data presented by Ohkawa-Rosovsky and Watanabe document a remarkable stability in the wage differential between agriculture and manufacturing up to World War I.[8] This suggests an efficiently operating labor market up to

1919 in spite of the massive disequilibrating conditions generated by growth during the Meiji era. Apparently conditions reversed after World War I, for increasing "wage dualism" is far more evident in the 1920s and afterwards (Watanabe 1968; Taira 1970; Noda 1972). However, our focus is on the period up to 1915, when, as we have seen, our mobility specification appears to command empirical support.

We turn now to the theory of factor pricing embodied in our model. Our framework assumes that efficiency factors are paid their marginal value products, provided that the marginal product of efficiency labor is sufficient to allow every member of the labor force to consume a certain quantity of agricultural output, γ. We interpret γ to be a "subsistence" level of consumption of agricultural output per capita which is considered by the society to be essential for the welfare of its members. This minimum bundle of agricultural goods, which is the same for all laborers in the economy, is assumed in the Meiji case to be somewhat above the caloric minimum at which starvation occurs. The research by Oshima (1970, p. 119) and Hayami-Yamada (1970) on average caloric intake during the decade 1878–87 is roughly consistent with this assumption.

Defining $w(t)$ to be the current wage per efficiency laborer equalized across sectors, then from the sectoral production functions the efficiency wage functions can be derived as

$$w(t) = P(t)\,(1-\xi)A_1^{\frac{\sigma_1 - 1}{\sigma_1}} \left[\frac{Q_1(t)}{y(t)L_1(t)}\right]^{\frac{1}{\sigma_1}}, \qquad [3.3]$$

$$w(t) = \alpha_L \frac{Q_2(t)}{y(t)L_2(t)}, \qquad [3.4]$$

where $P(t)$ is the current price of industrial goods in terms of agricultural goods. Note that wage income and wage rates are not the same in our model (or, as we shall see, in historical fact): wage *income* per laborer is $w(t)y(t)$. We require that efficiency factor payments in the ith sector exhaust the output of that sector at each point in time, so that

$$r(t) = P(t)\,\xi A_1^{\frac{\sigma_1 - 1}{\sigma_1}} \left[\frac{Q_1(t)}{x(t)K_1(t)}\right]^{\frac{1}{\sigma_1}}, \qquad [3.5]$$

$$r(t) = \alpha_K \frac{Q_2(t)}{x(t)K_2(t)}, \qquad [3.6]$$

and

$$d(t) = \alpha_R \frac{Q_2(t)}{R(t)}, \qquad [3.7]$$

where $r_i(t)$ is the current rental rate of efficiency capital in the ith sector, and $d(t)$ is the rental rate on agriculture land.

In view of our assumption of constant returns to scale and perfect factor mobility, capitalists maximize their profits by equating the marginal rates of substitution of efficiency capital for efficiency labor between sectors. Such profit-maximizing behavior determines the allocation of factors between sectors. However, if the marginal value product of efficiency labor implied in this distribution of factors does not permit a per capita consumption of the minimum subsistence, our model is undefined. We have therefore imposed a restriction on the model by requiring that $w(t)y(t) > \gamma$. That is, income per laborer must be equal to or greater than the socially determined minimum subsistence level. This wage constraint satisfies the inequality $Q_2(t) \geq \gamma L(t)$, given that $r_2(t)$ and $d(t)$ are positive. This inequality is equivalent to Jorgenson's phase of dualistic development when an agricultural surplus appears (1967, pp. 301–2). It is confirmed by historical evidence drawn from the 1870s and 1880s.

Since so much debate has been aroused by the merits of alternative factor pricing schemes in theorizing about Meiji development, some discussion of the so-called classical and neoclassical frameworks might be instructive.[9] The classical approach, emphasized by Lewis and Fei and Ranis, assumes that one sector (typically agriculture) is characterized by overt or disguised unemployment of labor such that the prevailing wage is more than labor's marginal product.[10] In extreme versions of this model, a reserve army of unemployed exists and labor's marginal product is zero. Since marginal productivity theory cannot explain the distribution of income under the assumed classical conditions, an alternative income distribution framework, an "institutionally" determined wage, is offered as a substitute. When the marginal product of labor rises above the institutionally determined wage at some "turning point," the classical and neoclassical models merge. Much of the recent literature on Japan's modern economic growth has been devoted to identifying this "turning point" in her history. Fei and Ranis (1964, chap. 4) place the date at World War I, while Minami (1968, pp. 380–402) prefers to set the date during the early 1960s.

A choice between the classical and the neoclassical framework can be made on either empirical or theoretical grounds. The empirical relevance of the models has occupied the center of attention. As in all tests of model veracity, quantitative investigation may focus on assumptions—and in this case, the existence and nature of unemployment—or on the model's predictions. The relative failure of empirical studies to discriminate between the two competing models can be illustrated by comparing the conclusions of those supporting the classical interpretation with the neoclassical protagonists. Lewis (1958, p. 1), the earliest modern exponent of the classical dualistic model, asserts that "more than half of the world's population (mainly in Asia and in Eastern Europe) lives in conditions which correspond to the classical and not the neoclassical assumptions." Adding to this inventory of countries, Fei and Ranis (1964, p. 6) conclude, "The empirical support of both our theory and policy conclusions draws heavily on the experience of nineteenth century Japan and contemporary India." The Lewis-Fei-Ranis interpretation of the empirical record is in sharp contrast to Jorgenson's reading. Jorgenson (1966, p. 53) forcefully argues that "the scope and applicability of the classical approach to the development of a dual economy is severely limited. More specifically, the classical assumptions do not apply to Latin America, Africa, Southern Europe, India, China, or the remainder of Southeast Asia." Our own review of the debate reveals that neither side has provided persuasive evidence to support its view. Jorgenson and others, for example, have shown that the annual marginal productivity of labor (adjusted for seasonality of employment) is positive in almost all areas, and thus the extreme version of the classical model, which assumes redundant labor, is at variance with the historical record (Oshima 1958, pp. 686–87). However, the most relevant case of the classical framework, where the marginal productivity of labor is positive but less than the institutional wage, is also consistent with the Jorgenson findings. Furthermore, as Marglin (1966, p. 63) has correctly pointed out, "the relevant question . . . is whether or not the industrial wage reflects the product foregone by adding another man to the ranks of the employed in industry." While there may be *seasonal* unemployment, the average *annual* return to labor in agriculture may be less than, equal to, or greater than the institutional wage. In any case, as Sen (1966) has shown, the existence or nonexistence of disguised unemployment is not a necessary nor a sufficient condition of the classical theory.

The classical model possesses an illusive defense since the determinants of the institutional wage are seldom articulated rigorously. Similarly, the neoclassical theorist can always fall back upon a modified theoretical formulation where labor force unemployment is due to labor market adjustment lags, thus permitting temporarily underutilized factors (frictional unemployment). It should be stressed, however, that overt unemployment was not manifested secularly in the Meiji Japanese economy. Even during the 1930s the unemployment rate never rose above 1.5 percent (Odaka and Ishiwata 1972, p. 27).

Similar ambiguity has resulted from the early attempts to test alternative model predictions. Jorgenson (1966, p. 54) has argued that "the hypothesis of a constant real wage in the agricultural sector where disguised unemployment exists is the most important assumption underlying the classical approach. . . . The classical approach stands or falls on this hypothesis." Partly based on his finding that Japanese development shows rising real per capita labor income in agriculture during the so-called classical period of growth, Jorgenson asserts that "the classical approach must be rejected" (ibid., p. 60). But as Marglin has shown, the Jorgenson conclusion rests on a restrictive assumption that production in the agricultural sector is characterized by a Cobb-Douglas production function. Since this is not a necessary assumption in the classical model, and since, for example, a CES production function yields predictions similar to those found by Jorgenson for Japan, the evidence is again inconclusive. It might also be noted that even if production in the agricultural sector were described by a Cobb-Douglas function, constancy of real wages is not sufficient to reject the marginal productivity theory. This empirical result may merely reflect a stagnating phase of growth.

Perhaps the most telling evidence in favor of the neoclassical position can be found in econometric studies of Japanese agriculture during the interwar period. A crucial test of the neoclassical view of Japanese agriculture would be the conformity between estimated output elasticities and historically observed factor shares. If labor's output elasticity is far lower than labor's reported output share, then there is a presumption that the real wage is in excess of labor's marginal product and the classical hypothesis would be vindicated. The studies using farm data drawn from the 1930s suggest no such result. Ohkawa, Tsuchiya, Shintani, and Akino-Hayami all find evidence consistent with the neoclassical hypothesis (cited in Akino and Hayami 1972, pp. 18–23).

We have chosen to develop a model of economic dualism within the tradition of neoclassical economics. This decision was based on several considerations. First, we have yet to identify persuasive theoretical arguments or empirical findings which reject the validity of marginal product pricing as being applicable to Meiji Japan. Second, marginal product pricing is founded on well-established postulates of economic behavior. In contrast, formulations of the determinants of the institutional wage which are equally well founded in theory have not yet emerged in the economics literature. While we admit that the institutional wage is a plausible notion, until a theory can be derived to establish the analytical foundations of this formulation, and/or until this theory is established to conform with fact, then we are reluctant to discard one of the most powerful weapons in the economic arsenal—the marginal productivity theory of distribution. Third, and more important, our focus is on the low-income, growing Meiji economy in which stagnation, below-subsistence conditions and Malthusian "traps" were not key features. Finally, our approach to an analysis of the Meiji economy parallels that of all who seriously engage in formal model construction—protagonist and adversary alike. The predictions of our formulation will be confronted by evidence; the relative success or failure of our model will be judged in part by the historical record. While such a comparison of a simple dualistic model with the historical record will not be sufficient to establish its unique validity, a movement in this direction appears more productive at this point than entering further into an already muddled debate.

3.2.4. Consumption Demand

The next step is to introduce a meaningful demand system into our characterization of the Meiji economy. Theoretical and historical considerations suggest that the demand system must possess the following characteristics: (i) it must produce Engel effects; (ii) it must predict a rise in the expenditure elasticity for food over time; (iii) it must recognize dualism in consumption behavior between rural and urban areas; (iv) it must provide a role for demographic influences; and (v) it must capture the notion of "subsistence requirements." We shall see below that each of these characteristics has been identified explicitly in quantitative descriptions of Meiji consumption. In addition, the demand system must satisfy the technical requirements of "adding-up."

Demand theory has focused most recently on attempts to incorporate a complete system of demand equations into general equilibrium models. The demand equations must encompass all commodities and satisfy the "adding-up criterion." From among those models which meet these criteria,[11] we have selected the Stone-Geary system to apply to Japan. There is considerable empirical support for this choice. The most recent is the research of Parks (1969) and Yosihara (1969*a*). Following earlier work by Stone, Parks introduces greater flexibility into the linear expenditure system by allowing the demand parameters to vary systematically with exogenous variables. In his empirical analysis of Swedish historical consumption patterns, Parks finds the linear expenditure system superior to the competing models for the two commodity groups that concern the present study: agricultural and manufactured goods. The superiority of the linear expenditure system is also shown by Yosihara's examination of Japanese consumption from 1902 to 1960.

Our model assumes that each laborer possesses a utility function of the Stone-Geary form (Geary 1950–51; Stone 1962, 1964, 1965, 1966). At each point in time consumers allocate their budget so as to maximize the utility they derive from the consumption of agricultural and industrial goods. As Goldberger (1967) has pointed out, the Stone-Geary expenditure system aggregates perfectly over individuals in a group, given that each group member has the same utility function. We further assume that there is a difference in consumption behavior in the two sectors. Dualism in consumption behavior is reflected in the hypothesis that the residents of a sector have a relatively strong demand for the goods which originate in that sector. Recent work by Ohkawa and Kaneda on prewar Japan suggests that consumption behavior in rural and urban areas was significantly different. Their work demonstrates a greater preference for urban goods among urban households than among rural households.[12] The existence of substantial differences in consumer preferences is implicit in the notion of dualism, although we do not insist that demand dualism persists into very late stages of Japanese Modern Economic Growth. We do assume, however, that urban immigrants adopt urban consumption behavior immediately, with no habit persistence lags. Kaneda's research on Japan over the period 1878–1964 shows a gradual elimination of dualism in demand; nevertheless, sectoral differences in demand parameters persisted during most of the first half century of modern Japanese development.

The parameter γ_{ij} is the minimum acceptable amount of the ith commodity per capita required by laborers in the jth sector. In keeping with the interpretation of industrial output as being a nonessential consumer good and Ohkawa's observation of the persistence of Japanese demand for "traditional" commodities and services, $\gamma_{1j} = 0$ and $\gamma_{2j} = \gamma > 0$.

Given wage income per laborer, $y(t)w_j(t)$, and the commodity price ratio, $P(t)$, the Stone-Geary system postulates that each member of the labor force first purchases the minimum required quantity of agricultural ("traditional") output, γ. At the given relative price this costs γ, which may be termed subsistence income. He is left with $y(t)w_j(t) - \gamma$, which may be called supernumerary income; this he distributes among the goods in the proportions β_{ij} where i refers to the commodity and j the sector of residence. As noted above, our model does not make any predictions about the behavior of a consumer whose income is insufficient to meet minimum subsistence standards. Thus, only when $Q_2(t) > \gamma L(t)$ is the model defined. This condition corresponds to Jorgenson's phase where an agricultural surplus emerges. It seems clear that successful Meiji growth satisfies these conditions, since an agricultural surplus was forthcoming after the 1870s and earlier. Furthermore, we have already noted that caloric intake exceeded the minimum required as early as the 1870s.

The laborers' demand system can be summarized as follows:[13]

$$\frac{D_{1j}(t)}{L_j(t)} = \frac{\beta_{1j}}{P(t)}[y(t)w(t) - \gamma], \qquad [3.8]$$

$$\frac{D_{2j}(t)}{L_j(t)} = \beta_{2j}\, y(t)w(t) + [1 - \beta_{2j}]\gamma. \qquad [3.9]$$

Now define the current elasticity of demand for the *i*th good with respect to per capita income of laborers in the *j*th sector to be

$$\eta_{ij}(t) = \frac{\partial[D_{ij}(t)/L_j(t)]}{\partial[y(t)w_j(t)]}\,\frac{y(t)w_j(t)}{D_{ij}(t)/L_j(t)}.$$

It follows from equations [3.8] and [3.9] that

$$\eta_{1j}(t) = \frac{y(t)w_j(t)}{y(t)w_j(t) - \gamma},$$

$$\eta_{2j}(t) = \frac{\beta_{2j}y(t)w_j(t)}{\beta_{2j}y(t)w_j(t) + [1 - \beta_{2j}]\gamma},$$

from which it is seen that $0 < \eta_{2j} < 1 < \eta_{1j} < +\infty$ irrespective of the values of β_{ij} and γ. In short, the model exhibits behavior consistent with that attributed to "Engel effects" for any combination of theoretically feasible demand parameters.

This section began by noting that the demand system utilized in characterizing pre–World War I Japan should have five properties consistent with the descriptive evidence. (i) Although the size of expenditure elasticities is still debated, elasticities for food less than unity is common to all Japanese studies. The model is consistent with these documented Engel effects. (ii) Kaneda argues that food elasticities rose in twentieth-century Japan. Our model makes a similar prediction. (iii) Ohkawa, Kaneda, and Kuznets all document rural-urban dualism in demand, and, once again, the model is consistent with these observations. (iv) Demographic influences are normally thought to be important in influencing demand patterns (Kelley 1969). Our model emphasizes this effect too, but it is not directly felt through family size. Rather, the effect is indirect. That is, demographic variables have an impact on income distribution and, in particular, $w(t)y(t)$. Increased population growth tends to lower $w(t)$ and wage income; thus the share of expenditures devoted to foodstuffs increases. In addition, we have the impact of urbanization on demand composition embedded in our model.

(v) Finally, the concept of "subsistence" plays a prominent role in all classical labor surplus models. As we have seen, it plays an equally prominent role in our neoclassical paradigm.

3.2.5. Investment Demand, Savings, and Capital Formation There is both empirical and theoretical justification for focusing on sources of income as a basis for considering aggregate savings behavior in the growing Meiji economy. Analysis of data from contemporary low-income countries in East Asia (including Japan) indicates that savings functions which ignore long-run changes in functional income distribution will invariably be inaccurate (Williamson 1968). Lewis (1954, pp. 156–66) has argued that the profit-making entrepreneurs are the significant savers in society and that landlords (*except* in the Japanese case), wage earners, peasants, and salaried middle classes contribute relatively little. According to Fei and Ranis (1966, pp. 3–7), the essence of the difference between agrarianism and dualism lies in the motivation of the owners of the "surplus" in agriculture (see also Ranis's classic study [1970]). In this connection, Fei and Ranis have placed considerable emphasis on the savings behavior of the landlord as a crucial determinant of the economy's growth.

In our model of the Meiji economy we assume that property income recipients save a fixed share of income. Given the limited data, we make no distinction between industrial capitalists, agricultural "capitalists," and landlords. All property income recipients behave in an identical manner, and they allocate their investment goods to both sectors. Wage income recipients consume all of their income. Thus, investment demand is given by

$$I(t) = \frac{s}{P(t)}\{r(t)x(t)K(t) + d(t)R(t)\}. \qquad [3.12]$$

The gradual increase in the aggregate Meiji savings rate documented in chapter 4 is explained in our model by a shift in factor shares in favor of capitalists and landlords. Unfortunately, there is very little evidence on functional income share trends in Meiji Japan.[14] While not specificially explaining the rising trend in savings during the early stages of Japanese growth, Ohkawa and Rosovsky (1965, pp. 77–79) conclude that the expansion subsequent to 1905 was due to a movement away from traditional production and toward the more capital-intensive techniques in the modern sector. In the early period they emphasize the rate of agricultural surplus creation which, through government taxes (primarily the land tax), was channeled into nonprimary production (ibid.; see also Ohkawa and Rosovsky 1960; Rosovsky 1961, 1968 p. 360; Sinha 1969, p. 110). The economywide savings rate thus depended upon a rapidly growing agricultural surplus.[15]

Nakamura's (1966, pp. 151 and 155–69) interpretation of aggregate savings behavior is quite different. He places much greater emphasis on the distribution of income as a determinant of aggregate savings. In his framework the agricultural sector remains the main source of investment resources; however, savings growth depends primarily on capturing an increasing share of the existing surplus. This contrasts with the Ohkawa-Rosovsky interpretation where increased savings is based mainly on obtaining a share of a rapidly expanding surplus product (Rosovsky 1968, p. 360).

According to Nakamura, the Restoration transferred income from the high-consuming ruling class (including the samurai and daimyo)[16] to a new group of lower-consuming landowners. Decreases in the Meiji land tax coupled with the erosion of the tax burden through inflation distributed income to the relatively higher savers. Not only did the landowners save, but "the rural landlord-merchant played a major role in early Meiji financing by establishing and operating banking institutions and industrial and commercial enterprises" (Nakamura 1966, p. 167). Sinha supports the Nakamura interpretation. He qualifies the primacy of government-taxed agricultural surplus, noting "in the land tax the Meiji rulers did not find a new source of revenue, they merely rationalized it," and "the land tax was not even adequate to meet the armament expenditures of the regime" (Sinha 1969, pp. 125–27). On the other hand, while Sinha regards the Nakamura thesis of increased savings based on changes in the income distribution as substantially true, he notes that landowners likely invested some of their earnings in land improvements and other forms of agricultural enterprise.

In sum, the savings mechanism which Nakamura and others find supported by qualitative evidence is consistent not only with our own theoretical framework and with Japanese savings trends, but also with the hypothesis that the labor share in Japan was declining over time. Even though the Tokugawa ruling class can be considered as early capitalists, the income distribution relevant to the present discussion took place *after* the Meiji land reforms. In this case the capitalists and the landowners enjoyed substantial windfall gains through the lower tax burden and inflation. If this is accurate—and we find this a plausible interpretation of Meiji Japan—then an overall decline in the labor share, causing a gradual rise in the economywide savings rate, appears consistent with the historical record. While the descriptive literature appears to lend some support to this interpretation, the relevant quantitative evidence from the Meiji period is as yet much too fragmentary for forming definite judgments on these issues.

The data *after* 1907 is available to test these propositions; moreover, the results are consistent with our savings specification. For example, Minami and Ono (1972, p. 15) find the following for the period 1907–37:

> A negative coefficient of the wage income-nonwage income ratio implies that the propensity to save from wage income is less than that from nonwage income, and, therefore, the lower relative share of wages results in the larger aggregate savings available for investment expenditures.

A similar result was found by Klein and Shinkai (1963, p. 9) for the period 1930–59.

Note that in equation [3.12] the relative industrial (investment) goods' price, $P(t)$, plays a prominent role. The specification implies unitary elasticity of gross investment with respect to price. Even should the aggregate national savings rate *in current prices* be stable, the ratio of fixed price gross investment to GNP may rise if $P(t)$ falls over time. We shall have more to say about this relationship in chapters 6 and 8, since its implications for understanding Meiji Japanese experience with capital formation rates are profound. Finally, current net investment in the Meiji economy is taken as simply total gross investment less replacement, where replacement is proportional to the aggregate capital stock. Current net investment is given by

$$K(t) = I(t) - \delta K(t). \qquad [3.19]$$

No mention has been made thus far of "investment spurts" or

of the role of government in financing Meiji Japanese development. Before considering these complexities, it seems fruitful to exhaust first the potential of simple dualistic models which provide an endogenous explanation for savings and capital formation rates. The issue can be clarified by rewriting [3.19] and using [3.12]:

$$\frac{\dot{K}(t)}{K(t)} = \frac{I(t)}{K(t)} - \delta = [1 - \alpha_L(t)]s\left\{\frac{P(t)K(t)}{G(t)}\right\}^{-1} - \delta,$$

where $\alpha_L(t)$ is the economywide labor share and $G(t)$ is gross national product. Thus, rates of capital accumulation may accelerate over time for the following reasons: (i) The savings parameter, which is fixed and exogenously given in our model, may in fact rise, thereby producing an "investment spurt"; (ii) the capital-output ratio in *physical terms* may fall; (iii) the relative price of capital goods may fall; (iv) the functional distribution may shift favoring nonlabor income. Chapter 6 decomposes Meiji Japanese experience into these sources of trend acceleration in rates of capital accumulation.

3.3 Potential Extensions of the Model

In section 3.2 and in the formal statement that follows, the model developed has two attributes which the Japanese economic historian may find especially objectionable. First, the dualistic model is closed to trade, and commodity prices are determined endogenously. In contrast, Meiji Japan is sometimes characterized as an economy where trade was an "engine of growth" and, further, as an economy which relied heavily on the importation of agricultural products very early in the Meiji period. Our closed-economy specification is critically examined in chapter 12, where the potential role of foreign trade in Meiji growth is confronted in detail. When the special attributes of Meiji Japanese trade are carefully considered and the impact of world market conditions on growth is evaluated in depth, we argue that the evidence is far from sufficient to reject our closed-economy characterization on the grounds of "lack of realism." Second, the model excludes an explicit government sector, while governmental activity appears to have played a prominent role in qualitative accounts of Meiji development. The Meiji government had a notable impact on the economy in at least two dimensions: (i) capital formation rates through redistributive policies; (ii) technical progress through education, "pilot" experiments in industry, and public activity in research and dissemination of new agricultural technologies. While we shall not formally include a government "sector" in our model, our paradigm of Japanese development will indeed be interpreted to take into account the potential importance and roles of the public sector. The impact of government on capital formation rates is examined in chapter 7; the nature of government-fostered technical progress, in chapter 11.

3.4. A Model of Dualistic Development: A Mathematical Statement

The formal static model is composed of seventeen endogenous variables: $Q_i(t)$ = outputs, $K_i(t)$ = capital, $L_i(t)$ = labor force, $w(t)$ = wage rate of efficiency labor, $r(t)$ = return on efficiency capital, $d(t)$ = land rental rate, $P(t)$ = the relative price of industrial goods, $D_{ij}(t)$ = workers' demands for consumption goods, $C_i(t)$ = capitalists' and landlords' demands for consumption goods, and $I(t)$ = gross investment. There are five exogenous variables: $K(t) = \bar{K}$, $L(t) = \bar{L}$, $x(t) = \bar{x}$, $y(t) = y$, and $R(t) = R$, the land stock.

Production

$$Q_1(t) = A_1 \{\xi[\bar{x} K_1(t)]^{\frac{\sigma_1 - 1}{\sigma_1}} + (1-\xi)[\bar{y} L_1(t)]^{\frac{\sigma_1 - 1}{\sigma_1}}\}^{\sigma_1/\sigma_1 - 1}, \quad 0 < \sigma_1 < 1. \qquad [3.1]$$

$$Q_2(t) = A_2 \{[\bar{x} K_2(t)]^{\alpha_K} [\bar{y} L_2(t)]^{\alpha_L} [\bar{R}]^{\alpha_R}\}, \quad 0 < \alpha_K, \alpha_L, \alpha_R < 1, \alpha_K + \alpha_L + \alpha_R = 1. \qquad [3.2]$$

Factor Demand

$$w(t) = P(t)\,(1-\xi) A_1^{\frac{\sigma_1 - 1}{\sigma_1}} \left\{\frac{Q_1(t)}{y L_1(t)}\right\}^{1/\sigma_1} \qquad [3.3]$$

$$w(t) = \alpha_L \frac{Q_2(t)}{\bar{y} L_2(t)} \qquad [3.4]$$

$$r(t) = P(t)\, \xi A_1^{\frac{\sigma_1 - 1}{\sigma_1}} \left\{ \frac{Q_1(t)}{\bar{x} K_1(t)} \right\}^{1/\sigma_1} \qquad [3.5]$$

$$r(t) = \alpha_K \frac{Q_2(t)}{\bar{x} K_2(t)} \qquad [3.6]$$

$$d(t) = \alpha_R \frac{Q_2(t)}{\bar{R}} \qquad [3.7]$$

Commodity Demand

$$\frac{D_{1j}(t)}{L_j(t)} = \frac{\beta_{1j}}{P(t)} [\bar{y} w(t) - \gamma],\ (j = 1,2) \qquad [3.8]$$

$$\frac{D_{2j}(t)}{L_j(t)} = \beta_{2j} \bar{y} w(t) + [1 - \beta_{2j}]\gamma,\ (j = 1,2) \qquad [3.9]$$

$$C_1(t) = \frac{\beta_{11}}{P(t)} \{[1-s] r(t)\, \bar{x} \bar{K} + [1-s] d(t)\, \bar{R} - \gamma\} \qquad [3.10]$$

$$C_2(t) = \beta_{12}[1-s]\{r(t)\, \bar{x} \bar{K} + d(t)\, \bar{R}\} + (1 - \beta_{12})\gamma \qquad [3.11]$$

$$I(t) = \frac{s}{P(t)} \{r(t)\, \bar{x} \bar{K} + d(t)\, \bar{R}\} \qquad [3.12]$$

Factor Employment

$$\bar{K} = K_1(t) + K_2(t) \qquad [3.13]$$

$$\bar{L} = L_1(t) + L_2(t) \qquad [3.14]$$

Market Balancing Equations

$$Q_1(t) = D_{11}(t) + D_{12}(t) + C_1(t) + I(t) \qquad [3.15]$$

$$Q_2(t) = D_{21}(t) + D_{22}(t) + C_2(t). \qquad [3.16]$$

Five equations summarize the dynamic properties of the system.

Dynamic Equations

$$x(t) = x(0) e^{\lambda_K t} \qquad [3.17]$$

$$y(t) = y(0) e^{\lambda_L t} \qquad [3.18]$$

$$\dot{K}(t) = I(t) - \delta K(t) \qquad [3.19]$$

$$\dot{L}(t) = nL(t) \qquad [3.20]$$

$$\dot{R}(t) = \dot{\bar{R}}(t), \text{ exogenously given.} \qquad [3.21]$$

4

Theory and the Quantitative Historical Record

4.1. The Model's Plausibility: Some Methodological Issues

Two methods can be used to judge the plausibility of our model as a framework for analyzing early Japanese economic growth. The first is to examine the assumptions underlying the model's structure both on theoretical and empirical grounds. Chapter 3 contains a defense of those assumptions. There we considered in detail such critical model components as the concepts of demand and production dualism, the mechanism of factor pricing and factor transfer between sectors, the bias and intensity of technical change, the framework of equilibrium analysis, and so forth. Evidence from contemporary development studies and from an extensive historical literature on Japanese growth was assembled to support the veracity of the model's key assumptions. Additionally, considerable attention was devoted to aspects of the paradigm which might be considered by some as weaknesses by omission: the absence of a government sector, failure to capture factor and commodity market disequilibria, and the omission of elements causing economic instability. We have argued in defense that our framework was designed to focus on a specific set of development problems, and the omitted elements were considered, a priori, to be less important than the included model components in addressing these issues. We have cautiously avoided the common methodological pitfall of increasing the model's complexity solely to add greater "realism." Increased realism is always associated with a more intricate model structure, and indeed it can often yield real benefits. Yet, the costs of incorporating greater detail into a model of growth from low income levels may exceed the benefits. The demands on data for model testing and analysis increase enormously; as a result, added measurement errors may be introduced. This is an especially important consideration in analyses of early industrialization. Chapters 6 and 11 and Appendixes A and B should make this point abundantly clear. Moreover, the model becomes less susceptible to qualitative analysis since the linkages within the theoretical structure increase more than in proportion to the number of new elements introduced. In short, we have attempted to defend with evidence those major components included and excluded from the framework, realizing that ours is a model which addresses a specific set of issues, and that the success or failure of this model must be judged by the extent to which it generates useful insights into these problems. Our paradigm of Japanese growth and structural change is in no sense definitive. As in any modeling attempt of this type, such a history "will today be no more than a *parable* agreed upon."[1]

But the proof of the pudding lies in the eating. This brings us to the second method of judging any model of Japanese historical development. When assigned the quantitative characteristics of the Japanese economy during the period being considered, does the framework yield a believable empirical characterization of Meiji economic growth and structural change? It is this comparison of "fact" and "fiction" which we confront in the present chapter. Here we examine an empirical representation of the dualistic model developed in chapter 3. The model is given quantitative content by the assignment of specific numerical initial conditions and parameters. The model is then capable of generating a set of "predictions" of the historical record. Can these predictions be characterized as a successful attempt to rewrite Meiji Japanese economic history?

Two difficult methodological problems underlie a comparison of these simulated trajectories with "history." First, while we would hardly expect a precise correspondence between our model and history, what criteria should be employed to assess whether the quantitative characterization of Japanese development is sufficiently accurate to merit subsequent analysis? Second, in those areas where the model is found to be deficient in reproducing the empirical record, to what are we to assign the "error": errors in model specification? errors in the "estimates" of the Japanese parameters and initial conditions? or—and this should be emphasized—errors in the quantitative historical record itself? The reader must be continually alert to the possibility that where deviations in the model's predictions from the quantitative historical estimates occur, the assignment of the labels of "fact" or "fiction" to the model, on the one hand, or to the data, on the other, cannot always be made unambiguously given the current stage of Japanese historiography.[2] Both the data and the model possess elements of "fact" and "fiction," and which should be used as the norm in judging the other becomes, on occasion, a difficult decision indeed.[3] With this word of caution we take the position in the pages which follow that the quantitative historical record represents the norm in judging the model's veracity, realizing that the comparisons must be qualified where known deficiencies in the data exist.

This brings us to another critical methodological issue in comparing the model's predictions with history—the criteria employed to judge the acceptability of the absolute level of the comparisons. Even if the data are assigned a "factual" status, we still require a norm for appraising whether the model's predictions are close enough to the historical record to merit its use in quantitative analysis. Possibly the only acceptable norm is to compare our model's ability to rewrite history with those of alternative theoretical frameworks. Unfortunately there are only two such competitors available in the literature: one is provided by our own research in a recent preliminary excursion into Japanese economic history; the other by Minami and Ono in their application of the labor-surplus model to Japanese development.[4] By these two standards, our present effort is unequivocally successful. This gives us little comfort, however, since modeling of general equilibrium systems is still in an early stage of development. The number of studies in this area is limited.

The most prevalent method employed by economists in appraising a model's performance is to compare summary statistical predictions in terms of probability norms. This procedure compares the model's predictions to a probability distribution in order to establish the possibility that the results could have happened by chance. Regression models typically employ a "normal" or a "t" distribution in assigning the chance probabilities. Unfortunately, no such statistical methods and standards are available to summarize and compare the results of general equilibrium model predictions. Admittedly many descriptive statistics are available, ranging from those pioneered by the National Bureau of Economic Research (diffusion indexes, conformity indexes) to the more complex information-loss statistic proposed by Theil. But, it must be emphasized each of these statistics is merely descriptive, and whether the specific computed value is in some sense "acceptable" is still a matter of judgment. An adequate assessment of the acceptability of a specific computed diffusion index, conformity index, or Theil statistic can only be performed by a comparison of the results with those of previous studies—a comparison which should suggest whether the current model is or is not *relatively* successful. Again, the literature is too small for such statistical comparisons, for the present at least, to have any meaning.

With these limitations clearly stated, we can now outline the procedures employed in this chapter to analyze the veracity of our quantitative characterization of the model outlined and defended in chapter 3. The only reasonable approach to appraising the model's simulations is to compare them with the quantitative record on a variable-by-variable basis. Judgments on the degree of conformity will be based on an evaluation of the limited number of simulations of general equilibrium systems found in the literature. Our analysis will also take into account an appraisal of the quality of the Japanese historical data. Moreover, the results will be qualified for those components of the quantitative historical record which the model is not designed to confront; for example, economic instability. We shall present a sufficient amount of supporting data and statistics in this chapter and in Appendixes A through C to provide the reader an opportunity to judge the empirical relevance of our model for himself.

4.2. Japan at the Beginning of Modern Economic Growth

The specific numerical representation of Japanese economic growth depends critically on the initial conditions and parameters assigned to the dualistic model developed in chapter 3. Considerable detail on the derivation of these initial conditions and parameters is provided in Appendix B. Attention is focused in this section only on the overall quantitative characteristics of the modeled economy. A more detailed evaluation of the simulated economy can be found in part 3, where the leading issues of Meiji economic growth are confronted.

As noted in chapter 2, the model we have constructed to characterize early Japanese development is designed to describe what Simon Kuznets has denoted as "Modern Economic Growth." This stage of development possesses four characteristics: (1) the application of modern scientific thought and technology to industry; (2) a sustained and rapid increase in real product per capita,[5] usually (but, as we shall see in chapters 8 and 11, not always) accompanied by high rates of population growth; (3) rapid rates of transformation of the industrial structure (changing sectoral output, labor force and capital stock distributions); and (4) the emergence of or expansion in international contacts (Kuznets 1959, lecture 1). Henry Rosovsky finds these conditions to have been fulfilled around 1887. He describes the period 1868–85 as one in which Japan entered a "transition" to Modern Economic Growth (Rosovsky 1966, pp. 91–139; see also Ohkawa and Rosovsky 1965, pp. 47–66). We begin our comparisons of the model structure with the Japanese economy in 1887, the first year for which the recently revised *LTES* estimates are available for several critical economic magnitudes, including output and gainfully employed labor.

The Meiji economy in 1887 can be described as predominantly rural. Approximately 85 percent of the gainfully employed labor force producing commodity output was in the primary sector—agricultural and mining industries. The primary sector's output comprised almost 68 percent of the economy's commodity production.[6]

The transition to an urban, modern economic structure can be considered as an important attribute of Meiji development. The nature of this transformation can be better understood by an examination of the "differential structure" of the urban and rural sectors in 1887. A proportionately greater share of the economy's capital stock was engaged in producing industrial commodities, with the industrial capital-labor ratio being several times larger than that of agriculture. This representation can only be taken as approximate, however, since the *LTES* agricultural estimates exclude the potentially important component of farm-formed capital (notably, the irrigation and drainage infrastructure). Associated with the disproportional allocation of capital between sectors is a higher labor productivity in industry. The urban laborer produced approximately two and one-half times more output than his rural counterpart. In terms of average labor productivities at least, dualism was clearly evident at the beginning of the Meiji period.

Production dualism was not restricted to the allocation of factors between sectors; it was incorporated in the underlying technology as well. There was a tendency over time for the rate of technical change to proceed somewhat more rapidly in industry. Estimates of the early figures place the agricultural and industrial rates of total factor productivity growth at 1.2 and 1.4 percent per annum, respectively. These rates, coupled with the assumption of narrower factor substitution possibilities in industry, resulted in a notable labor-using bias in agriculture and a labor-saving bias in industry. The elasticity of factor substitution in industry is assumed to be 0.8; in agriculture 1.0. While there may have been a tendency for this bias to change over time, and especially after World War I, the bias is assumed to be constant and substantial during the Meiji period. (The rates of capital and labor augmentation through technical change assumed in the model are 1.14 and 1.94 percent per annum, respectively.) Given the relatively greater size of the rural sector, overall labor-augmenting technical change characterized the Meiji period.

Demand dualism has long been heralded as a critical attribute of early Japanese growth. Rosovsky and Ohkawa have highlighted the propensity of Meiji Japanese households to demand "traditional" goods, which required relatively little capital in their production. This demand pattern has been hypothesized as an important explanation of the overall expansion of aggregate per capita output and capital utilization. These demand attributes can be formally described in terms of a relatively high proportion of "primary" products in the Japanese household's expenditures, and the tendency for farm households to demand these "traditional" goods in higher proportions. Any study which fails to include these demand relationships may omit one of the potentially most important features of Japanese development during its industrialization process. In Appendix B we establish estimates of the demand parameters for food by rural and urban residents: the slope coefficients in the Stone-Geary linear expenditure system are .477 and .541, respectively, for urban goods.

During isolated periods of Meiji development the level of national saving was substantial. Nevertheless, significant portions of this savings effort were dissipated on military durable expenditures. If one excludes military expenditures from the investment totals, Meiji Japan is more accurately characterized as achieving a relatively modest average savings rate at the beginning of Modern Economic Growth. Ohkawa and Rosovsky provide estimates of saving at around 12.2 percent of gross national expenditure. Contrary to what is generally believed, unusually high savings rates were not a primary attribute of early Japanese development. Fortunately, labor force and population growth were also modest. The annual population growth rate was somewhat less than one percent for the economy as a whole. Restricting our attention to the gainfully employed labor force in commodity producing sectors, the growth rate was closer to 0.29 percent.

4.3. The Model's Plausibility: Selected Series

In this section the key predictions made by the simulation model are compared with the Japanese quantitative historical record. The comparison highlights those aspects of the model which appear to be particularly successful in reproducing history. It also emphasizes those aspects where data or model deficiencies merit qualifications to the analysis which follows in subsequent chapters. The comparisons are typically made with historical series smoothed by seven-year moving averages, thereby attenuating the short-run variations due to data irregularities or economic instability. The smoothed series is more appropriate for analysis, for the model was never intended to confront instability. Comparisons are made at four-year intervals, since the *LTES* income and employment data are normally available only in that form. In any case, annual comparisons would be somewhat inappropriate since our interest is in long-run Meiji development.

4.3.1. Aggregate Growth of Real per Capita Commodity Output

Table 4.1 displays the predicted and actual output per worker growth performance from 1887 to 1915. These three decades cover all of the Ohkawa-Rosovsky phase of initial Modern Economic Growth and the first decade of their phase associated with the creation of differential structure. The historical data, in constant 1934–36 prices, are compared with the model's predictions, in 1915 prices.

Overall conformity between the output-labor ratios in table 4.1A is close for the entire period, although there is a consistent

Table 4.1

Aggregate Growth Performance

4.1A Commodity Output Per Worker Levels (1887 = 100.0)

Year	Japan (1934-36 prices)	Model (1915 prices)
1887	100.0	100.0
1891	108.6	111.0
1895	121.8	123.7
1899	134.9	138.5
1903	146.5	155.8
1907	156.8	176.2
1911	181.8	200.5
1915	215.4	229.0

4.1B Commodity Output Per Worker Growth Rates

Period	Japan (1934-36 prices)	Model (1915 prices)
1887-1903	2.42	2.81
1899-1915	2.97	3.19
1887-1915	2.77	2.99

Sources: Appendix Table A.8; the simulation.

tendency for the simulation to overpredict the Japanese experience. Furthermore, one of the key features of Meiji Japanese performance—trend acceleration—is clearly reproduced in the simulation. When the period is bisected into two overlapping sixteen-year segments, the annual growth rate of the Japanese labor productivity rises by 0.55 percentage points; a similar trend acceleration is traced out by the simulation, 0.38 percentage points. The sources and implications of this trend acceleration are explored in chapter 6.

4.3.2. Structural Change in the Dualistic Economy

Tables 4.2, 4.3, and 4.4 provide an overview of several measures of structural change in the dualistic economy: the rate of labor force redistribution (urbanization), the mix of output between urban and rural production (industrial output share), and a summary measure of sectoral productivity gaps (comparative output-labor ratios). Clearly, in assessing the model's veracity, the ability of the dualistic model to reproduce the key elements of structural change are as important as, if not more important than, its ability to reproduce aggregate growth rates and phases of output growth.

Labor force redistribution. Consider first table 4.2, which presents a key measure of economywide structural change, the rate of

Table 4.2

Urbanization and Sectoral Labor Force Growth

Year	Labor Force Growth						Urbanization ($u = L_1/L$)	
	Japan			Model			Japan	Model
	L	L_1	L_2	L	L_1	L_2		
1887	100.0	100.0	100.0	100.0	100.0	100.0	100.0	100.0
1891	101.9	117.4	99.2	101.2	112.6	99.1	115.2	111.3
1895	103.4	129.7	98.8	102.3	124.9	98.4	125.3	122.1
1899	104.7	139.7	98.5	103.8	137.4	97.6	133.4	132.7
1903	105.5	148.0	98.1	104.7	149.6	96.8	140.0	142.8
1907	105.7	153.6	97.3	105.9	161.9	96.1	145.2	152.8
1911	106.9	162.5	97.1	107.2	174.3	95.4	152.0	162.6
1915	108.2	186.1	94.5	108.4	186.4	94.7	172.1	171.9

1887 = 100.0

Sources: Appendix Table A.6; the simulation.

"urbanization." Our empirical analysis focuses exclusively on commodity output, and thus the sectoral labor force distribution does not correspond precisely to the rates of Japanese urbanization. The historical series utilized for comparison are the gainfully employed in secondary and primary production, figures consistent with the commodity output series used to establish the initial conditions for the simulation.

The extremely close correspondence of aggregate labor force growth between the simulation and the actual Japanese data found in table 4.2 is of no consequence since the Japanese performance was used as the basis for deriving the aggregate labor force parameter used in the simulation. Of far greater importance is the remarkable similarity between sectoral labor force growth rates in Meiji history and in the model. Not only is the urbanization summary measure of labor transfer almost identical in the two series for the entire period (172.1 in Japanese history, 171.9 predicted by the model), but both series exhibit an absolute *decline* in the labor force residing in agriculture (94.5 in Japanese history, 94.7 in the simulation). The latter attribute of early Meiji experience has long been a puzzle to economic historians, and chapter 11 will dwell on it at length. These results are a marked improvement over those found in our earlier and preliminary excursion into Japanese economic history, where we examined a model which excluded land from the agricultural production function (Kelley and Williamson 1972). The industrial employment share was significantly underpredicted in the earlier study. Presumably the addition of land to the agricultural production function has contributed to the ability of the simulated economy to accord more closely with the Japanese historical record of structural change.

Industrialization. Industrialization proceeded at a rapid pace over the Meiji period. The industrial output share rose from an 1887 base of 100 to 215.6 in 1915 (table 4.3); this compares with

Table 4.3

The Industrial Output Share

Year	Japan (1934-36 prices)	Model (1915 prices)
1887	100.0	100.0
1891	108.9	112.2
1895	126.1	124.7
1899	145.2	137.2
1903	145.8	149.8
1907	181.1	162.5
1911	196.2	175.0
1915	215.6	187.6

1887 = 100.0

Sources: Appendix Table A.7; the simulation.

a somewhat lower level of 187.6 predicted by the model. The conformity of Japanese industrialization and the model is strongest in the first half of this period; in 1903 the indices stand at 145.8 and 149.8, respectively. In the decade following, a marked spurt in Japanese industrialization takes place which is not fully captured in the model. The nature of this spurt, and its relation to the output trend acceleration noted above, is explored in chapters 6, 7, and 11.

Labor productivity gaps. A popular measure of the "differential structure" in the dualistic economy is the labor productivity gap—the average labor productivity differentials between the secondary and primary sectors. This differential structure is summarized in table 4.4. Here it is seen that for the first half of the period there is a gradual rise in the relative labor productivity prevailing Japanese industry. An average of 1899 and 1903 yields an index of 115.0. A quantitatively similar rise is produced by the simulation, where the average index for the period 1899–1903 stands at 113.1. After this period the historical data record a sharp jump in industrial productivity, a discontinuity absent in the model predictions.

Table 4.4

Sectoral Labor Productivity Gap

Ratio of Average Labor Productivities in Constant Prices: Industry Over Agriculture

Year	Japan	Model
1887	100.0	100.0
1891	94.4	102.8
1895	104.1	106.7
1899	118.2	110.6
1903	111.8	115.5
1907	151.1	120.8
1911	164.1	125.5
1915	166.5	132.7

1887 = 100.0

Sources: Computed from Appendix Table A.8; the simulation.

Labor productivity gaps are inevitable in neoclassical models like the one developed in chapter 3. They can be explained by the existence of differential sectoral production parameters, the inelasticity of land supply, and the higher rates of technical change prevailing in industry. Yet the model is not capable of generating *discontinuities* in the relative sectoral labor-productivity trends. The discrepancy must be explained either by a change in production characteristics around the turn of the century (a view emphasized by Ohkawa and Rosovsky) or by a change in sectoral rates of total factor productivity growth. Possibly the increased deviation in the model's predictions and Japanese history in the last portion of the period may in part reflect a transition to a new "epoch" in Japanese technological conditions. For example, an alteration may have occurred in the bias embodied in new technology. Japanese historians have suggested that such a change may have occurred shortly before World War I. Chapter 9 explores this hypothesis in greater depth. Chapter 11 examines an alternative hypothesis, the retardation in agricultural total-factor productivity growth, while chapters 7 and 10 explore the impact of demand attributable to government expenditures.

4.3.3. The Rate of Capital Formation

The estimates for which we have the least confidence—not only for Japan, but for most other countries as well—are those relating to the aggregate and sectoral capital stock. Appropriate price weights, exclusion of major components (e.g., farm-formed capital in agriculture), and identification of reliable depreciation parameters are especially difficult problems, which plague the national income statistician in constructing capital stock estimates. Some of these problems are particularly acute with reference to the Japanese series (see Appendix A). It is for this reason that we place somewhat less weight on the year-to-year comparisons of Japanese historical experience in capital formation than we do in some of the other comparisons, where the data base is more credible. Furthermore, it seems likely that the agricultural capital-stock has the greatest underestimation. As a result, capital stock growth rates are underestimated especially early in the period. Furthermore, the capital-output ratio in agriculture has a more serious downward bias. With these qualifications, we now turn to table 4.5, where capital-output and capital-labor ratios over the Meiji period are presented.

In terms of the broad trends, and even their general magnitudes, the modeled economy appears to perform fairly well even in this dimension. Consider first the major trends in the Japanese capital-output ratio. There we observe a decline in both the agricultural and industry ratios, with a mild rise in the aggregate, as capital shifts to the sector in which it is utilized more intensively. These trends are reproduced in the simulations. However, the relatively more precipitous decline in the industrial capital-output ratio compared to agriculture is not reproduced in the simulation. We wonder to what extent this can be explained by the low quality of the agricultural capital stock estimates.

Table 4.5

Capital-Output and Capital-Labor Ratios

Year	Japanese Capital-Output Ratios (1934-36 prices)			Model Capital-Output Ratios (1915 prices)			Japanese Capital-Labor Ratios (1934-36 prices)			Model Capital-Labor Ratios (1915 prices)		
	Total	Ind.	Agr.	Total	Ind.	Agr.	Total	Ind.	Agr.	Total	Ind.	Agr.
1887	100.0	100.0	100.0	100.0	100.0	100.0	100.0	100.0	100.0	100.0	100.0	100.0
1891	101.6	100.9	92.8	104.1	96.4	93.3	108.4	103.9	103.9	115.6	107.9	109.1
1895	97.8	97.1	87.4	108.5	93.1	93.7	118.8	117.3	118.4	134.1	117.6	120.6
1899	97.7	93.0	82.7	112.6	90.1	91.4	139.5	136.6	139.8	156.0	129.0	134.4
1903	99.8	101.8	76.3	116.9	87.4	89.8	157.1	155.0	158.5	182.0	142.8	151.3
1907	107.5	94.9	82.4	120.9	84.8	88.3	184.8	185.5	191.9	213.0	158.9	171.5
1911	109.5	96.8	74.8	124.8	82.5	87.0	223.0	227.1	233.8	250.2	178.0	196.1
1915	109.9	93.1	70.9	128.7	80.3	86.2	266.5	251.4	258.7	294.6	200.7	226.1

1887 = 100.0

Sources: Computed from Appendix Tables A.5, A.6, and A.7; the simulation.

Rapid capital deepening is a phenomenon widely associated with successful economic growth; Japan is no exception. Moreover, there is a tendency for the pace of capital deepening to occur somewhat more rapidly in agriculture. The simulation model predicts these general trends and their magnitudes. It also yields a similar pattern in terms of relative sectoral capital deepening. It should be noted, however, that the simulations overstate the rise in the Japanese capital-labor ratio, a result consistent with the comparisons of aggregate output growth where a modest overestimate by the model was also identified. Once again we are not convinced that the overestimate represents a liability of the model rather than a weakness in the capital stock data.

Table 4.6 presents the economywide capital stock growth rates

Table 4.6

Capital Formation Rates
(in percent)

Period	Japan	Model
1887–1903	3.22	4.11
1899–1915	4.33	4.35
1887–1915	3.91	4.24

Sources: Computed from Appendix Table A.5; the simulation. The underlying series refers to the net stock of capital.

for Japan and the model. The most pronounced feature of the Japanese experience in capital stock growth appears to be the marked acceleration over the period, although some of the acceleration must surely be spurious and related to poor estimates of purchased inputs in agriculture. While the overall capital stock growth rates appear to be somewhat higher in the simulations, they are almost exactly the same for the period 1899–1915. Note too that the modeled economy also generates an increase in the pace of capital formation. The acceleration has been noted by development economists as a prerequisite or key feature of the development process; it is commonly associated with stages of economic growth and development. Discontinuous stages play no role in our model. Nevertheless, the model also generates endogenously this important growth experience. The ability of the model to capture the phenomenon increases its credibility as a viable framework for analyzing the development process in general, and that of Japan in particular.

The Japanese savings-rate estimates represent the share of gross domestic capital formation in gross national expenditure. They are in current prices and have been adjusted to exclude spending on military durables. Comparable current price series can be obtained from the simulations; both series are presented in table 4.7.

Table 4.7

Average Savings Rates
(in percent)

Year	Japan	Model
1887	12.2	12.2
1897	14.1	12.6
1904	12.3	12.8
1913	14.8	12.9

Sources: Appendix Table A.9; the simulation.

The model is not fully successful in capturing aggregate savings-rate movements. The predicted shares rise by less than 1 percent over the period; the Rosovsky estimates for Japan increase by about 2.5 percent. This discrepancy does not merit too much attention, however, since the increase in the economywide savings rate was modest in both series. Moreover, our inability to reproduce this aspect of history is in large part related to the "investment spurts" in the early 1890s and the middle of the first decade of the twentieth century. These are widely acknowledged to be associated with long swings, or long-run variations in output and employment. Since our model is designed to examine variations and levels in the long-run trend, the appropriate historical series with which to compare the model would be one which abstracts from these elements of instability. Chapters 6 and 7 explore investment spurts in greater detail.

4.3.4. Input and Output Prices

In contrast to the capital stock data, estimates of input and output prices are perhaps the most reliable components of the Meiji historical record. We therefore place greater emphasis on the price comparisons in evaluating the model's correspondence with history. In addition, real wage movements have been of particular interest to Meiji economic historians. The explanation for this attention can be found in the debate between adherents of the neoclassical and the labor-surplus models of development. Close attention must therefore be devoted to the model's wage rate predictions, since chapter 9 will enter the debate in depth.

Wage rates. A variety of wage rate series are available for Japan. These are presented in table 4.8. The first three indices are taken from the revised *LTES,* while the last column represents the daily wage for female silk-reeling operatives in the Yamanashi prefecture—a relatively homogeneous labor force over the period examined. Silk reeling also constituted a major industrial activity during the Meiji era. Each of the wage-rate series is expressed in real terms. Discussion of the construction of these series is postponed to chapter 9.

The general prediction of the labor-surplus models—relative stability in the real wage rate—appears to hold throughout most of this period. This is true not only of agriculture, where male daily wage rates rose decisively above their period average only in the first decade of the twentieth century, but also of manufacturing wages. Similarly, only a modest upward movement was experienced in silk reeling. It is therefore notable that the neoclassical model's predictions correspond closely to those in Japanese history: an extremely modest rise in the wage rate, sufficiently slow, in fact, to be considered virtually constant. Constancy in the real wage is hardly the exclusive property of the labor-surplus framework; it is evident in our neoclassical system as well. In chapter 9 we shall explore the sources of this real wage stability.

Earnings. An equally relevant series related to the real wage per man hour or day is the index of annual earnings, adjusted to capture variations in the annual utilization of labor. The earnings variable in the model is the efficiency-augmented wage. We shall argue in chapter 10 that the efficiency factor can be interpreted to reflect increased utilization of labor over time. To our knowledge, only one such historical series is available—the annual earnings index of female silk-reeling workers. Both series are presented in table 4.9.

The Japanese earnings index increased substantially over the period, even though the wage rate itself was relatively constant. The Japanese earnings index for silk reeling and the model's $y(t)w(t)$ stood at 176 and 171, respectively in 1908–11, which compares with wage rates in the same industry of 113 and 108. The model is thus able to capture the phenomenon of this fundamental price and income allocation in Japanese history. A de-

Table 4.8

Real Wage Rates

Period	Japan			Model	Period	Japan
	Male Daily Labor in Agriculture	Common Labor	Male Labor in Manufacturing			Female Silk Reeling
1885–87	100.0	100.0	100.0	100.0	1885–87	100.0
1888–92	92.7	92.3	88.4	100.6	1888–92	102.0
1893–97	88.8	96.3	82.5	101.6	1893–97	122.0
1898–02	100.6	113.2	95.5	103.1	1898–02	108.0
1903–07	94.9	109.9	94.0	104.6	1903–07	109.0
1908–12	106.2	128.7	109.6	107.3	1908–11	113.0

1885–87 = 100.0

Sources: Appendix Table A.2; the simulation.

Table 4.9

Annual Labor Earnings

Period	Japan	Model: y(t)w(t)
1885–1887	100	100
1888–1892	110	107
1893–1897	130	119
1898–1902	128	132
1903–1907	133	148
1908–1911	176	171

1885–1887 = 100.0

Sources: Appendix Table A.2; the simulation.

tailed analysis of the relationship will be undertaken in chapter 9.

Sectoral terms of trade. The Japanese historical literature emphasizes the secularly rising relative price of agricultural commodities in accounting for the induced productivity changes in the farm sector. Indeed, the labor-surplus model stresses the importance of these productivity improvements in moderating the price rise, thereby forestalling the "turning point." Given the common use of simple labor surplus models in analyzing Japanese history, the emphasis makes considerable sense. But it may have diverted our attention from an equally critical issue: Japan developed under conditions of sharply declining capital goods prices. In chapter 6 we shall see how the price movement fostered the secular rise in capital formation rates. Commodity price relatives are determined endogenously in our model, and the model predicts a rise in the relative price of primary products during periods of capital deepening. In the light of the emphasis which historians and development economists have placed on the terms of trade, a comparison of the model's predictions with history takes on added importance.

The price series predicted by the model is not in terms of current yen. Rather, the model predicts relative price changes: an index of industrial output prices in terms of agricultural goods. The most closely comparable historical index is the ratio of industrial goods' prices to an all-commodity index of agricultural product prices. This series and the corresponding price index for the model are presented in table 4.10. The relative price of industrial goods (and producer durables) declines sharply over the Meiji period,

Table 4.10

P(t): Output Price Relatives

Year	Japan	Model
1887	100.0	100.0
1891	85.4	96.3
1895	81.6	91.9
1899	82.5	87.5
1903	83.3	82.6
1907	87.5	77.9
1911	77.5	73.3
(1915)	(93.4)	(68.5)

1887 = 100.0

Sources: Appendix Table A.1; the simulation.

reaching a low of 77.5 in 1911. This compares with a level of 73.3 in the simulation. The marked increase in the price of industrial goods between 1911 and 1915 (based on the five-year period 1913–17) is the result of wartime demands and should be considered as an outlier to the long-period trend. As in most price series, the Japanese figures manifest considerable short-term variation, especially during wartime. If one ignores the wartime conditions, the direction and magnitude of the relative commodity price movements are very close indeed.

Real interest rates. To complete our price-series comparisons, table 4.11 presents indices of real interest rates for Japan and the

Table 4.11

Real Interest Rates

Year	Japan			Model
	Tokyo Discount Rate	Tokyo Time Deposit Rate	Bank of Japan Discount Rate on Commercial Bill	
1887	100.0	100.0	100.0	100.0
1892	105.4	115.4	128.1	94.1
1897	26.5	- 21.5	- 1.4	92.4
1902	78.9	101.5	83.1	91.7
1907	48.3	16.9	25.4	72.1
1912	55.1	13.8	15.5	64.9

1887 = 100.0

Sources: Appendix Table A.3; the simulation.

model. Since the model does not predict general price level movements, there is no difference between the nominal and the real rate of interest. In contrast, the three Japanese interest rate series—the Tokyo discount rate, the Tokyo time deposit rate, and the Bank of Japan discount rate on commercial bills—are available only in nominal terms. To provide a conversion of these series to real terms, we have adjusted the nominal series to account for the average rate of price inflation for the preceding three years (see Appendix A, table A.3). This assumes, somewhat arbitrarily, that the current price change is known with certainty. The resulting real interest rate series can be taken only as very crude approximations to the corresponding figure in the model.

Given the marked variation in both the interest rate and in inflation experience during the Meiji period, the computed real interest rate series displays significant period-to-period movement. The apparent instability is partly due to our inability to smooth the nominal interest rate figures (see Appendix A, table A.3), which are presented only on an annual basis for the indicated years. The long-period secular decline in the real interest rate in Japan is evident, however, irrespective of which series is examined. The Tokyo discount rate, which shows the least instability over the period, declines to a level of 55.1 in 1912. This compares favorably with the model's prediction, since the real interest rate index stood at 64.9 in the same year.

4.4 Summary

From a variable-by-variable comparison of the model predictions with history, we conclude that for those series which are of particular analytical importance (prices, wages, earnings, output, labor force, and productivity indices), and abstracting from those comparisons where the underlying Japanese data are particularly suspect (the capital stock series), the model tracks the Japanese historical record quite well. There appears to be a slight tendency for the model to overstate the rate of Japanese economic progress. Furthermore, the model tends to underpredict structural change, particularly toward the end of the Meiji period—probably because of factors exogenous to the underlying structure of the Meiji economy. The exogenous factors are important and deserve the special attention reserved for them in the chapters following.

Key economic variables yield particular credibility to the

modeled economy. These include the ability of the system to capture the stability of the real wage; the persistent secular expansion in wage earnings; and the acceleration in both the rates of output growth and capital formation. Each of these factors has been highlighted by Japanese economic historians. In combination with the broad conformity of the model predictions with the Japanese historical record, and with the model defense with reference to the Japanese literature undertaken in chapter 3, the results thus far set forth provide a sufficient basis, we believe, for launching into a more detailed analysis of our dualistic model of the Meiji economy.

5

The "New" Economic History and Counterfactual Analysis

5.1. Counterfactual Analysis in Economic History

5.1.1. An Overview

Chapter 3 constructed a model of Meiji Japanese development which we think is relevant for historical analysis. Chapter 4 attempted to establish the empirical plausibility of the dualistic model by comparing its predictions with historical fact from 1887 to 1915. How will the model be used to analyze early phases of Modern Economic Growth in Japan? The present section evaluates the counterfactual as a means of historical analysis. Section 5.2 briefly reports the recent use of general equilibrium models in economic history. Section 5.3 concludes with a discussion of the appropriate mode of analysis when general equilibrium models are applied to economic history. First, conventional comparative static analysis is discarded as too restrictive. Second, the steady-state emphasis of the growth theorist, a method recently applied to early Japan by Jorgenson, is rejected as inappropriate. Finally, we defend our comparative dynamic approach to Japanese history. We then indicate how the counterfactual can be utilized to uncover the lessons of early Meiji development.

5.1.2. Counterfactual Analysis in Economic History

The methodology employed in part 3 of this book can perhaps best be understood by an example. Consider just one issue of fundamental interest to both economic historians and development economists: the sources of industrialization. Structural change in the form of industrialization can be measured either in terms of output or input distribution between sectors. By convention, changes in the relative share of industry value added in GNP is normally termed "industrialization" in the two-sector format. This statistic has been central to historical analysis since the British

Industrial Revolution began; most recently it has been assigned a dramatic nomenclature in Rostow's (1966, 1960) description of the "take-off." Measurement of industrialization in Japanese Modern Economic Growth has been equally active (for example, Ohkawa and Rosovsky 1968). The most ambitious empirical effort in identifying the "sources" of industrialization in Japan was made by Chenery, Shishido, and Watanabe (1962).

Measurement of structural change from the input side has usually dealt with employment distribution, because of the greater abundance of labor force data compared with information on the capital stock. Furthermore, changes in the relative share of industrial employment in the total labor force, $u(t)$, is often equated with urbanization. The behavior of $u(t)$ is at the core of the dual economy tradition. Fei and Ranis (1964) refer to $u(t)$ as a measure of the "center of gravity" of an economy. They tend to judge the success or failure of a national development effort on the behavior of $u(t)$ over time, and the rate of labor transfer out of traditional agriculture is the key in their analysis.

Comparative static analysis of the dualistic model developed in chapter 3 is quite explicit regarding the impact of capital accumulation on $u(t)$.[1] An increase in the economywide capital stock per worker through capital formation tends to raise the relative price of labor. As a result, substitution against labor takes place in both sectors as firms attempt to save on the now more expensive factor input. By assumption, industry finds it more difficult to substitute capital for labor than traditional agriculture, since the elasticity of substitution is lower in industry. Consequently, there is a relative "push" of labor off the farm. In summary, a rise in the capital stock per worker tends to foster a rise in $u(t)$, and thus industrialization takes place. In formal terms, this result can be expressed as

$$\frac{\partial u(t)}{\partial k(t)} > 0,$$

where $k(t)$ is the economywide capital-labor ratio. As long as industry remains the more capital-intensive sector, and given the relative difficulty of factor substitution there, increases in $k(t)$ will always foster a labor transfer from agriculture to industry. The economic historian, however, is interested in the *quantitative* dimensions involved for a specific economy. He wishes to know how government policy, the elasticity of land supply, production characteristics, technical change, and demand might have influenced the impact of capital formation on industrialization. The economic historian has an intuitive understanding that the *magnitude* of this rate of labor transfer depends crucially on the structural parameters in the economy and on initial conditions. For example, since industry has more limited substitution possibilities in our dualistic model, agriculture should undergo more rapid rates of "mechanization" (that is, the relative importance of purchased inputs in agriculture should increase more rapidly). Granted, the level of capital-intensity may be initially so low in agriculture (as it was in Meiji agriculture in the 1870s) that the higher *rate* of "mechanization" may be scarcely noticeable. But as long as the differential in substitution elasticities persists, "factor reversal" will take place at some point in time, and agriculture will in fact become the more capital-intensive sector. The closer these sectoral capital-intensities (the less marked is observed production dualism), the less potent will a given increase in $k(t)$ be on $u(t)$. In summary, the elasticity of $u(t)$ in response to $k(t)$

$$\frac{\partial u(t)}{\partial k(t)} \cdot \frac{k(t)}{u(t)}$$

will vary both with the structural parameters unique to a given economy and with the conditions prevailing at some point in historical time when the elasticity is being computed (i.e., given the initial values of $u(t)$ and $k(t)$). Finally, the observed rate of industrialization at any point in time depends on the size of the "shock" to the economy being considered; in our example, it depends on the magnitude of $\dot{k}(t)/k(t)$.

The impact of capital formation on industrialization can be viewed formally as a combination of these three effects:

$$\frac{\dot{u}(t)}{u(t)} = \frac{k(t)}{u(t)} \cdot \frac{\partial u(t)}{\partial k(t)} \cdot \frac{\dot{k}(t)}{k(t)}.$$

The theorist may be very wary in evaluating the impact of a small change in $\dot{k}(t)/k(t)$ on $\dot{u}(t)/u(t)$, since his result may be sensitive to both initial conditions and structural parameters assumed in the dualistic model. Indeed, he may wish to know precisely how the structural parameters influence the impact.

Chastened by the theorists' warnings, the empirical economist therefore takes care in evaluating the sensitivity of his conclusions by performing what is known as "parametric analysis." The economic historian is even more pragmatic. First, he has little interest in an abstract evaluation of a modeled economy's behavior. Second, he is not particularly concerned with the fact that the elasticity of $u(t)$ with respect to $k(t)$ is influenced by initial conditions and structural parameters. After all, his interest is centered on a particular economy at a particular point in time: in our case, the Japanese economy, 1887–1915. Indeed, the modern economic historian wishes to explore *how an economy would have behaved under alternative historical conditions.* Suppose the rate of capital accumulation had been raised by 1.5 percentage points had Japan followed a peacetime course between 1894 and 1905 rather than the militaristic path which in fact she chose—a question posed in chapter 7? How would the rate of industrialization, $\dot{u}(t)/u(t)$, have been affected? An answer to this question would yield an explicit measure of the industrialization foregone during a period of militarism, and would help identify the sources of Meiji Japanese industrialization. This experiment is called an *historical counterfactual,* and it illustrates the methodology used in part 3 to uncover the lessons of Japanese history.

5.1.3. Counterfactual Analysis in American "Cliometric" History

Although the counterfactual is now a common mode of analysis in American economic history, our reading of Japanese economic history has uncovered few examples of its use.[2] Explicit counterfactual analysis in American economic history did not reveal itself fully until the appearance of Robert Fogel's (1964) research on the railroads.[7] Fogel argued that the impact of the railroads on late nineteenth-century American development could not be adequately appreciated unless one asked how the development of the economy would have been altered by its absence. It is evident that a quantitative answer to that question requires the development of an economic model. The appearance of explicit models, like the one in chapter 3 of this book, was greeted with uneasiness by many practitioners in the discipline: "It has been asserted that the models which underlie the answers to such questions are 'figments' and that they cannot be verified. Consequently, counterfactual models are held to be a direct threat to the integrity of economic history as an empirically confirmed description of the economic development of nations" (Fogel 1967, pp. 283–84). Parenthetically, we agree with the critics that some effort should be made to verify these "figments" before proceeding with counterfactual analysis. This in fact was the goal in chapter 4: to convince the reader that our "figment" in chapter 3 is a plausible description of Meiji Japanese development. Nevertheless, "The real difference between the new economic historians and their predecessors lies in the approach to the specification of models rather than in the frequency with which models are employed" (ibid, p. 284). With the appearance of explicit counterfactual analysis, American economic historians have made notable strides in determining the economic effects of the antebellum tariff, slavery, railroads, the Bessemer converter, the reaper, the Revolutionary War, and the availability of a frontier.[3] These effects could not have been isolated without considering how the American economy would have progressed in the absence of such institutions, processes, and artifacts (Fogel 1967, p. 285).

Part 3 applies the counterfactual to Meiji Japan by considering how her development would have been altered in the absence of the following factors considered by some to be critical in early Japanese development: slow population growth, inelastic land supplies, rapid technical progress in agriculture, the labor-saving bias embodied in imported Western technology, military adventurism from 1894 to 1905, and consumer demand favoring industrial goods. When explicit counterfactuals like these are posed of the Meiji Japanese economy, the answers are often at variance with conventional wisdom.

5.2. General Equilibrium Models and Historical Analysis

Following the introduction of counterfactual analysis in American economic history a decade or so ago, a new but inevitable revolution began to take place within the ranks of the cliometricians themselves. What was the appropriate mode of historical analysis? Should the railroads be evaluated in a partial equilibrium vacuum —that is, restricted to the transport sector itself, or should the analysis of such an important historical event be evaluated in a general equilibrium framework—that is, by exploring the interdependent impact throughout the economy? (Williamson, 1972.)

Should the impact of the frontier on American development be evaluated by partial equilibrium analysis of agriculture alone, or should we trace its impact throughout the economy in a general equilibrium framework? (Fogel 1967, pp. 297–308; Passell and Schmundt 1971; Williamson, forthcoming.) Can the impact of American tariff policy be effectively captured using partial equilibrium analysis, or must we rely on general equilibrium analysis in deriving an accurate understanding of its impact? (Pope 1972; Green 1970.) The more recent research in American economic history has shown quite convincingly that a general equilibrium approach is essential for many, if not most, of the problems of interest to economic historians. We believe the analysis contained in part 3 warrants the same conclusion regarding historical research on Meiji Japan.

5.3. Modes of Analysis: Comparative Statics versus Comparative Dynamics

5.3.1. Comparative Static Analysis: Critique

The use of general equilibrium models in economic history has two inherent weaknesses. The first relates to their inevitable *simplicity;* the second to the conventional mode of analysis—a heavy reliance on *comparative statics.* While the first pitfall cannot be avoided, the second can.

All models are "simple" in the sense that they abstract from elements in the real world thought to be unimportant. Without a judicious use of simplification, no understanding of an economic process would be possible, and a useless chronicle of events would be the only bequest made by the historian. Instead, the art is to develop models of historical development which capture the essential and suppress the trivial. Even those aspects of an economy thought to be absolutely fundamental can often be taken as exogenous, thereby simplifying the model yet allowing subsequent analysis of the excluded activity by treating it as a parameter change. For example, we need not explicitly introduce Meiji governmental activity into our model to explore the impact of Meiji fiscal policy on the economy. As long as the rate of technical change in agriculture can be identified as having been influenced by government policy, the impact of that policy can be readily evaluated using our model. Similarly, if Meiji fiscal policy can be shown to have had a pronounced influence on Japanese capital formation, the impact of that policy can be easily estimated using our model. In any case, only by explicit theorizing can economic historians really expect to uncover the sources of growth and development. Only then are the underlying assumptions made sufficiently clear so that the burden of proof can be shifted onto others who may choose to approach history with a competing model of the economy. Nor is it necessarily the case that a more complex model will more closely conform to reality. Complexity and realism are hardly synonymous when it comes to developing models of historical development.

An issue far more important than simplicity is *efficiency:* "The attempt to transform economic history from a discipline based on implicit, weakly specified, and untested theories to one based on rigorously specified and empirically warranted theories is a prodigious and frustrating enterprise. The greatest obstacle is the paucity of data" (Fogel 1967, p. 297). While researchers on the interwar and postwar period of twentieth-century Japanese development have enjoyed the luxury of evaluating large equation systems (Klein and Shinkai 1963; Minami and Ono 1972; Odaka and Ishiwata 1972; Ueno and Kinoshita 1968), those of us interested in the pre-1915 period have no such option. As the discussion in chapter 4 and Appendixes A and B indicate, the historical data for the Meiji period is still of limited quantity and quality in spite of the impressive efforts of Professor Ohkawa and his associates. The dualistic model in chapter 3 was developed with an eye on data availability. The model was made as efficient as possible with respect to the available historical data. The simplicity of the model was in fact an explicit goal so as to minimize the number of parameters for which quantitative information was required.

Let us turn to the second and, in our judgment, the more serious weakness of "general equilibrium" histories. With very few exceptions, these histories rely on *comparative static analysis.*[4] These studies evaluate the impact of a given "institution, processes or artifact" under the assumption that the resource endowment, subsequent technology and even commodity prices are fixed. Development economists would hardly be satisfied with such an approach. Nor would "traditional" historians. Can the dynamic effects associated with exogenous changes in the land stock, military expenditures, importation of labor-saving western technologies, or labor force growth be ignored in any meaningful analysis of the Meiji economy? Certainly not. However primitive, some theory of resource growth and technological change must be appended to the static model. Comparative static analyses which identify the historical impact of exogenous variables on income distribution, factor prices, and output mix are of limited usefulness if these endogenous variables have an impact, in turn, on rates of capital formation or technological progress. Yet in confronting dynamic issues, we must also take care to avoid the pitfalls presented by growth theory.

5.3.2. Asymptotic Properties and Growth Theory: Critique[5] The potential limitations of growth theory are best displayed by the debate between Jorgenson and Fei and Ranis. In his review of the classical labor surplus model of economic dualism, Jorgenson (1967) specifies a Cobb-Douglas production function in manufacturing. Given the classical assumptions that the terms of trade and the nominal wage are fixed, Jorgenson shows that average labor productivity in manufacturing must also be constant. Moreover, the capital-output ratio in manufacturing declines over time at a constant rate in the labor surplus model. The model also predicts increasing rates of growth in manufacturing output, employment and the capital stock. This follows if the classical savings hypothesis is invoked and in addition no capital is utilized in agriculture.

Jorgenson then proceeds to explore the predictions of his own neoclassical model of economic dualism. However, his predictions are derived from an analysis of the long-run (or steady-state) behavior of the model, where it is assumed that the capital-labor ratio is constant. Under the assumption of steady-state growth—a condition this book rejects as uninteresting—the rate of capital stock and output growth are equal in the long run. Apparently the Fei-Ranis and Jorgenson models generate conflicting predictions: the classical model has the capital-output ratio declining while the neoclassical model predicts constancy. Furthermore, since manufacturing employment growth approaches that of the total labor force in the long run, Jorgenson's special case of dualism predicts, *in a steady state,* that manufacturing employment will grow at a slower rate than both output and the capital stock. It appears that there are appreciable differences in the predictions of these competing models regarding the behavior of industrial labor productivities and industrial capital-output ratios. Jorgenson (1966) then examines early Japanese economic history to discriminate between the two models.

Unfortunately, Jorgenson's historical test is spurious since his mode of analysis is inappropriate for historical testing. Dixit (1970) has shown that the two models are *not* in conflict when they are analyzed in their short-run disequilibrium phases—rather than in steady state. Dixit's exercise is instructive and we may do well to dwell on it. He shows that under Jorgenson's assumptions, the manufacturing labor force follows a short-run growth path as in figure 5.1. Let the rate of capital stock growth be denoted by ϕ and let the rate of technical change in labor-augmenting form be λ_L, as in our model in chapter 3 (but $\sigma_1 = 1$ and $\lambda_K = 0$). The rate of employment augmentation in Jorgenson's

FIGURE 5.1

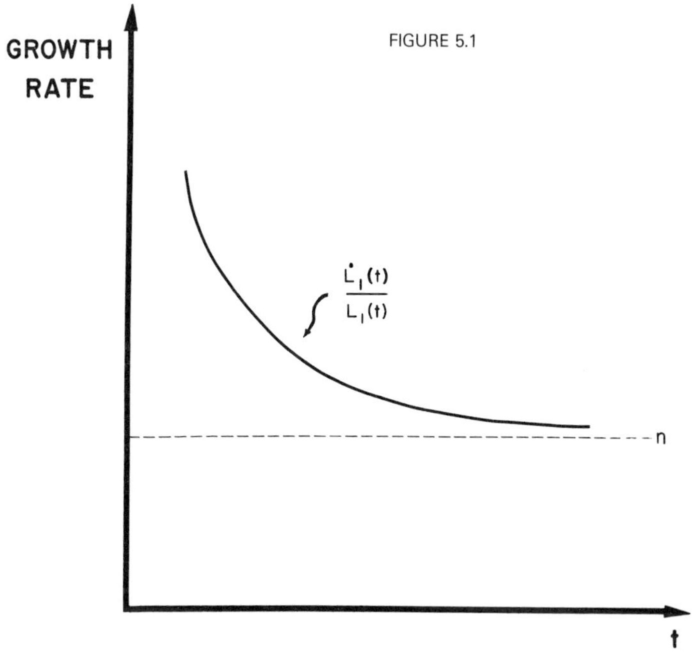

manufacturing sector, $\dot{L}_1(t)/L_1(t) + \lambda_L$, and the rate of capital stock growth are both exhibited in figure 5.2. Two paths of $\phi(t)$ are feasible, and both rise over time. The first, $\phi_1(t)$, continues to increase until $\phi_1(t) = n + \lambda_L$, where $\dot{\phi}_1(t) = 0$. The second, $\phi_2(t)$, rises more rapidly until $\phi_2(t) = \dot{L}_1(t)/L_1(t) + \lambda_L$ where $\dot{\phi}_2(t) = 0$ and $\dot{L}_1(t)/L_1(t) > n$; $\phi_2(t)$ declines thereafter. Up to $t = t^*$, the capital-output ratio is *declining* and the rates of capital stock growth are *rising*. Thus, up to t^*, Jorgenson's neoclassical model makes the same predictions as the classical model. Dixit estimates that the period up to t^* falls into a range of from two to six decades. Since our focus is on a period of three decades—1887–1915—the short-run rather than the asymptotic properties of our model (and Jorgenson's) are clearly the appropriate frame of reference for historical analysis. Accordingly, we conclude that the predictions derived from steady-state properties of the dualistic model are inappropriate, and the simulated behavior in a

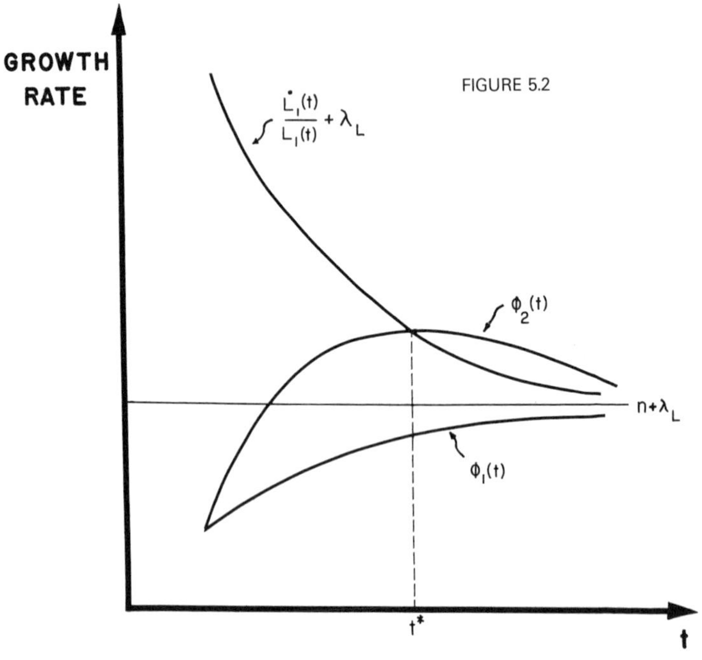

FIGURE 5.2

short-run disequilibrium phase of early development is the relevant one for historical analysis.

5.3.3. Comparative Dynamics, the Counterfactual, and Meiji Japanese History

The simulation reported in chapter 4 is our approximation of the developing Meiji economy between 1887 and 1915. The correspondence between this simulated history and fact is hardly perfect, but it is sufficiently close, in our judgment, to warrant use of the model in historical analysis. In part 3 we label this simulation "actual." What we propose to do in part 3 is to compare our "actual" simulation with a sequence of "counterfactual" simulations. The discrepancy between these pairs of simulations can then be explicitly attributed to whatever parameter has been changed in each counterfactual. For example, in chapter 8 we pose the following counterfactual: What would have been the nature of Japanese economic growth had she sustained the high population growth rates prevailing in the contemporary developing world? The "actual" simulation assumes a specific value of n, population (labor force) growth, estimated from Meiji demographic data. Contemporary developing economies have experienced population pressure at some three times that rate. Thus, the "counterfactual" simulation examines Meiji Japanese performance 1887–1915 under the alternative world where the revised rate of labor force growth, n^*, is $n^* = 3n$. The actual and counterfactual histories are then compared. Divergence in output per capita growth, sectoral productivity gaps, real wages, and industrialization rates can then be explicitly attributed to $(n^* - n)$. The experiment allows us to identify in quantitative terms just how much of Japanese growth experience can be attributed to these demographic factors. Similar counterfactual analysis is applied to other parameters: the rate of technical progress in agriculture (chapter 11), the elasticity of land supply (chapter 11), the impact of military activity (chapter 7), the role of the bias embodied in imported western technology (chapter 9), the impact of demand (chapter 10), and the role of savings (chapters 6 and 7).

Each of these counterfactuals is an exercise in comparative dynamics. The results are enlightening and very often conflict with *expost* accounting of Meiji economic growth. We turn now to these lessons of Japanese history.

PART THREE

The Lessons of Meiji Economic Development

6

Aggregate Growth Performance: Trend Acceleration and Miracles?

6.1. The Japanese "Miracle" and Contemporary Aspirations

We have come to refer to Japanese growth performance as "miraculous" and to the Japanese "model" of development for so long that it may come as a surprise to some readers just how ordinary the Meiji aggregate growth experience was. Professor Kuznets, for example, has told us that Japan's 2.4 percent annual growth rate of product per capita from 1879/81 to 1959/61 was matched or exceeded only by Sweden and Soviet Russia. Indeed, Western Europe from the mid-nineteenth century was able to achieve only half that rate while America and Canada maintained rates between 1.6 and 1.7 percent over the same period (Kuznets 1966, table 2.5, pp. 64–65). On the basis of evidence such as this it "is easy to see why a number of Asian and other underdeveloped countries . . . are keenly interested in learning how Japan did it" (Oshima 1970, p. 111). In fact, the aggregate growth performance of the Meiji economy up to 1915 (a period of modern economic growth which excludes, however, the notable interwar performance) is no more impressive than that of most contemporary developing economies. How did we arrive at this revisionist position?

The statistics on early historical experience with industrialization and growth are fragmentary and of doubtful quality.[1] This generalization holds for many contemporary developing nations, for American growth in the antebellum period, for British industrialization experience in the late eighteenth century, and, of course, for Meiji Japan. Indeed, the attempts to reconstruct modern Japanese economic history have been shrouded in an unusually intense data controversy since so much is at stake. This debate has been concerned with such fundamental facets of Japanese development as the role of agriculture in modern economic growth. The history of Western economies suggests that an agricultural revolution and a subsequent rise in agricultural productivity may often be viewed as prerequisites for modern economic growth and industrialization.[2] This has been termed the "prerequisite" hypothesis. With the appearance of quantitative Japanese research by such scholars as Ohkawa and Rosovsky, the prerequisite thesis has been vigorously challenged. Based on official agricultural statistics, Johnston, Ohkawa, Rosovsky, and others have argued that Japanese experience was unique, although it is currently being reproduced in the form of a "green revolution." Not only did the Meiji record, when based on the 1957 Ohkawa estimates, suggest miraculous growth performance, but the rapid expansion of agricultural productivity from levels comparable to contemporary monsoon Asia took place simultaneously with industrialization (Ohkawa et al. 1957). These results diminished the importance of an agricultural revolution as a prerequisite to modern economic growth and stressed instead the concurrent growth of agriculture and industry. An index of the widespread acceptance of the early Johnston-Ohkawa-Rosovsky characterization of Meiji economic history is the frequent reference to the "Japanese model" of development.

In the light of the early income estimates, Nakamura and Oshima sharply questioned the uniqueness of Japanese growth experience both in relation to the miraculous overall rates of progress and in relation to the Johnston-Ohkawa-Rosovsky interpretation of agriculture's role in Asian development.[3] Nakamura argued that the early Ohkawa estimates greatly understated the level of agricultural production beginning in 1878–82; moreover, this understatement, resulting from biases in official government statistics due to tax evasion practices, diminished over time.[4] The result was a significant overstatement of the growth rate of Japanese agriculture. Nakamura's competing estimates showed agricultural output expanding at a far more modest annual rate of around 1 percent from 1878/82 to 1913/17; the comparable figure compiled from the early Ohkawa series was 2.4 percent (Nakamura 1966, p. 12): that is, two and one-half times as fast. Even though Nakamura did not assemble new estimates for secondary and tertiary production, he asserted that the growth rate in these sectors was also overstated due to the widespread monetization of production during the Meiji period.[5] Given the importance of the agricultural sector, Nakamura's competing estimates reduced the Ohkawa aggregate annual growth rate from 4.0 to 2.8 percent. If possible biases in secondary and tertiary production were also taken into account, Oshima (1965, p. 356) argued that the aggregate growth rate would be even lower, perhaps as low as 1 or 2 percent.

Since their pioneering research, upon which most of our contemporary impressions of early Japanese economic development are based, there has been significant progress by Ohkawa's group in improving the output series. The results, appearing as the *LTES,* constitute the quantitative input to this book. All participants in the data debate agree that the *LTES* estimates are a significant improvement over the earlier series, and that the *LTES* implied growth rates in agriculture are much lower and the initial agricultural productivity levels substantially higher. The most recent estimates of per annum rates for the Meiji economy as a whole are as follows:[6]

GNP per capita	1.14
GNP per worker	1.68
Commodity output per capita	1.93
Commodity output per worker	2.77

The discussion in Appendix A should make evident that we believe the quality of the improved historical data to be such that the service sector is at present best ignored in analysis. Nevertheless, the Japanese miracle seems to have disappeared if these GNP per capita and per worker growth rates are fairly close to the mark. They are roughly comparable to the long-term rates achieved by the North American and Western European nations. Furthermore, they are *less* than the rates achieved in the noncommunist, less developed economies between 1955 and 1965; that figure was 1.9 percent. The rate for contemporary underdeveloped Asia was 2.1 percent.[7] In short, "the dates usually given for a supposed 'take off' in Japan had more to do with the development of Japanese statistics than with the facts of economic growth" (Hagen and Hawrylyshyn 1969, p. 46).

6.2. Meiji Japan and the Nineteenth-Century World Economy

We have also been taught that Meiji Japan was undergoing trend acceleration long before the impressive twentieth-century climb in

Japanese growth rates (Ohkawa and Rosovsky 1960, p. 43; 1965; 1968, pp. 10–12). This characterization has held firm throughout the debate and in the revisions. Even in the *LTES* commodity output data there is no evidence of growth retardation: for the period 1887–1903, the annual rate per worker is 2.4 percent while for 1899–1915 it is 2.96 percent (Appendix A). Thus, there is substantial evidence of an acceleration in growth rates before the interwar period. Indeed, it could be argued that the "unusually" rapid post World War II experience is not independent of preceding decades but instead is part of a long secular trend acceleration which had its source in the Meiji period.

The Japanese historical experience with growth acceleration prior to World War I is in striking contrast to that occurring elsewhere in much of the world economy (Williamson, 1973). Most of the world economy was undergoing growth retardation at the end of the nineteenth century. English experience from the 1860s to the turn of the century has been the source of continued research, and the debate has been at least as active as that over Meiji performance. The period has been identified in the literature as the "Great Depression," characterized by declining general price levels, declining nominal interest rates, and a retardation in aggregate real output growth. Between the periods 1870–1890 and 1890–1910, English GNP per worker growth rates decline from 1.44 percent to 0.46 percent per annum (McCloskey 1970, pp. 457–58). Trends in American performance were very much like that of Great Britain. Output-per-worker growth in 1860 prices declines from 1.71 to 1.24 percent per annum between the periods 1869/78–1884/93 and 1884/93–1899/1908 (Williamson, forthcoming, chap. 5).

The growth experience taking place outside of Meiji Japan during this period is relevant to the present study for two reasons. First, the comparison highlights the unusual character of Japanese growth prior to World War I. Second, it illustrates the limitations of conventionel growth theory. Recent research cited above on Great Britain and America has illustrated the usefulness of simple neoclassical paradigms in accounting for the "Great Depression" in England and America. Postulating fixed national savings rates, these models of late nineteenth-century Anglo-American growth are fully capable of explaining the marked retardation in these economies. The Meiji Japanese economy, it appears, was being driven by somewhat different forces, since she not only avoided retardation but enjoyed growth acceleration. What were these forces?

6.3. Meiji Japanese Performance and Economic Theory

6.3.1. An Overview

Growth models which hypothesize stability in aggregate savings rates and in the functional distribution of income may be useful for explaining modern economic growth, but they appear to be inadequate when confronted with early economic development. Given the initial disequilibrating shock centered on the Restoration which apparently produced a rise in aggregate savings rates and in the intensity of technical progress, conventional theory would predict a *retardation* in capital stock and output growth rates as the economy seeks a higher equilibrium capital-output and capital-labor ratio. Yet the *LTES* net capital stock series imply a significant *increase* in the rate of capital stock growth between 1887 and 1915: the average per annum rate 1887–1903 was 3.22 percent, while that of 1899–1915 was 4.33 percent (Appendix A, table A.5). The simulation also generates an acceleration in capital stock growth rates, although not as marked: over the same period, they rise from 4.11 to 4.35 percent per annum.[8] The accelerating rate of capital formation has commonly been explained by an appeal to exogenous "investment spurts" centered around 1905. Before considering this possibility (chapter 8), it might prove fruitful first to exhaust the potential of simple models which provide an *endogenous* explanation for the capital stock growth acceleration.

The issue can be clarified with the use of some simple accounting identities. Define $G(t)$ as gross national product and $[1-\alpha_L(t)]$ as the variable nonlabor income share. Furthermore, recall the assumption that all of wage income is consumed. From the gross investment-gross savings identity, where $P(t)$ is the relative price of capital goods, we get

$$\frac{\dot{K}(t)}{K(t)} = \frac{I(t)}{K(t)} - \delta = [1 - \alpha_L(t)]\,\bar{s}\left\{\frac{P(t)K(t)}{G(t)}\right\}^{-1} - \delta \quad [6.1]$$

Rates of capital accumulation may accelerate over time if the savings parameter rises, thereby producing an "investment spurt." The trend acceleration may also occur for the following reasons:

(i) the functional distribution of income may shift favoring nonlabor income; (ii) the capital-output ratio in *physical terms* may fall; (iii) the relative price of capital goods may decline. We shall consider each of these contributing factors in turn.

The central element of the dualistic models is a rise in the nonlabor (profit) share (see, for example, Kelley, Williamson, and Cheetham 1972*b*, pp. 118–21). This interpretation has strong roots in most of Japanese historiography, whether written by Marxian, classical, or neoclassical economists. For example, the labor-surplus models generate a rising profit share in *manufacturing* and then stability after the turning point when neoclassical conditions are satisfied. Jorgenson's framework predicts an improvement in the overall share of property income even in the neoclassical case, since the larger share in manufacturing produces an overall increase as industrialization takes place (Jorgenson 1961, 1967). Certainly the coincidence of relatively stable real wages reported in chapter 10, coupled with commodity output-per-worker rates of 2–3 percent, suggests a rise in the nonlabor share and thus in the rate of accumulation. In chapter 9 we show that this interpretation of Japanese growth may be wide of the mark and that the real wage stability has little to do with labor *earnings* and thus distributional patterns. It should suffice here to point out that our model predicts only a marginal rise in the nonlabor share from 1887 to 1915: from 0.58 to 0.61. Unfortunately, the work by Ohkawa only covers the period of factor shares *after* 1920, so we cannot directly confirm or deny this analysis for the pre-1915 period. Yet, Rosovsky and others have presented extensive evidence suggesting that aggregate national savings shares rise only very moderately during the Meiji period: between 1887 and 1913, $s^*(t)$ rises from 0.122 to 0.148 (Appendix A, table A.9). It seems likely that the labor surplus models cannot explain the trend acceleration in capital stock growth by an appeal to distributional factors alone, for the rise in historical rates of capital accumulation far exceed the secular increase in national savings rates.

The second potential source of accelerating rates of capital accumulation may lie with a fall in the capital-output ratio in *physical* terms. In the Solow-Swan models, a retardation in capital stock growth rates occurs as the economy approaches a higher equilibrium capital-output ratio (Solow 1956; Swan 1956). This is not the case in most dualistic models. Consider the industrial sector in the labor surplus framework. Here

$$\frac{\dot{K}_1(t)}{K_1(t)} - \frac{\dot{Q}_1(t)}{Q_1(t)} = \frac{-\lambda(t)}{\beta_1}, \qquad [6.2]$$

where $\lambda(t)$ is the rate of total factor productivity growth and β_1 is the output elasticity of capital in a Cobb-Douglas production function (Jorgenson 1967). The Fei-Ranis model then predicts a *decline* in the industrial capital-output ratio over time ("capital shallowing"). Dixit (1969, 1970) has recently shown that Jorgenson's model makes the same prediction in its disequilibrium phase. In contrast with the Fei-Ranis and Jorgenson analysis, the industrial capital-output ratio can move in *either* direction in our model. We have shown elsewhere that in our dualistic model (Kelley, Williamson, and Cheetham 1972*b*, p. 91)

$$\frac{\dot{K}_1(t)}{K_1(t)} - \frac{\dot{Q}_1(t)}{Q_1(t)} = [1 - \alpha_K(t)]\frac{\dot{k}_1(t)}{k_1(t)} - \lambda_K, \qquad [6.3]$$

where α_K is the output elasticity with respect to capital and λ_K is the rate of capital augmentation through technical change. Thus, the secular movement in the industrial capital-output ratio depends on the size of λ_K compared with $[1-\alpha_K(t)]\ \dot{k}_1(t)/k_1(t)$.

The Meiji data presented in Appendix A (tables A.5 and A.7) and chapter 5 contradicts the Fei-Ranis and Jorgenson models. The (net) capital-output ratio in industry *rises* from 3.86 to 3.95 between 1887–99 and 1903–15. The same is true for the economy-wide capital-output ratio, which *rises* from 1.91 to 2.17 over the same time period. Yet these results are consistent with the simulation discussed in chapter 4: the predicted capital-output ratio rises from 1.51 to 1.73. It seems clear that the trend acceleration in capital accumulation during the Meiji period cannot be explained by a decline in the physical capital-output ratio.

6.3.2. The Role of Capital Goods Prices

Consider again our expression for capital accumulation rates in equation [6.1]. Note that a third source of accelerating capital formation rates may be a fall in the *value* capital-output ratio. In both historical fact and the simulation the ratio declines (although only modestly): starting from a base of 100 in 1887, the simulation predicts a level of 98.0 by 1915. Offsetting movements in relative prices and the physical capital-output ratio produce this result. The relative price of industrial products normally declines in our dualistic model. That is, we know

$$\frac{\dot{P}(t)}{P(t)} = [\alpha_{2K}(t) - \alpha_{1K}(t)]\frac{\dot{\omega}(t)}{\omega(t)}.$$

As long as industry is more capital intensive, $\alpha_{1K}(t) > \alpha_{2K}(t)$, and successful capital deepening takes place fostering a rise in the wage-rental ratio, $\omega(t)$, then $P(t)$ declines. With rising wage-rental ratios the relative price of industrial products (and producer durables) falls. Unless the labor-augmenting bias is very strong, increases in the physical capital-labor ratio insures a rise in $k(t)$ and $\omega(t)$, and therefore a fall in $P(t)$. In fact the simulated relative price of industrial commodities declines from an 1887 base of 100 to an average index of 74.5 twenty-three years later, on the eve of World War II and concomitant food shortages. The comparable *LTES* index is 77.0.

Not only does the relative price of industrial goods decline over the period before wartime conditions have their influence, but the relative price of producer durables exhibits an even more dramatic fall. The relative price index for manufactured investment to manufactured consumer goods stands at 63.9 by 1910.[9] The capital goods' relative price decline throughout the Meiji period was very favorable for accelerating capital formation rates. Without this sharp relative price decline, the rate of accumulation would have been retarded, perhaps seriously enough to attenuate or even eliminate the acceleration in capital formation rates, and thus the observed rise in per capita output growth.

6.3.3. Savings and Capital Formation

That data presented in Table 6.1 illustrate the relevance of our emphasis on capital goods' prices. The secular increase in the investment share in GNP and the investment "spurt" following 1904–5 are both apparent in the revised Ohkawa-Rosovsky series. It is generally assumed that both the secular increase and the short run spurts reflect a comparable shift in the capital accumulation rate. Although the requisite annual data were not available to us at the time of this writing, we suspect that a significant portion of the acceleration in capital formation rates can be attributed to the secular decline in capital goods prices rather than to an increase

Table 6.1

Predicted and Actual Gross Savings Rates: Japan, 1887 to 1919

Year	Model		Japan	Actual Less Predicted:
	Current Relative Prices	1915 Relative Prices	(Current Prices)	Col. (3)-Col. (1)
	(1)	(2)	(3)	(4)
1887	.122	.093	.122	.000
1897	.126	.105	.141	+.015
1904	.128	.115	.123	-.005
1913	.129	.127	.148	+.019
1919	.130	.130	.166	+.036

Sources: Col. (3) from Appendix A, Table A.9; col. (1) and col. (2) are seven-year moving averages from the simulation.

in the national savings rate. Certainly the model's predictions bear this out. While the aggregate savings share in current income rises by the very modest rate of 0.8 percentage points over three decades, the constant price share rises by 3.7 percentage points, more than four times as much.[10]

This accounting for the secular rise in Japanese capital formation rates is especially attractive, being consistent with the recent research by Hayami and Ruttan on Japanese agriculture which we shall discuss in chapter 11. As is now well known, the bias (and rate) of Japanese agricultural productivity growth is consistent with an induced innovation hypothesis in which the ratio of fertilizer to rice (and land service) prices plays a critical role.[11] The rate of increase in purchased working capital inputs in Meiji Japanese agriculture is remarkable. Given the impressive decline in the prices of those inputs, it is not all clear that a profound change in the current price share of those inputs in the gross value of farm output was required to produce impressive labor productivity and yield improvements.

Although the mild secular increase in the current price historical savings rate can be adequately explained in our model by the gradual rise in the nonlabor income share, a significant residual between the predicted and actual savings rate persists. From 1887 to 1919, the predicted share (table 6.1, col. (1)) rises by only 0.8 percentage points while the revised Ohkawa-Rosovsky series (table 6.1, col. (3)) increases by 4.4 percentage points. This residual of 3.6 percentage points accounts for a small portion of the discrepancy between the sharp rise in historical capital formation rates and the much more moderate rise predicted by a dualistic model which assumes parameter stability. Furthermore, note that all the discrepancy between the predicted and observed national savings rates is generated by two unusual periods: 1887–97 and after 1905. While we can offer a plausible endogenous explanation to the Ohkawa-Rosovsky (1968, p. 23) question as to "why [the] ratio [of capital formation] to total output should continue to rise secularly," we find ourselves confronted with not one but *two* unexplained "investment spurts." One of these is well known and begins after 1905. Because the investment spurt is not reversed after World War I, this is not a long swing movement in the usual sense. Although the investment spurt after 1905 has been extensively discussed in the literature, we confess our inability to capture it in our model. Furthermore, descriptive statements like "The years 1905–19 are particularly associated with increased social overhead investment, the modernization of the cotton textile industry, and especially with the development of the large integrated spinning-weaving establishments" (Ohkawa and Rosovsky 1968, p. 24) are not very helpful in accounting for these discontinuities. In any case, if the investment spurt in the period just prior to World War I is to be explained by, say, government policy toward social overhead investment, how do we account for the low and declining savings rates during the 1890s, and for the "spurt" between the mid 1880s and mid 1890s? Chapter 7 will confront these spurts in Meiji performance by analyzing fiscal policy and military expenditures during the period.

6.4. Summary

To the extent that we have successfully identified a historically plausible paradigm of Meiji development, two inferences appear to emerge from this chapter. (i) Having identified the periods in which the savings rate appears to reveal an upward shift due to forces exogenous to our model, we are in a position to perform counterfactual experiments which may shed light on the impact of capital formation on Meiji economic growth. We can now explore the quantitative impact of exogenously induced savings rate changes (investment spurts) on Meiji Japanese development. This is the subject of chapter 7. (ii) Since the primary source of savings in the late 1880s was still agriculture, and given the broad empirical plausibility of our model, then there may be little scope for a functional-distribution-in-agriculture thesis in explaining the investment spurts during the Meiji period. While the agricultural surplus (nonlabor income in agriculture) continues to grow, it cannot explain the *discontinuity* in the economywide savings rate in the two periods cited. Chapters 7 and 11 will have more to say on this issue.

7

Investment Spurts, Military Expenditures, and Meiji Fiscal Policy

7.1. The Long Swing and Investment Spurts

7.1.1. The Investment Spurt, 1905–19, and Contemporary Analogies

The post-World War II rate and acceleration of Japanese growth has excited frequent comment. Quite naturally, economic historians have searched earlier Japanese experience to establish whether the recent "economic miracle" is unique. Ohkawa and Rosovsky (1968) have devoted perhaps the most effort in determining whether the postwar performance represents a radical shift in Japan's trend rate of growth. With the Japanese defeat, the 1946 GNP had fallen abruptly to the 1917–18 level, and the prewar 1939 peak was not resumed until 1954 (ibid, p. 6). The interesting experience is that of subsequent years:

> Movements of the postwar growth rate are clear: a decline from the very high levels of the early postwar years reaching a turning point near 1954; after that the rate of growth accelerates. Our interpretation of this is that the high rates of the immediate afterwar years were heavily influenced by recovery factors which tended to fade away in the middle 1950's. The subsequent growth spurt must therefore be attributed to "new" factors. [Ibid., p. 7]

The growth rates during the 1954–61 period are truly impressive: investment expanded at 20.9 percent per annum; GNP in constant prices at 10.9 percent per annum; and average labor productivity at 9.1 percent per annum. It seems apparent that it was an "investment spurt" which gave rise to this growth pattern: "The term 'investment spurt' has been used to imply an explosive increase in the rate of fixed capital formation, accompanied by an accelerated rate of output growth (ibid, p. 20; see also the excellent paper by Bronfenbrenner [1965]). Of course, it is one thing to identify accelerating rates of capital formation as the dynamic force behind Japanese Modern Economic Growth, and quite another to explain why capital formation should have proceeded in discrete phases. The present chapter intends to supply a tentative explanation for these discontinuities in growth performance and investment spurts.

The post-World War II experience is not unique. Indeed, there are two investment spurts in the pre-1915 period. Table 7.1 documents their magnitude and timing. Of special interest in this chapter is the episode from around 1905 to 1919. While the decade ending in 1905 is one of relatively poor growth performance, it should be emphasized that the period is not one of excess capacity and unemployment in the sense that the 1890s were depressed years for the American or British economies. But it is a decade of unimpressive growth compared with the three decades preceding World War I taken together. From 1905 onwards, conditions reversed. What was the cause of this investment spurt? What explains the lackluster performance between 1895 and 1905? Can the explanation of the investment spurt following 1905 also account for part of the "miracle" following 1954?

Table 7.1

Growth Instability in the Japanese Economy, 1887-1931

Period	Ohkawa-Rosovsky per Annum Growth (Constant Prices) in		Period	LTES per Annum Growth in Commodity Output
	Gross Domestic Fixed Investment (1)	GNP (2)		(3)
1887-1898	na	4.33%	1887-1895	2.76
1898-1905	3.53%	2.27	1895-1907	2.43
1905-1919	6.67	4.21	1907-1915	4.35
1919-1931	4.99	3.56		

Sources: Cols. (1) and (2) from K. Ohkawa and H. Rosovsky, "Postwar Japanese Growth in Historical Perspective: A Second Look," Tables 1-1, 1-3 and 1-7, pp. 9, 12 and 22. Col. (3) from Appendix A, Table A-7.

7.1.2. Long Swings and Meiji Growth Instability

As is often the case in economic history, Japanese historians have looked to the experience of other economies in searching for an explanation of the discontinuities in Meiji growth. In this case, their attention has turned to American nineteenth- and twentieth-century experience with long swings or Kuznets cycles (Kuznets 1930; Burns 1934; Abramovitz 1959, 1961, 1964). Simon Kuznets and Moses Abramovitz have established the existence of secular fluctuations in American history with durations of between fifteen and twenty-five years. These fluctuations appear in demographic variables, investment components, output, prices, employment, and even the balance of payments. Although there is continued debate as to their causes—and in particular whether these are to be found in exogenous or endogenous factors—there is much less disagreement regarding their existence and timing.

Economic instability appears to be equally pervasive in Japan. Table 7.1 documents a wide variance in GNP growth rates up to 1931: 1887–98 and 1905–19 are phases of rapid growth, while 1898–1905 and 1919–31 are periods of retardation. The growth in gross domestic fixed investment traces out a similar pattern. Furthermore, in chapter 9 (tables 9.1 and 9.2) it can be seen that real wages tend to rise up to 1898–1902, fall to 1903–7, and rise again sharply to World War I. Similar secular movements are found in all of the historical series presented in chapter 4. Evidence such as this has led Ohkawa and Rosovsky to treat the investment spurt 1905–19 as only one episode in a long-swing chronology which can be traced from the late 1870s to the contemporary postwar period.[1]

Confirmation of the Ohkawa and Rosovsky position has come from many sources. A recent paper by Shinohara (1972*a*, p. 3) estimates the average duration of the Japanese long swing at between twenty-one and twenty-two years. Shinohara finds pronounced cycles in manufacturing gross output which conform rather closely with the Ohkawa-Rosovsky dating: 1882–88 is viewed as an upswing; 1888–1902 as a downswing; and 1902–15 as another upswing. He notes that "this seems to be associated with [the] investment-GNP ratio which has been recognized by Ohkawa, Rosovsky, [and others]" (ibid., p. 5). Shinohara also finds a close association between balance of payment conditions in general, the trade balance in particular, and the domestic long swing in manufacturing. Fujino (1968, 1966) has uncovered similar evidence for the case of construction. Producer durables, structures, and nonfarm residential buildings all exhibit long swings with similar timing from the late 1880s to World War II.

There seems no doubt that Japan exhibited significant secular instability in her growth performance throughout the Meiji period.

The cause of this growth instability is an unresolved issue:

> In saying that real forces are dominant in [Japanese] Kuznets cycles, I take it that Professor Shinohara means that the long swings reflect chiefly *a fluctuation in the growth-rate of potential output* and not a fluctuation in the rate of change in the intensity of resource utilization, the latter implying growth of demand relative to potential output. In the USA, there are many reasons to believe that both processes were at work and, indeed, that a central element in the US Kuznets cycles was an interaction, or feedback, between change in intensity of resource use and growth rates of potential output based on growth of stocks of resources. If something similar were not the case in Japan, it would, indeed, constitute a very important difference between the long swings in the two countries. [Abramovitz 1972, p. 3; italics ours.]

Abramovitz's emphasis on potential output variation is examined in the present chapter. We shall suggest that the long swing up to 1915, and the 1905–15 investment spurt in particular, is in large part explained by a savings constraint on capital formation. This view is in contrast with that of Ohkawa, Rosovsky, and others, who stress the forces inducing instability in investment demand. For example, Ohkawa and Rosovsky (1968, p. 24) postulate that the investment spurt after 1905 was induced by a "higher-than-average rate of return on capital so that the incentive to invest remain[ed] strong." They then confront the critical issue: Why was the investment incentive so strong? First, borrowed technology flooded Japanese industry after 1905. (Its timing is not wholly explained.) This had two effects. On the one hand, the new technology raised potential rates of return and induced new investment. On the other hand, investment demand was reinforced by the increased capital-intensity inherent in the new technology. Ohkawa and Rosovsky (ibid., p. 24) view the cotton textile industry, with its modernization and the development of large integrated spinning-weaving establishments, as a prime example of the process. Second, the investment spurt "during the 'teens' of this century was certainly affected by the bonanza atmosphere" of the Japanese economy around World War I (ibid., p. 23). Some difficulties with this argument should be noted. Why 1905? Why the sluggish growth performance from the mid-late 1890s up to 1905? Why is there no evidence of notable secular unemployment from the mid-late 1890s up to 1905? (Odaka and Ishiwata 1972, p. 27.) Why are prices stable during the crucial phase of this investment spurt, 1905–11?[2]

A partial answer to these questions is supplied by explicitly focusing on the supply constraints to Meiji growth and, in particular, on the availability of savings for capital formation. If savings are treated as an active constraint on Meiji growth rather than as a passive response to unstable investment demand, a somewhat different interpretation of investment spurts and Meiji growth instability is suggested.

7.1.3. Savings Rates in the Model and Meiji Japan: Secular Trends and Investment Spurts

In the preceding section it was suggested that it may be inappropriate to apply the Western long-swing framework to Meiji Japan, since Japanese instability may in fact largely reflect variations in potential GNP growth rather than departures from full employment due to variation in aggregate demand. The Japanese scholar normally treats investment spurts as demand-induced. With the possible exceptions of Emi (1972*a*, 1972*b*) and Shinohara (1972*a*), little mention is ever made of a possible saving constraint on growth. This section attempts to establish the plausibility of this alternative view of Meiji experience. To do so, the Ohkawa-Rosovsky saving-ratio series (gross domestic fixed capital formation as a share in current price GNP), $s^*(t)$, will be imposed exogenously onto our model. A comparison between this new simulation (labeled "$s^*(t)$ exogenous") with the simulation discussed in chapter 6 (labeled "$s^*(t)$ endogenous") and with the actual historical growth experience should be instructive. First, the comparison will distinguish in yet another way (chapter 6) the secular trends in the saving ratio from investment spurts. Second, it should reveal whether our model is capable of generating investment spurts when the hypothesized saving constraint is allowed to vary exogenously. Third, and most important, the experiment will establish whether our model generates long swings in GNP growth whose timing and amplitude correspond to Japanese historical experience. If it does, then the plausibility of the savings constraint approach to explaining Meiji instability would at least be partially established. It should be apparent, however, that our savings-constraint interpretation cannot be conclusively vindicated by such a simulation experiment. The reason, of course, is that variations in the exogenously given savings rate may have been caused by investment-demand forces not captured in our model.

The results of this experiment are displayed in table 7.2. The

Table 7.2

Investment Spurts and Instability, 1887-1915: Ohkawa-Rosovsky and the Model Compared

7.2A Per Annum Growth in Gross Domestic Fixed Capital Formation (Constant Prices)

Period	Model		Ohkawa-Rosovsky
	s*(t) Endogenous	s*(t) Exogenous	
1887-1898	4.35%	5.74%	na
1898-1905	4.57	3.16	3.53%
1905-1915	4.73	6.89	6.67

7.2B Per Annum Growth in Constant Price GNP

Period	Model (Commodity Output GNP)		JAPAN (Commodity Output GNP)
	s*(t) Endogenous	s*(t) Exogenous	
1887-1895	2.95%	3.04%	2.76
1895-1907	3.29	2.38	2.43
1907-1915	3.63	3.88	4.35

Sources: The Ohkawa-Rosovsky Gross Domestic Fixed Capital Formation series is taken from their "Postwar Japanese Growth in Historical Perspective: A Second Look," Tables 1-1 and 1-7, pp. 9 and 20. The terminal date on the Ohkawa-Rosovsky series is actually 1919. The Japanese GNP growth rates are from Table A.7, Appendix A.

"$s^*(t)$ exogenous" series is generated in the following fashion: the Ohkawa-Rosovsky current price savings ratio is inserted into our model by extrapolating the annual $s^*(t)$ series between the moving average figures centered on the dates given in Appendix A, table A.9. The annual growth rates in constant price gross domestic fixed capital formation predicted by the model are then compared with a similar historical series in table 7.2A. The "$s^*(t)$ exogenous" model reproduces the investment spurt 1905–19 rather closely: the historical growth rates are 3.53 and 6.67 percent per annum in 1898–1905 and 1905–1919, respectively; the comparable "$s^*(t)$ exogenous" model rates are 3.16 and 6.89 percent. Note, too, the predicted decline in these growth rates between 1887–98 and 1898–1905. This instability in the growth of gross domestic fixed capital formation is in sharp contrast with the gradual rise produced by the model when $s^*(t)$ is determined endogenously. Although the overall growth rate in gross domestic fixed capital formation for the period 1887–1915 is roughly the same in both models, the model with $s^*(t)$ endogenous produces only a gradual secular rise from 4.35 to 4.73 percent between 1887–98 and 1905–15. If one employed these figures to represent the underlying trend rates, then the growth rate in gross domestic fixed capital formation during 1898–1905 was some 1.4 percent below the secular rate, while during 1905–15 it was some 2.2 percent above it.

Table 7.2B displays the implied behavior of GNP. The dating is slightly different, because the *LTES* commodity output figures (Appendix A, table A.7) are moving averages centered on years which are not quite comparable with those available for gross domestic fixed capital formation. Nevertheless, long swings in GNP growth rates are apparent in the "$s^*(t)$ exogenous" model. While the long run secular growth rate in the $s^*(t)$ endogenous model rises by 0.34 percent from 1887–95 to 1895–1907—reflecting trend acceleration (chapter 6), the growth rate in the "$s^*(t)$ exogenous" model *declines* by almost 0.70 percent. The difference is significant—about one percent per annum. Furthermore, the predicted short-run retardation in GNP growth between 1887–95 and 1895–1907 is roughly comparable with that of the historical series: the latter falls by 0.30 percent in the smoothed data, while the former declines by 0.70 percent in the unsmoothed data. The spurt following 1907 is also reproduced in this experiment. The $s^*(t)$ endogenous model predicts a secular acceleration in GNP growth from 3.29 to 3.63 percent between 1895–1907 and 1907–15. When exogenous short-run investment spurts are introduced into the model, the growth rate accelerates far more sharply over the same period, from 2.38 to 3.88 percent. The historical series exhibits a comparable acceleration, from 2.43 to 4.35 percent.

This exercise provides a quantitative illustration of an alternative interpretation of the poor growth performance of the Meiji economy during the mid-late 1890s—an interpretation which focuses on a diminution in the savings ratio rather than with a deterioration in investment demand hypothesized in the long-swing literature. The investment spurt after 1905–7 may be explained in a similar fashion. What is now required to support this interpretation is an explanation for the short-run variance in the savings rate which is independent of investment-led effects. The remainder of this chapter will search for the explanation in terms of Meiji fiscal policy and military adventurism.

7.2. Sake versus Swords: Capital Formation and Military Expenditures

7.2.1. The Role of the Military

With few exceptions, recent quantitative economic histories of the Meiji period fail even to mention the heavy Japanese commitment to international military adventurism between 1894 and 1906. They appear to have forgotten Lockwood's firm reminder of the less pleasant lessons of Meiji history from 1895 to 1935: "The drain of empire building went far to nullify the more constructive use of state power to mobilize savings for investment in productive enterprise. . . . Significantly, the war which profited Japan the most was World War I, when she remained neutral in all but name" (Lockwood 1954, pp. 577–78). Since military expenditures play only an incidental role in modern quantitative accounts of Meiji development, especially in the long-swing literature, it might be helpful to refresh our memories as to the potential importance of militarism in limiting Japanese growth performance during the Meiji era. Lockwood makes the point rather strongly: "The whole fiscal policy of the Meiji government, beginning with the Land Tax Reform of 1873, might be characterized as designed to extract the maximum amount of revenue from agriculture . . . to forward the industrial and military ambitions of its ruling groups" (ibid., p. 293). In Landes's words, "In the last analysis political and military considerations had precedence. The economy was an instrument in the service of the nation, rather than the reverse" (Landes 1965, p. 175). Indeed, in the 1890s and afterward the Meiji ruling class did not hesitate to sacrifice economic interests to further the goals of state building, military strength, and prestige (ibid., p. 504). If one is seeking a justification for the favorite slogan "Fukoku kyōhei" (a rich country, a strong army), one need only recall the events of the 1860s and 1870s. In 1862–63, the bombardments by American and British warships of Shinonseki and Kagoshima taught Japan the advantages of Western military power. In addition, the opposition of dissident clan leaders after 1868 suggested the wisdom of developing a strong counterrevolutionary military force. Expenditures for law and order became especially compelling with the Satsuma Rebellion in 1877.[3]

In our period of analysis, military outlays by the Meiji government do not rise sharply until 1894. Table 7.7 documents a moderate share of military expenditures in GNP between 1887 and 1893, a level approximating 3 percent of GNP. This figure triples in 1894 and remains at high levels until 1906. The military expenditure share averaged 4.3 percent in GNP during the periods 1887–93 and 1907–15. The share in 1894 was almost 10 percent, while that of 1904–5 was an astounding one-fifth of GNP. The impact of these military expenditures on Japanese long-term development does not receive adequate attention in contemporary quantitative accounts of Meiji growth. The sources of the increased military expenditure are not difficult to uncover. A successful war with China was concluded in 1894–95. Not only did Japan receive the Liaotung Peninsula as a result, but she also received £38.1 million in indemnity. These funds were utilized in part to build up an international reserve and made possible the adoption of the 1897 gold standard. The victory and financial bounty also gave Japan sufficient prestige to terminate humiliating economic treaties with Western powers. After acquiring Formosa and the Pescadores, the Meiji government redoubled her armament program and successfully challenged Russia in 1904–5. Although the Russo-Japanese war was financed extensively by foreign loans, it still placed a heavy burden on the Meiji economy.[4]

It seems improbable that the correspondence between the poor growth performance and heavy military outlays during 1895–1907 is coincidental. Similarly, the correspondence between the "investment spurt" after 1905–7 and the diminished military expenditures was unlikely to have been dictated by sheer chance either. A long-swing framework may not be required to account for a quantitatively important trade-off between sake and swords ("butter and guns"). This view of Japanese development also partially accounts for the rapid expansion of the economy during and following the period of World War I neutrality. Even by 1938, when Japanese war preparations began anew, the share of military outlays in central government revenues was only 35.5 percent; this compares with 51.2 percent in 1898 (Lockwood 1954, p. 292).

To adequately account for the halt in growth due to Meiji military adventurism between 1894 and 1905, it becomes necessary to examine Meiji fiscal policy in somewhat greater detail.

7.2.2. A Reinterpretation of Meiji Fiscal Policy

It is generally agreed that Meiji fiscal policy was successful in fostering Japanese development. Japanese experience has often been cited as an example of how contemporary developing economies might stimulate their own growth by using the same fiscal tools (Smith 1955; Patrick 1961; Ranis 1970). With the notable exceptions of Oshima and Lockwood, most analysts are content to judge Meiji fiscal policy a success on the basis of two attributes. First, the government was effective in increasing the tax yield as a share of GNP. No doubt, but what is the virtue of a large tax-expenditure component in GNP without an explicit evaluation of its impact on efficiency and growth of the entire economic system? Second, a significant share of Japanese capital formation was directly financed by the Meiji government. True, but what share of the large tax revenues were devoted to "productive investment," and would these investments have been forthcoming by private interests in the absence of Meiji fiscal action? These are some of the questions this section will explore. Our own position will be closer to the less enthusiastic evaluation of Japanese fiscal policy contained in the research of Oshima and Lockwood.

Meiji government expenditures (current prices) are presented in table 7.3, which includes expenditures by all governments, central and local. There is a steady secular rise in nonmilitary expenditures throughout the period 1887–1915, and this is true of both capital outlays as well as "other" nonmilitary expenditures. Yet military outlays were from one-quarter to one-fifth of government expenditures even during peacetime periods: in 1887–93 the share is 20 percent, and in 1907–15, 23 percent. The share devoted to military outlays is, of course, much larger during war years: 55 percent in 1894 and 61 percent in 1904. During the period 1894–1906, the average share is 40 percent, almost twice as large as that reached during the prior and subsequent periods of lesser military activity and preparation. Thus, not only is a large proportion of government expenditures allocated to the military

Table 7.3

Meiji Military and Non-Military Government Expenditures
(million ¥, current prices)

Year	Total (1)	Military (2)	Non-military: Total (3)	Non-military: Capital Outlays (4)	Non-military: Subsidies to Enterprises (5)	Non-military: Other (6)
1887–1893	817	161 (19.7%)	656 (80.3%)	123 (15.1%)	28 (3.4%)	505 (61.8%)
1894–1906	6094	2440 (40.0%)	3654 (60.0%)	831 (13.6%)	83 (1.4%)	2738 (45.0%)
1907–1915	7448	1720 (23.1%)	5728 (76.9%)	1546 (20.8%)	123 (1.7%)	4059 (54.4%)

Sources: Col. (1): Sum of cols. (2) and (3). Col. (2): Military outlays from LTES (Vol. 7), Table 14a plus Table 4, cols. (6) and (7). Col. (3): sum of cols. (4), (5) and (6). Col. (4): nonmilitary capital outlays by government from LTES (Vol. 7), Table 14b. Col. (5): subsidies paid to enterprises by government from LTES (Vol. 7), Table 14b.

throughout the period, but major variations in this military expenditure share are clearly in evidence. The 1894–1906 episode is one of unusually heavy commitment to military outlays. Furthermore, table 7.7 confirms the importance of these expenditures in GNP. The government expenditure share rises from 15 to 25 percent between 1887–93 and 1907–15, but the proportion from 1894 to 1906 is far higher, reaching a remarkable 40 percent in 1905.

Meiji revenue sources (table 7.4) are well known, and detailed descriptions can be found in the excellent accounts by Ranis (1970), Lockwood (1954, chaps. 5 and 10), and Oshima (1965). Land taxes decline in relative importance throughout the period from more than 50 percent of government revenues in 1887–93 to less than 15 percent by 1907–15. The decline as a share in GNP (table 7.7) is also precipituous over these three decades. Although income from public enterprises rises sharply, this source is unimportant until after 1906 and railroad nationalization. The main source of the secular increase in government revenues comes from the residual—what we label "consumption

Table 7.4

Meiji Government Revenues
(millions ¥, current prices)

Year	Land Taxes (1)	Income From Public Enterprises (2)	Consumption Taxes: Residual (3)	Total (4)
1887–1893	421 (50.1%)	58 (6.9%)	361 (143.0%)	840
1894–1906	992 (25.3%)	393 (10.0%)	2535 (64.7%)	3920
1907–1915	1062 (14.6%)	1252 (17.2%)	4981 (68.2%)	7295

Sources: Col. (1): revenues from real estate taxes from Hundred-Year Statistics of the Japanese Economy, p. 136, applying 50 percent increase for local surcharge. Assumes all real estate taxes are land taxes. Col. (2): income from public enterprises from LTES (Vol. 7), Tables 7b and 7d plus surplus of the national railroads from LTES (Vol. 7), Table 3. Missing years in LTES supplied by H. Moulton, Japan: An Economic and Financial Appraisal, p. 454. Col. (3): derived as a residual, col. (4) minus cols. (1) and (2). Col. (4): total government current revenues from LTES (Vol. 7), Tables 7b and 7d plus surplus of national railroads from LTES (Vol. 7), Table 3.

taxes." The label seems appropriate in view of the regressivity of th Meiji tax structure, its dependence on indirect taxation, and its avoidance of significant taxation on property income (Ranis 1970; Oshima 1965). Yet the wartime expenditures were hardly financed by current revenues alone. Between 1894 and 1908, the Meiji government deficit was large and, with few exceptions, increasing. Table 7.5 documents these debt operations and separates domestic from foreign borrowing. The foreign borrowing component includes indemnities (a "benefit" from military aggression); increased official specie holdings are subtracted from the series. Up to 1893, net domestic borrowing is insignificant—in fact, three of these years are ones of debt retirement financed from government surpluses. The same is true after 1906: net debt retirement and surpluses were typical from 1910 to 1914. From 1894 to 1905, government deficits were the order of the day, and in spite of large scale foreign financing in London and Paris, especially during the Russo-Japanese conflict, the burden on the domestic capital market was apparent. With the exception

Table 7.5

Meiji Debt Operations and Debt Service
(million ¥, current prices)

Period	Government Deficit (-) (1)	Domestic Borrowing (+) (2)	Foreign Borrowing (+) (3)	Domestic Debt Service (4)
1887–1893	23	-18	-5	131
1894–1906	-2174	937	1237	557
1907–1915	-153	-403	556	1079

Sources: Col. (1): government deficit from Table 7.4, col. (4) minus Table 7.3, col. (1). Col. (2): government surplus (- government deficit, col. (1)) minus foreign borrowing (col. (3)). Col. (3): net foreign borrowing equals increase in foreign debt plus indemnities (Hundred-Year Statistics of the Japanese Economy, p. 158) minus increased official specie holdings (derived from Hundred-Year Statistics of the Japanese Economy, pp. 169 and 192). Col. (4): national debt service (LTES (vol. 7), Table 146) minus foreign debt service (LTES (vol. 7) Table 7c).

of 1896, each of those years registered net domestic borrowings in the private capital market. The impact of these debt operations on the domestic capital market merits close attention.

Tables 7.6 and 7.8 yield evidence in quantifying the cost of Meiji military adventurism. First, an index of the impact of debt operations on the domestic capital market is presented. Domestic debt service is treated as a net transfer from private nonsavers to private savers. This may seem to be an extreme position, but the Meiji tax structure is known to have been highly regressive, and most students of the period feel that revenues can be treated as a consumption tax. Thus, as a first and exploratory approximation, debt servicing may be viewed as a transfer from low-income wage-earning consumers to high-income property-holding savers. The total impact on the domestic capital market is then the sum of retirements and (domestic) interest payments on government debt. Given a regressive tax structure favoring property income recipients in the extreme, this impact represents the ability of Meiji fiscal policy to augment the flow of investible funds available for private capital formation. Whether that potential flow is in fact entirely diverted to private capital formation

Table 7.6

Indices of Government Impact on Capital Formation and Private Savings
(millions ¥, current prices)

Year	Impact of Debt Operations on Domestic Capital Market (1)	Net Government Impact on Capital Formation (2)	New Government Railroad Investment (3)
1887	18	32	0
1888	14	28	0
1889	13	30	0
1890	17	39	25
1891	22	52	-4
1892	30	52	3
1893	35	67	2
1894	-48	-22	0
1895	-98	-73	2
1896	173	222	6
1897	-27	48	16
1898	-55	14	0
1899	-20	61	26
1900	-62	34	1
1901	-35	64	11
1902	-84	5	14
1903	-66	27	1
1904	-132	-79	3
1905	-68	2	0
1906	142	233	10
1907	64	234	26
1908	90	296	34
1909	121	278	47
1910	317	496	56
1911	206	433	84
1912	276	473	103
1913	219	417	83
1914	177	359	85
1915	12	165	69
1887–1893	149	300	26
1894–1906	-380	536	90
1907–1915	1482	3151	587

Sources: Col. (1): Domestic debt service (Table 7.5, col. (4)) minus domestic borrowing (Table 7.5, col. (2)). Col. (2): Impact of debt operations on domestic capital market, col. (1), plus government capital outlays (Table 7.3, col. (4)) plus subsidies to enterprises (Table 7.3, col. (5)). Col. (3): new government railroad investment from LTES (vol. 7), Table 3 and H. Moulton, *Japan: An Economic and Financial Appraisal*, p. 454.

Table 7.7

Government Revenue and Expenditure
Shares in GNP

Year	Total Expenditures	Military Expenditures	Capital Outlays	Land Tax	Consumption Taxes
1887	.171	.033	.018	.097	.068
1888	.172	.034	.018	.092	.067
1889	.172	.033	.020	.091	.072
1890	.145	.021	.019	.064	.049
1891	.124	.029	.032	.066	.063
1892	.125	.027	.021	.063	.067
1893	.124	.027	.022	.064	.066
1894	.174	.096	.021	.052	.055
1895	.223	.085	.019	.049	.061
1896	.167	.059	.039	.046	.082
1897	.213	.074	.048	.038	.074
1898	.174	.054	.031	.027	.069
1899	.274	.064	.042	.045	.094
1900	.206	.066	.044	.034	.100
1901	.192	.048	.042	.034	.104
1902	.253	.044	.041	.037	.125
1903	.199	.061	.037	.031	.105
1904	.333	.205	.021	.039	.110
1905	.404	.233	.030	.054	.147
1906	.306	.135	.027	.048	.145
1907	.262	.069	.047	.041	.145
1908	.270	.068	.062	.041	.153
1909	.252	.058	.047	.043	.164
1910	.283	.063	.057	.039	.178
1911	.244	.057	.060	.032	.174
1912	.211	.048	.045	.027	.151
1913	.200	.045	.044	.027	.148
1914	.216	.036	.042	.029	.148
1915	.191	.050	.037	.029	.148
1887–1893	.145	.029	.022	.075	.064
1894–1906	.249	.100	.034	.040	.103
1907–1915	.233	.055	.048	.033	.050

Source: GNP in current prices used in denominator from Hundred-Year Statistics of the Japanese Economy, p. 32. Government expenditure and revenue components can be found in Tables 7.3 to 7.6.

Table 7.8

Government Impact on Capital Formation and Savings Rates

Year	Impact of Debt Operations on Domestic Capital Market as Share in GNP (1)	Net Government Impact on Capital Formation as a Share in GNP (2)	Period	s*(t) (3)	Net Government Impact on Capital Formation as a Share in GNP (4)
1887	.027	.048			
1888	.021	.041			
1889	.019	.043			
1890	.018	.042			
1891	.026	.062			
1892	.033	.058	1884-1890	.122	.044
1893	.037	.072	1894-1900	.141	.027
1894	-.041	-.019	1901-1907	.123	.025
1895	-.080	-.060	1910-1916	.148	.106
1896	.140	.036			
1897	-.018	.032			
1898	-.027	.007			
1899	-.011	.035			
1900	-.031	.017			
1901	-.017	.030			
1902	-.044	.003			
1903	-.029	.012	1887-1898	na	.042
1904	-.056	-.034	1898-1905	na	.009
1905	-.031	.001	1905-1915	na	.090
1906	.053	.087			
1907	.021	.075			
1908	.029	.095			
1909	.040	.092			
1910	.108	.169			
1911	.058	.121			
1912	.067	.114	1887-1915	na	.054
1913	.052	.098			
1914	.045	.091			
1915	.003	.043			

Sources: See note to Table 7.7 for cols. (1) and (2). Col. (3) is from Appendix A, Table A.9. Col. (4) contains averages from col. (2).

is, of course, a separate issue. In any case, table 7.8 shows that Meiji debt operations augmented the investable resources in the private domestic capital market between 1887–93 and 1906–15. The conditions reversed markedly from 1894 to 1905. With the exception of the indemnity year 1896, this wartime period was one in which resources available for private capital accumulation were diminished. This does not imply coercive action. As long as government debt is being offered under conditions competitive with private debt, individual savers must have been quite willing to augment their portfolios with government debt. Furthermore, as a share in GNP, this impact was quite significant (table 7.8). The more relevant issue is the potential impact of Meiji fiscal action on capital formation (excluding military durables) as a share in GNP. This estimate is presented in table 7.8 (col. (2)) and figure 7.1. The figure shows what happens when government

FIGURE 7.1 NET GOVERNMENT IMPACT ON CAPITAL FORMATION AS A SHARE IN GNP (NGICF)

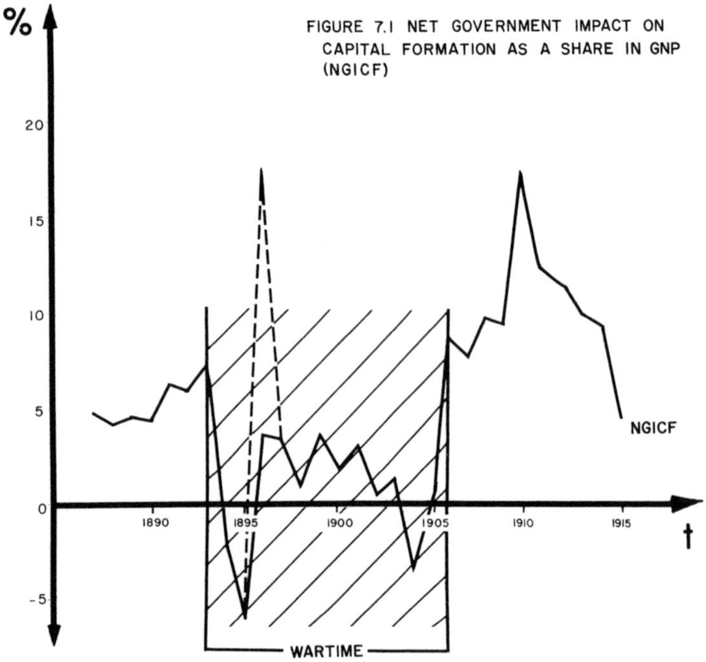

capital outlays are added to the impact of debt operations in the domestic capital market (plus subsidies to private enterprises). Our approach is apparently consistent with the now conventional position on the burden of the national debt, especially during wartime. The recent literature (Modigliani 1961; Bowen, Davis, and Kopf 1960; Diamond 1965) focuses on private capital formation foregone when governments induce potential investors to increase the share of government debt in their portfolios rather than in private debt which represents claims on "productive" assets, that is, private capital formation. In table 7.8 and figure 7.1 we have refined this accounting to include capital formation by Meiji governments, since some of the government debt issue surely financed social overhead investment during the period; in other words, some of the government debt issue represented a substitution of public for private capital accumulation.

From 1887 to 1893, the net government impact on capital formation as a share in GNP was 5.2 percent. The figure is 9.9 percent from 1906 to 1915. Compare these figures with that of the wartime years, 1894–1905: 1.7 percent. Perhaps we need search no farther for the causes of the investment "spurt" after 1905. While it appears that (public and private) capital formation rates were suppressed by fiscal policy during the wartime years, the opposite was true after 1904–5. The magnitude of the fluctuation is striking.

7.3. Military Adventurism and Investment Spurts: A Counterfactual

The issue we now confront is the cost of international military aggression on the Meiji economy. In terms of figure 7.1, we could ask the following question: If the government impact on capital formation as a share in GNP (NGICF) between 1893 and 1906 had followed a smooth, secular trend rise, rather than exhibiting a wartime drag, what would have been the influence on Meiji growth performance 1887–1915? This counterfactual raises technical difficulties. Although we have shown that Meiji military expenditures between 1894 and 1905 tended to diminish the share of investable resources available for productive capital formation, the figures presented in table 7.8 and figure 7.1 cannot be used directly to estimate capital formation foregone by wartime activity. There are at least two reasons for this. First, although the Meiji tax system was regressive, to assume it was completely regressive would be much too extreme; we would overestimate the impact on capital formation by simply adjusting the observed $s^*(t)$ by NGICF. Second, we have no firm evidence on the savings behavior of those who held government debt and received interest payment on those holdings. We pose instead an alternative counterfactual which should serve as a useful first approximation for the impact of the diminution in NGICF on capital formation during the wartime years. The counterfactual employs a simple device in evaluating the wartime drag on development: an alternative $s^*(t)$ series is introduced into our model of the Meiji economy. The experiment, labeled $s_u^*(t)$, adopts a relevant counterfactual, one suggested by Oshima.[6] The $s_u^*(t)$ series is derived by assuming that Meiji Japan could have maintained a peacetime strategy by holding the share of military outlays in GNP at the levels prevailing from 1887 to 1893. That share was just short of 3 percent. The difference between the actual share of military outlays in GNP, and the 3 percent, is then used to augment the savings rate. The difference between $s_u^*(t)$ and $s^*(t)$ provides an upper estimate of additional capital formation which could have been forthcoming in the absence of the "unusual" military commitments from 1887 to 1915. No doubt some of the resources released from military activity under peacetime conditions would have been used for consumption purposes. Indeed, many Japanese scholars have argued that external military victories were used to minimize the discontent at home generated by austere economic policies (Lockwood 1954, pp. 18–19; Oshima 1965). Oshima, believing that the causation ran in the opposite direction, advocates a view closer to ours. He thinks that the more rapid growth resulting from a peacetime strategy would have reduced the rural unrest which *contributed* to the militarism of the Meiji era (Oshima 1965, p. 381). Thus, some readers may choose to view the $s_u^*(t)$ series as an upper limit in evaluating the impact of war on Meiji development; our own position would lie close to $s_u^*(t)$. As a final qualification, our analysis makes no effort to evaluate the economic "benefits" associated with the victories over China and Russia.

The results of the counterfactual are presented in table 7.9. The growth rate in GNP (commodity output) per worker would have been raised by almost 0.5 percentage points under the "peacetime" counterfactual conditions: that is, growth rates for the period as a whole would have been raised from 3.1 to 3.6

Table 7.9

The Impact of Military Adventurism on Meiji Economic Growth: A "Peacetime" Counterfactual

Variable	"Actual" $s^*(t)$	Counterfactual $s^*_u(t)$
1. Index in 1915 (1887 = 100)		
Constant Price GNP	257	292
Industrial Employment Share	181	200
Industrial Output Share (Constant Price)	198	242
Real Wage	112	121
Real Earnings	191	208
Constant Price GNP per Worker	237	269
2. Growth in Constant Price GNP per Worker	3.13%	3.60%

Source: See text for description of the counterfactual experiment.

percent. This is one explicit estimate of the trade-off between economic growth and military adventurism, and a qualification to the slogan "Fukoku kyōhei"—a rich country, a strong army. By our accounting, GNP per worker in 1915 was six-sevenths of the GNP per worker which would have been achieved had a peacetime strategy been pursued. One cannot help but speculate what the result would have been had the wars been lost, as was the case in World War II. This counterfactual experiment with $s^*_u(t)$ confirms the wisdom of Lockwood's statement: "Significantly, the war which profited Japan the most was World War I, when she remained neutral in all but name. Had she again stayed on the side lines in World War II, she might once more have reaped fabulous gains" (Lockwood 1954, p. 578).

Our results suggest that the stress which Ohkawa and Rosovsky place on the interwar period must be qualified. They have emphasized the impressive growth performance of the Japanese economy *after* 1905–19, and have viewed the period 1905–19 as transitional to modern twentieth-century experience with the higher growth rates. According to the 1957 Ohkawa GNP estimates, upon which much of their earlier analysis is based, growth rates rose from 3.4 percent per annum during the period 1885/98–1905/19, to 3.9 percent during 1905/19–1919/31, and to 4.1 percent during 1919/31 to 1931/38 (Ohkawa and Rosovsky 1968, table 1–2, p. 10). By their accounting, the trend acceleration in Japan is primarily a post-World War I phenomenon. We disagree. Not only did we find evidence in chapter 6 of trend acceleration during the early Meiji period, but the $s_u^*(t)$ counterfactual suggests that the acceleration would have been even more marked had Japan avoided military conflict. Indeed, if the Ohkawa pre-1905/19 growth rates are raised by 0.5 percentage points—an upper estimate of the domestic expansion foregone by war (table 7.9), the growth performance prior to World War I would have been almost identical to that following the war. A key distinction between the late nineteenth-century aggregate growth experience and that of the pre-1938 twentieth-century experience is the lack of military adventurism. There is certainly a lesson for contemporary Asia in this: "The well-known militaristic . . . features of prewar Japanese society suggest that Japan's pattern of growth is more to be guarded against than emulated" (Lockwood 1954, p. viii).

Two issues remain. What was the impact of military expenditures on industrialization and real wages? Table 7.9 provides an incomplete assessment of these issues. Our model fails to yield a complete assessment, because Meiji fiscal policy enters only as an influence through $s^*(t)$ and thus on the relative importance of investment demand. While current military outlays tended to suppress private and public investment, they were composed primarily of demands for industrial goods. The counterfactual focuses only on the dynamic capital formation effects, and excludes the comparative static effects of a shift in current demands from agricultural commodities, which loomed large in Meiji households' budgets, to industrial commodities, which loomed large in government military outlays. While we find that the industrial employment share would have been some 10 percent higher, and the industrial output share some 22 percent higher, had peacetime conditions prevailed, the comparative static effects may have tended to dampen or reverse these dynamic effects. Much more research is necessary to assess fully the impact of military expenditures on Meiji industrialization.

There is considerable indirect evidence to support the view that military expenditures during the Meiji period had profound implications for the relatively slow "trickling down" of the gains from Japanese expansion to the common laborer in the form of improvements in workers' living standards. Chapter 9 will explore the real wage issue in detail. The counterfactual analysis presented here, however, has some bearing on the results. First, table 7.9 documents that military expenditures retarded growth in the Meiji economy and thus retarded improvement in real wage and earnings as well. Second, the comparative static impact of wartime demands must have reinforced these dynamic effects, for the increased military expenditures fostered a relative shift to industrial output. Industrial production was less labor-intensive, so that the comparative static effect must have tended to suppress the derived demand for labor and the real wage. The evidence presented in chapters 4 and 9 is consistent with this hypothesis since the upward trend in real wages is interrupted between 1893/97 and 1903/07. Furthermore, the analysis in chapter 10 documents a powerful impact of demand on real wages, earnings, and labor's share in Meiji Japan. Third, the regressive tax structure surely implied a deterioration in workers' living standards during the wartime period given the concomitant heavy tax burden. In summary, the slow improvement in workers' living standards during the Meiji period may have been explained as much by Japanese military imperialism as by the underlying structural characteristics of secular growth. Ashton's insight on the British Industrial Revolution seems applicable to Meiji Japan as well: "The misery and unrest which attended the Industrial Revolution in England during the early nineteenth century were not so much the product of the factory system as of the Napoleonic Wars."[7]

8

Demographic Change and Meiji Economic Development

8.1. Population and Japanese Economic Growth

It is ironic that while contemporary population pressure in the developing world is widely cited as possibly *the* critical constraint to economic progress, analysts of Meiji growth performance have conspicuously avoided almost any mention of demographic factors in Japanese development. This schizophrenia is illustrated by such statements as the one provided by the highly regarded Pearson Commission: "No other phenomenon casts a darker shadow over the prospects for international development than the staggering growth of population" (cited in World Bank 1972, p. 3). A recent World Bank report places a more specific, yet equally dismal quantitative dimension on the assertion: "Typically, if fertility is halved in a generation, by the end of that period per capita incomes can be 20% to 40% higher than if fertility had remained constant. The indicated benefits become more impressive as projections are extended into the future" (ibid., p. 15). If these estimates are correct, there is indeed cause for concern. Population growth in the developing countries approached 2.7 percent in the 1960s; in the developed world the figure was closer to 1.2 percent. The "population bonus" to the economic progress in the advanced countries, employing the World Bank predictions, must have been enormous.

Using the same reasoning, early Japanese growth should have been notably influenced by her demographic situation. On the eve of the Restoration, Japan was supporting population growth rates even lower than those in the advanced countries of today. The best estimates place the aggregate population growth rate in Meiji Japan at around .9 percent (Appendix B). Employing the contemporary quantitative estimates on the relation between aggregate population growth and the rate of economic progress, we would be led to conclude that the Japanese success in economic development was explained in large part by unique demographic conditions inherited from the past. For example, using the World Bank predictions, per capita income levels in one generation would be around 50 percent higher as a result of reducing population growth rates from 2.7 to .9 percent; the per-capita income levels could well be raised by 75 percent over a longer period of time. Do demographic factors therefore fully account for the "Japanese miracle?" Why have Japanese economic historians ignored, or at least notably underplayed, the role of population in Meiji economic development?

Possibly the Japanese economic historian is correct: Japanese demographic conditions, while unusual by contemporary standards, may not have exerted a significant quantitative impact on the rate of Meiji economic progress. Unfortunately, such a case has never been made; and even if it had, the interesting issue would be *why* such a historical result prevailed in contrast to the findings relating to contemporary developing countries. Alternatively, the Japanese economic historian may have been focusing attention on relatively unimportant determinants of Japanese economic progress (technical change and the character of demand and production) at the expense of the quantitatively most significant factor—the unusually low population growth rates.

This chapter will attempt to place the role of demographic factors in Japanese economic development in perspective. Section 8.2 reviews the key analytical arguments giving rise to concern with population pressures in the developing countries. These are then compared with the postulates underlying our dualistic model for Japan. Section 8.3 analyzes the results of an historical counterfactual: what would have been the nature of Japanese economic growth had she sustained the high population growth rates prevailing in the contemporary developing world? The result of this counterfactual provides a resolution of the apparent schizophrenic analysis of the role of demographic factors in contributing to Japanese economic growth and structural change.

8.2. Population and Economic Development: The Traditional Arguments

While there are numerous connections between population and economic growth, those relating to population's impact on the pace of aggregate development in low-income countries are summarized well by J. J. Spengler (1951, pp. 350–51):

> In sum, population growth operates in four ways to retard the betterment of man's material condition. First, it increases the pressure upon a nation's land and resource equipment. . . . Second, it tends to accentuate this pressure through time by accelerating the rate at which the store of . . . natural resources is used up. Third, it diminishes the rate at which capital can be accumulated, and this diminution is greatly accentuated when . . . potential capital is utilized in maintaining for a few years children who eventually die before they reach a productive age. Fourth, given the rate of capital formation, the rate at which the equipment of the labor force can be increased is reduced.

The first two factors relating to natural resource constraints have, with the exception of Malthusian accounts, received relatively little attention by economists. It has commonly been assumed in growth studies that the pace of technology would compensate for much of the diminishing returns exerted by population on a limited resource base. Representative of this view is the analysis by George Stigler (1951, p. 61), who has argued that "a larger economy should be more efficient than a small economy: this has been the standard view of economists since the one important disadvantage of a large economy, diminishing returns to natural resources, has proved to be unimportant." While this hypothesis may not be as applicable to the future, it seems to be a reasonably useful assumption when applied to many historical accounts of economic development, including those of Meiji Japan. This does not mean that the relatively slow growth of Japanese arable land has played an unimportant role in the rate of output growth. Indeed, chapter 11 demonstrates that the opposite has been the case: aggregate output-per-laborer levels would have been notably enhanced had Meiji Japan experienced a rate of land-resource expansion or an elastic land supply comparable to some contemporary developing economies. Rather, it means that the land-resource constraint itself engendered offsetting factors—increased savings, technical change biased toward conserving land—such that population's impact through the resource-constraint connection was substantially attenuated. Such a case is also made in chapter 11, where a detailed examination of technical change and population pressures in Meiji agricultural development is provided. Our attention here will focus only on the population impact as it relates to capital formation, savings rates, and aggregate output performance.

The analytical story is straightforward. Given an incremental capital-output ratio and an economywide savings rate, an increase in population growth rates will reduce by a like amount the sustainable rate of per capita income growth. This represents the "production" impact of increased population growth, where population expansion diminishes the amount of capital available for each laborer and thus his average productivity. But, as Spengler and the World Bank predictions have noted, population growth may also exert a long-run dynamic impact on capital accumulation through its impact on the rate of savings. This connection occurs, of course, if the savings rate itself is believed to be associated directly with the level of per capita income. In addition, income distribution and dependency rates may play a role:

> High fertility can depress private savings in two ways: (1) by reducing the volume of savings by individual families when such savings are an important component of the national total; (2) by increasing the proportion of national income that must accrue to non-savers.[1]

A similar critical connection is highlighted in the "population-trap" models of Leibenstein (1957) and Nelson (1956, pp. 894–908). In summary, the magnitude of population's negative impact on the pace of per capita output growth in the traditional economic analyses depends critically on the size of the incremental capital-output ratio, and on the impact of population growth on the rate of savings through average family size. Analysts are generally agreed that larger family sizes are associated with lower household savings rates in developing countries, although this impact may be substantially attenuated as economic development takes place.[2] It certainly seems evident that the high dependency rates associated with rapid population growth tend to increase government expenditures on current welfare, health, and education items rather than capital outlays.

8.3. Population Growth in a Model of Economic Dualism

The impact of population growth in our dualistic model is somewhat more complex than that found in the traditional analyses cited above. While increased population growth produces an initial reduction in the growth of the capital-labor ratio—the widely analyzed impact on production—secondary effects are engendered which partially offset this initial impact. Specifically, the relative return to labor declines as it becomes more abundant. This leads to a reduction in labor's share which, given a savings specification where capitalists and landlords are the higher (and, in our case, the only) savers in the economy, results in an increase in the economywide rate of savings and capital formation. The positive impact on capital accumulation therefore partially offsets the retarding influence of accelerated labor force growth on capital-labor ratio growth. As a result, the net impact of increased population growth on the economywide rate of per capita output expansion cannot be determined analytically in this model; the issue is an empirical one.[3]

8.4. Population Growth and Meiji Economic Development

The impact of population on Meiji economic development can be most vividly analyzed by the use of the following historical counterfactual: *What would have been the speed of Japanese economic growth had she sustained the high population growth rates prevailing in the contemporary developing world?* Since Meiji population growth was around one-third of that experienced in the contemporary low-income countries, in the counterfactual we have tripled the Japanese population parameter, yielding a simulated history of Japan which, in the following tables, is denoted "contemporary population pressure." These series are compared with the economic trends found in our basic model which are labeled as "actual" Japanese performance.[4] The difference between the actual and counterfactual experiments represents a quantitative assessment of the role of demographic factors in Meiji economic development.

The impact of population pressures on aggregate Meiji development and structural change are summarized in table 8.1.[5] A somewhat surprising result emerges: contemporary population pressure would have exerted a small effect on Meiji economic development. After one generation (1887–1915), the level of output per capita would have declined by only 7.7 percent, from an index of 229 to 211. This is a result far short of

Table 8.1

The Impact of Population Pressure on
Aggregate Meiji Economic Growth
(1887 = 100)

Year	Output per Capita		Urbanization		Industrialization	
	"Actual"	Counterfactual: Contemporary Population Pressure	"Actual"	Counterfactual: Contemporary Population Pressure	"Actual"	Counterfactual: Contemporary Population Pressure
1887	100.0	100.0	100.0	100.0	100.0	100.0
1891	111.0	109.8	111.3	109.9	112.2	110.9
1895	123.7	120.9	122.1	119.3	124.7	122.1
1899	138.5	133.8	132.7	128.7	137.2	133.4
1903	155.8	148.6	142.8	137.7	149.8	145.1
1907	176.2	166.2	152.8	146.8	162.5	156.9
1911	200.5	187.0	162.6	155.8	175.0	168.7
1915	229.0	211.2	171.9	164.4	187.6	180.7

the reduction which the World Bank would have predicted using models and numerical estimates thought applicable to the developing world. Similar results are found for two key measures of Meiji structural change: the urbanization level would have been lower by only 4.4 percent, and the industrial output level would have been reduced by even less (3.7 percent). The smaller-than-expected impact of population on aggregate economic growth and structural change can in part be explained by the low initial level of the Japanese labor force growth rate. That is, the rate of labor force growth is augmented by 0.58 percentage points in the counterfactual. Yet the World Bank predictions are most appropriately applied to the case where population growth rates decline in the order of 1.0 to 1.3 percent. Even so, our results take into account both the short-run impact and the long-run dynamic effects, where the expected negative impact of population would have been largely revealed. A World Bank prediction for our counterfactual applied to Meiji Japan would have yielded a decline in output-per-laborer levels in 1915 of around 15 to 20 percent; this compares with our figure of 7.7 percent. Thus, the magnitude of the discrepancy between the conventional predictions and those forthcoming from the counterfactual is still notable.[6]

A part of this discrepancy can be reconciled by examining the impact of population growth on capital formation rates. Recall from equation (6.1) that in our model

$$\frac{\dot{K}(t)}{K(t)} = \frac{I(t)}{K(t)} - \delta = [1-\alpha_L(t)]\bar{s}\left\{\frac{P(t)K(t)}{G(t)}\right\}^{-1} - \delta$$

where $G(t)$ is constant price gross national product, $[1 - \alpha_L(t)]$ the variable nonlabor income share, $K(t)$ the physical capital stock, $P(t)$ the relative price of capital goods, $\bar{s}$ the marginal savings rate out of nonlabor income, and δ the rate of depreciation. In the "traditional" analysis of population's impact on economic growth, analysts either assume that the capital stock growth rate is invariant to population pressures, or that the economywide savings rate *declines* in response to larger average family sizes. In our formulation, the economywide savings rate *rises,* due to the impact of population on the distribution of income $[1-\alpha_L(t)]$. In addition, the rate of capital accumulation may be augmented by the impact on the relative price of capital goods, and the physical capital-output ratio, $K(t)/G(t)$.

The trends in the capital accumulation rate and its determinants are summarized in table 8.2 for both the actual and counterfactual regimes. Contrary to the usual expectation, we find that population pressure increases the rate of capital accumulation. While the magnitude of population's impact on the capital accumulation rate is not great, it is clear that population pressures *stimulate* growth through its dynamic impact on capital formation. The capital stock index (1887 = 100) in 1915 is 319.5 in the actual regime while it is 329.7 in the counterfactual.

The explanation for this result is complex, and derives from the interaction of the several quite distinct forces listed above. First, and most important, the physical capital-output ratio in the counterfactual world of contemporary population pressure rises at a significantly lower rate. This is a straightforward reflection of the increase in aggregate output levels in response to the augmented labor force. Of course, labor's *average* productivity declines, due to the pressure of population on the capital-labor ratio. But the population expansion tends to diminish the capital-output ratio and increase the productivity of capital. These forces

Table 8.2

The Impact of Population Pressure on the Sources of Meiji Capital Accumulation Rates (1887 = 100)

Year	Capital Stock Level		Constant Price Capital-Output Ratio		Non-Labor Share		Relative Price of Industrial Goods	
	"Actual"	Counterfactual: Contemporary Population Pressure	"Actual"	Counterfactual: Contemporary Population Pressure	"Actual"	Counterfactual: Contemporary Population Pressure	"Actual"	Counterfactual: Contemporary Population Pressure
1887	100.0	100.0	100.0	100.0	100.0	100.0	100.0	100.0
1891	117.0	117.1	104.2	103.0	101.4	101.4	96.4	96.6
1895	137.3	137.6	108.5	106.3	102.6	102.2	92.0	92.5
1899	161.5	162.5	112.6	109.5	103.3	103.3	87.5	88.3
1903	190.6	192.7	116.9	112.9	104.3	105.8	82.6	83.6
1907	225.7	229.5	120.9	116.1	105.2	106.5	77.9	79.1
1911	268.2	274.5	124.8	119.2	105.7	107.2	73.3	74.6
1915	319.5	329.7	128.7	122.5	106.2	107.7	68.5	69.9

exert a *positive* stimulus on capital accumulation rates. The magnitude of this stimulus is significant. In the actual regime, the capital-output ratio rises from an index of 100 in 1887 to 128.7 in 1915; the ratio rises only to 122.5 in the counterfactual experiment.

A second positive stimulus of population on capital accumulation is exerted through the shift of aggregate income to property income recipients, and away from the high-consuming laborers. By 1915 the nonlabor income share had risen to an index of 107.7 in the counterfactual, as compared to 106.2 in the actual Meiji series.

Counteracting these two positive stimuli is the behavior of $P(t)$, the terms of trade. While the relative price of industrial goods tends to fall in our model as economic development takes place, population pressures tend to attenuate this reduction. Indeed, had labor force growth rates in Meiji Japan been higher, the capital-labor ratio would have been initially suppressed. This would have generated a lower price of labor services compared with both capital and land services. Since agriculture is more labor-intensive, the relative price of agricultural goods would fall and the relative price of industrial goods would rise. In the thirty years considered here, the long run decline in industrial goods' relative prices is somewhat less marked in the counterfactual experiment of population pressure than in the actual regime.

Our results show that population's impact in a dualistic model of the type we have employed to describe Meiji economic development is by no means straightforward. Demographic influences operating in a general equilibrium framework must capture the simultaneous impact of population on (1) shifting income shares, (2) changing capital productivities, and (3) variations in the sectoral terms of trade. Models which focus only on "dependency" effects and thus abstract from any of these general equilibrium influences may be masking important (and offsetting) demographic-economic interactions. To return to the question posed by our counterfactual, we conclude that the unusual demographic conditions inherited from Tokugawa Japan do *not* appear to explain the rate of Meiji economic progress. Possibly the Japanese economic historian's preoccupation with nondemographic determinants of Japanese economic growth represents a well-placed emphasis. On the other hand, given the results of this chapter, it is equally clear that this de-emphasis of demographic factors in explaining Japanese development has been based on factors little understood. We have provided at least some analytical and empirical justification for searching elsewhere to obtain lessons from the Japanese growth successes.

Any economist who takes the effort to classify contemporary developing economies by per capita growth performance and population expansion rates will find a *positive* correlation. Such exercises clearly show that other factors are far more critical than population growth, and the high rates of population growth may, at low income levels at least, be more the result of economic success. Our historical counterfactual reported in this chapter leads to somewhat stronger conclusions. *If we hold other factors constant,* considerably higher rates of population growth in Meiji Japan would have made very little difference to her development performance.

9

Real Wages, Labor Slack, and Labor Surplus

9.1. Labor Surplus and Japanese Historiography

The economic history of Meiji Japan has become a battlefield for testing competing theories of the dualistic economy. No area of inquiry has generated more debate than the appropriate description of pricing and supply conditions in the Japanese labor market. The key adversaries in this academic encounter have been J. C. H. Fei and G. Ranis, supporting the labor-surplus interpretation, and D. W. Jorgenson, defending the neoclassical model (for example, Fei and Ranis 1966; Jorgenson 1966). In some respects this debate has been unnecessary and unfortunate. Not only have the "tests" of the theories often been either misspecified or misinterpreted, but the tests have frequently failed to explore the full implications of the competing models. The elements underlying the appropriate choice of wage specification in the dualistic models of growth can be best understood if the key unresolved aspects of the labor-surplus/neoclassical controversy are examined in some detail.

Consider first the Jorgenson framework of dualistic development. Because of the specialized form of Jorgenson's neoclassical dual economy model, the labor-surplus adherents have not been convinced that conventional neoclassical theory is a useful way of viewing Meiji Japanese development. Any economic historian, no matter what his position in the debate, must surely agree that "labor slack" must play a prominent role in an analysis of Meiji history. Yet there is no such role to be found in Jorgenson's neoclassical model of the dual economy (Jorgenson 1961, 1967). That overt and sustained unemployment is not allowed in the model is unimportant, since it is not applicable to Meiji Japan (chapter 3). But, more to the point, "underemployment" has no place either. We find it useful to define "underemployment" as a situation on which labor utilization rates or intensity of annual labor effort responds with a very high elasticity to real wages. Since labor is homogeneous and unaugmented by "intensity" or "efficiency" in Jorgenson's model, labor slack in the form of underemployment is not a characteristic of his dualistic framework. This seems to us an area where Jorgenson's model could be greatly enriched. We have shown in chapter 3, and will show in the present chapter, that labor slack can be readily introduced into the neoclassical model. As a consequence, it should become evident that much of the debate has been between Fei-Ranis and Jorgenson rather than between classical and neoclassical interpretations of Meiji Japanese history.

There is another special characteristic of Jorgenson's model which weakens his tests utilizing Japanese economic history. Jorgenson assumes an owner-operator tenure status in agriculture. In fact, only 54 percent of Japanese agriculture was in that form of tenancy by 1914 (Ranis 1970, table 4, p. 44). Under these conditions, Jorgenson's theory of intersectoral migration ties together the real wage in manufacturing and the *average* productivity of labor in agriculture. Presumably, average labor productivity in agriculture is the appropriate opportunity cost to potential off-farm migrants in Jorgenson's model. Having made this assumption, he attempts to show that, because average labor productivity grows at impressive rates between 1878–82 and 1913–17, it must follow that real wages rose, which would vindicate his version of the neoclassical model (Jorgenson 1966, pp. 53–55). Unfortunately, no mention is made in his account of the relative stability of real wages throughout the economy during the Meiji period.[1]

The tests of the labor-surplus version are in similar straits. The key assumption of the labor-surplus model is an institutionally fixed wage until the "turning point," after which neoclassical conditions prevail and wages become flexible. Unfortunately for the adherents to the classical model, substantial short-run wage variability over the long swing (chapter 7) can be documented for the Meiji economy prior to 1914 (table 9.1). Furthermore, while the overwhelming econometric evidence presented in chapter 3 argues that neoclassical input pricing conditions prevailed in interwar Japanese agriculture, at least two adherents to the labor-surplus thesis place the turning point well past this period into the post World War II years. Finally, the classical economists cannot agree on the timing of the turning point itself: Fei and Ranis place it at the end of World War I, while Minami (1970*b*, p. 270) and Lewis favor the 1950s! This is a rather imprecise prediction for a key aspect of the classical model. The turning point or the "commercialization point" is crucial in the Fei-Ranis model since it delineates the economy's movement out of a regime of surplus labor and wage fixing and into a modern neoclassical stage of marginal productivity pricing. Recall that this point is reached when, as agricultural development takes place, labor's marginal productivity finally exceeds the subsistence or institutional wage and as a result the real wage becomes a variable (Fei and Ranis 1964, p. 202).

Minami's (1970*b*) research is the most sophisticated attempt to quantify the turning point in Japanese history. Utilizing a Cobb-Douglas production function, Minami estimates the marginal productivity of labor in agriculture for the period 1905–65. He then compares real wages and marginal productivity in agriculture and finds equality only after World War II (Minami 1970*a*, table 12, p. 66). We have already noted that Minami's results are at variance with the econometric studies by Hayami and others (see Akino and Hayami 1972, pp. 18–23 and the extensive references within). Nevertheless, it may prove useful to note two telling implications of Minami's research. First, between 1905 and 1937, Minami's ratio of wages to marginal labor productivity are surprisingly *stable*. We doubt very much that the classical model would predict this result; on the contrary, Minami's finding looks suspiciously like a confirmation of the neoclassical hypothesis. Second, there is a fundamental difficulty in Minami's approach to measurement: "Labor productivity should be measured in terms of labor hours or labor days. As we have no reliable statistics for working days covering both pre- and postwar periods, we must use man-years in our denominator" (Minami 1970*b*, p. 272). Minami's inability to deal with labor utilization and intensity of annual work effort by employing man-year indices represents a fundamental flaw in his empirical analysis.

The time is ripe for a reconciliation between the classical and neoclassical adherents. This reconciliation can be made by showing that the neoclassical dualistic model developed in chapter 3 replicates real wage stability up to World War I. It does so by explicitly confronting the issue of "labor slack."

9.2. Workers' Living Standards, Wages, and Earnings: Problems with Measurement

Three measurement issues arise when we compare the predictions of the dualistic models with Japanese real wage experience. First, what is the appropriate deflator for constructing a real wage index? Since farm products are the numeraire in our model, the correct deflator for us is a price index of agricultural commodities. If instead our interest were in workers' living standards, an index weighted by variable budget shares would be more appropriate. Given wide historical variations in commodity price relatives, the divergence between real wages and living standards may be quite significant. Indeed, Appendix A documents a small secular rise in the relative price of agricultural products up to World War I, while Ohkawa's figures indicate a gradual decline in the food expenditure share between 1885 and 1910, from 47.3 and 44.3 percent (Ohkawa 1972*c*, table 7, p. 18). Thus, deflating by food prices tends to understate the true improvement in workers' living standards. However, the differences between food price and cost of living movements are not likely to be large enough to make our real wage an unreliable proxy for the standard of living. For qualitative confirmation, one need only recall the rice riots of 1918, which eventually encouraged a governmental commitment to "cheap rice" and importation from Korea and Formosa (Sawada 1965, p. 344; Hayami 1971, p. 460). Surely this important episode in Japanese social history confirms the importance of food (rice) prices in the workers' cost-of-living index.

Second, for model-testing purposes, care must be taken to identify an occupation or sectoral employment in which the "labor input" has been relatively homogeneous over long historical time periods. Alternatively, measurement devices must be employed which minimize age, sex, and skill compositional changes for the labor input whose wage is being analyzed over time. For the most part, the *LTES* wage data presented in Appendix A and analyzed in section 9.4 meet these requirements. The problem is far less serious during most of the three decades following the mid 1880s than in subsequent years. Aggregation problems become increasingly thorny with the appearance of wage dualism after World War I. Taira (1970), Watanabe (1968, pp. 122–34), Levine (1965, pp. 637–41), and Noda (1972, pp. 25–26) all seem to agree that wage differentials *within* industry do not really begin to appear until the growth in large-scale enterprise after 1905 or 1910. Of course, it could be argued that these wage differentials reflect labor market imperfections rather than skill differentials; in any case, they are relatively unimportant even as late as 1914. For 1909, Watanabe shows that manufacturing wages were identical between establishments employing between five and nine workers and those employing a thousand or more. By comparison, in 1951 the large enterprises were paying 2.7 times that of the smaller (Watanabe 1968, table 4–5, p. 125).

Third, and most important: Is the dualistic model making historical predictions about *wages paid* or *annual wage costs incurred* by the firm in producing an annual output? This issue appears to have been responsible for some of the confusion in the historical literature. Tussing (1970, p. 200) has noted that in Tokugawa times, as in agrarian economies everywhere, most manufacturing and service activities were produced by rural households engaged to varying degrees in cereal cultivation. Even though agricultural labor demand is highly seasonal, the daily wage is most often used as a measure of historical movements in labor's service flow price. Moreover, whether for agriculture, manufacturing, or construction, the daily wage is normally quoted at seasonal peak periods: "The activities in which the greater part of Meiji economic growth took place were largely rural occupations, depending for their labor supply on the slack time of the farm population, at least in the earlier years. . . . The main reservoir of labor supply was the excess (off-peak) labor time of the farm household" (ibid., p. 201). The estimated annual average wage paid in agriculture may therefore be a very poor index of labor costs to the extent that seasonal peak quotations are employed. Were the bias (the difference between daily and annual labor utilization) constant over time, such daily or peak season indices would still be useful in identifying real wage trends. Unfortunately for the historian, the bias is *not* constant. Tussing and others have emphasized that labor utilization increased during the year as Meiji development progressed. As a result, while peak seasonal wages grossly overstate average annual wage costs early in the period, the overstatement diminishes over time. Thus, agricultural wage series generally tend to bias downwards the measured increase in real wages during the process of Modern Economic Growth.

9.3. Wage Stability and Early Industrialization: An Alternative View

Meiji Japanese growth appears to be characterized by an increase in the average intensity of labor utilization during the full calendar year. This assertion is certainly confirmed by the experience of other nations embarking on early industrialization, past or present. Multiple cropping, field preparation, farm-formed capital accumulation, weeding, pest control, and the maintenance of a more extensive stock of durable inputs are all activities increasingly typical of a dynamic agricultural sector. The implication of this broadening of labor activities is a more intensive utilization of agricultural labor throughout the year. In addition, early industrial development in the form of small-scale enterprise presents the opportunity for off-farm employment during agricultural slack periods. Umemura's research brings strong support to the importance of "side" occupations in early Japanese development. In the early Meiji period, one-third of all the gainfully employed in Yamanashi and Yamagata Prefectures had side occupations (Umemura 1970, pp. 190–92). By 1920, the relative importance of "side-job" workers in manufacturing and service sectors had declined sharply, but they *rose* as a share in agriculture. In short, as industrialization took place: (i) labor worked longer during the year in nonagriculture; (ii) labor shifted into sectoral employments where the labor utilization rates had traditionally been less seasonal; and (iii) although the gainfully employed full-time workers in agriculture declined, the decline was in part offset by a rise in the use of part-time workers. All of this evidence suggests that real earnings are likely to rise far more than real wages in early stages of industrialization. Indeed, the case can be made even stronger. The real wage during seasonal peak periods may very well remain stable over protracted periods of early industrialization, but the annual earnings of labor may still rise significantly over time.

Our neoclassical dualistic model captures this characterization of Meiji Japanese growth by the simple expedient of incorporating labor-augmenting technical progress in the labor supply function. Recall from chapter 3 that technical progress in our model is consistent with a reading of Japanese history whereby technical change (in the Hicksian sense) was labor-using in agriculture while it was labor-saving in industry. More to the point, our labor-augmenting technical change specification yields two distinct wage rates. The first is an *efficiency wage,* which abstracts from labor's variable utilization rate as development takes place. This wage is payment to an efficiency labor unit and is best expressed by the quoted historical wage rates. The second is an *annual earnings index,* which, in our terminology, is the payment to labor embodying "efficiency improvement." We find it useful to interpret this rate of efficiency improvement, λ_L, as in part a measure of increased labor utilization. Thus, we view the annual earnings index as explicitly including *both* the impact of increased annual labor utilization *and* the wage rate.

Having made these distinctions, we are now in a position to confront the key analytical issue of this chapter. Is historical stability in the real wage a unique property of labor-surplus framework under conditions of Modern Economic Growth? If models? Can such stability be encountered in the neoclassical real wage stability is indeed typically observed in early stages of industrialization, is it necessary to construct a special model of institutional wage-setting to explain it? It has been shown elsewhere (Kelley, Williamson, and Cheetham 1972*b*, chap. 3) that the growth in (efficiency) wages in a dualistic model similar to the one used in this book, but excluding land, is given by

$$\frac{\dot{w}(t)}{w(t)} = \alpha_2 \frac{\dot{\omega}(t)}{\omega(t)},$$

where α_2 is the nonlabor share in agriculture and $\omega(t)$ is the economywide efficiency wage-rental ratio. That is, $\omega(t)$ is the ratio of efficiency wages to rates of return to efficiency capital. The efficiency wage-rental ratio is governed by the historical behavior of the efficiency-augmented capital-labor ratio:

$$\omega(t) = \psi[k(t)] = \psi\left[\frac{x(t)K(t)}{y(t)L(t)}\right] = \psi\left[\frac{x(t)}{y(t)}k^*(t)\right].$$

Even during industrial revolutions, or Modern Economic Growth, the labor-augmenting bias may be sufficiently powerful to produce only negligible increases in the *efficiency* capital-labor ratio, $k(t)$. At the same time the *observed* (physical) capital-labor ratio, $k^*(t)$, may be rising markedly. That is, although a crude index of the ratio of employed capital to labor stocks (of "gainfully employed") may be rising over time, the efficiency-utilization rate-adjusted capital-labor ratio may be growing at a much slower rate, if at all. Both $w(t)$ and $\omega(t)$ could exhibit relative stability while living standards and annual earnings, $y(t)w(t)$, could be increasing sharply. Under these conditions, the classical economist would observe historical increases in the crude capital-labor ratio and stable real wages, a set of predictions fully consistent with the labor surplus framework. But it would be erroneous to conclude that the economy must necessarily have been characterized by institutional wage-setting and "labor surplus," since a neoclassical model such as ours is capable of similar predictions. It becomes apparent that tests relating to the veracity of the neoclassical and classical models must account carefully both for the definitions of factor returns and, more importantly, for the possibility that a generalized neoclassical model may also generate wage stability.

9.4. Wages, Earnings, and Labor Slack: The Meiji Performance

Four historical real wage series are displayed in Tables 9.1 and 9.2. Three of these are revised indices reported in *LTES* while the fourth (table 9.2) is a real daily wage for female operatives in silk-reeling for Yamanashi Prefecture. This latter series was developed by Tussing and is especially attractive for our purposes, aggregation problems being largely absent. That is, female operatives in small-scale silk reeling underwent little skill improvement over time.[2] Each of these series exhibit similar cyclical movement and, with the exception of common labor, exhibit a very mild secular improvement in real wages of about 10 percent between the 1880s and 1910. The model is remark-

Table 9.1 Wages in Meiji Japan

Period	Real Wages: w(t)			Model
	Male Day Labor: Agriculture	Daily Wage: Common Labor	Male Wage: Manufacturing	
1885-89	100.0	100.0	100.0	100.0
1888-92	92.7	92.3	88.4	100.6
1893-97	88.8	96.3	82.5	101.6
1898-02	100.6	113.2	95.5	103.1
1903-07	94.9	109.9	94.0	104.6
1908-12	106.2	128.7	109.6	107.3

Source: Five year moving averages of cols. (6), (7) and (8), Appendix A, Table A.2.

ably accurate in predicting this very slow secular improvement: the predicted $w(t)$ in table 9.1 rises by slightly more than 7 percent over the same period. We could certainly debate whether the historical data exhibits "stability" given the wide cyclical variance associated with long swings in early Japanese development and the mild secular rise to 1910. Fei and Ranis (1964, p. 264) choose to interpret this performance as evidence of wage stability: "The virtual constancy before and rapid rise of the real wage after approximately 1918 is rather startling. We thus

Table 9.2 Wages and Earnings in Meiji Japanese Silk-Reeling

Period	Wages: w(t)		Earnings: y(t)w(t)	
	Japan	Model	Japan	Model
1885-87	100	100	100	100
1888-92	102	101	110	107
1893-97	122	102	130	118
1898-02	108	103	128	132
1903-07	109	105	133	148
1908-11	113	108	176	171

Source: Appendix A, Table A.2, averages for the years indicated.

have rather conclusive evidence in corroboration of our theoretical framework." Whatever the interpretation, it seems clear that wage "stability" is hardly the exclusive property of the labor-surplus model. Our neoclassical model predicts wage stability as well.

A more useful interpretation is that real wages do rise both in fact and in the simulation, but only moderately before World War I. This wage performance seems all the more striking when it is recalled (chapter 6) that gross national product per worker is growing at 1.7 percent per annum and commodity output per worker at 2.8 percent per annum over the same period. These figures do not, however, imply little improvement in living standards during early stages of Modern Economic Growth. Nor do they imply, as a consequence, major changes in functional income distribution away from labor.

Tussing's estimates of the real daily wage and real annual earnings for female operatives in silk-reeling are presented in table 9.2. Note the large discrepancy between real annual earnings and real wage behavior. While real wages rose by only 13 percent from 1885–87 to 1908–11, real annual earnings of female operatives rose by 76 percent! This corresponds to an average annual rate of growth of 2.4 percent, not far below the rate of 2.8 percent reported in chapter 6 for commodity output per worker. An almost identical result is forthcoming from the simulation which predicts an 8 percent rise in wages and a 71 percent rise in annual earnings over the same twenty-five years. Once again the correspondence is remarkable, supporting the plausibility of our neoclassical paradigm of Japanese progress. In short, "labor slack" in the Meiji economy may not be best described by surplus labor and institutional wage fixing. Instead, while "the incomes of the common people rose substantially [during the Meiji era] . . . the Japanese did it mostly by working longer and working harder" (Tussing 1970, p. 220). In the simulated economy, real *earnings* improve dramatically as they did in Japanese economic history. It is inconsequential that we label the trends as "efficiency improvements" in labor while Tussing calls them "more intensive labor utilization." The implications are far reaching in both cases.

One obvious implication is that the coincidence of wage stability and rapid productivity growth does *not* necessarily imply a massive income redistribution and thus a sharp rise in savings rates. The share of labor *earnings* in total income may have been far more stable. While this interpretation is consistent with the Ohkawa-Rosovsky estimates of national savings rates over the period (chapter 6), the labor-surplus model is not. Presumably the Fei-Ranis model would have difficulty reconciling stable wages with the very moderate rise in aggregate savings rates up to 1905–10. Indeed, the key progenitor to accelerating rates of capital formation in the labor surplus model is the relative increase in the profit share. The underlying source of the increased profit share in that framework is the postulated wage stability. Yet the revised Ohkawa-Rosovsky savings rates do not reflect major increases during the period prior to 1905–10, suggesting a notable qualification to the classical position which is based on pronounced shifts in the distribution of income.

9.5. Some Qualifications and a Counterfactual Experiment

It should be emphasized that we do not view our dualistic model as a competitor either to Jorgenson's model or to the labor-surplus formulation. Rather, ours restates in a more general manner the neoclassical model, which appears to be consistent with Japanese historical evidence. Stable wages are *assumed* to prevail in the labor surplus "phase" of the Fei-Ranis-Lewis models. The problem for them is to identify changes in institutional arrangements moving the economy from the labor surplus to the commercialization phase. Stage theories of any sort have always presented analytic difficulties to the theorist, although it is the great strength of the modern labor-surplus models that the movement from one phase to another—the "turning point"—is explained endogenously. Nevertheless, the labor-surplus advocates still have had difficulty in identifying the turning point in Japanese economic history; indeed, the Minami and the Fei-Ranis dating differs by almost forty years!

In our dualistic model, stable wages are determined *endogenously* rather than imposed by an arbitrary factor-pricing scheme. We are faced with a different but equally difficult problem: an explanation of the magnitude of the exogenously determined labor-augmenting bias. The term "magnitude" is to be emphasized here. While a labor-augmenting interpretation of Meiji

Japanese and contemporary Asian development appears to be generally accepted (chapter 3), why should the rate of labor-augmentation have been just sufficient to yield real wage stability during early phases of Modern Economic Growth? Furthermore, does the nature of the bias change after World War I so that real wages and real earnings grow more alike thereafter? If so, why? Does the marked increase in labor utilization rates during the Meiji period subside after 1915? If it does, how do we explain the retardation?

Based on the recent research by Ezaki and Jorgenson, it does seem possible that an "epochal" shift in the bias took place sometime during the interwar period, perhaps related to a concomitant development in the capital goods sector and a diminished reliance on imported technology. An examination of post-World War II Japan by Watanabe and others has shown that very little of the impressive rates of total factor productivity growth can be explained by improved labor quality or utilization. In fact, for the thirteen years 1951–64 as a whole, the labor "quality" index, $y(t)$ in our terminology, rises by only 1.5 to 3.3 percent.[3] Ezaki and Jorgenson confirm this result (Ezaki and Jorgenson 1972, pp. 64–74). Thus the bias for the period 1951–68 is the *reverse* of that assumed for the Meiji period: while we estimate (Appendix B) $\lambda_L = 1.7\ \lambda_K$ for the Meiji period, Ezaki and Jorgenson estimate $\lambda_K = 3.2\ \lambda_L$ for the 1960s. This striking contrast suggests a useful counterfactual experiment: *What would have been the behavior of real wages in Meiji Japan had the capital-augmenting bias of the post World War II years prevailed rather than the heavy labor-augmenting bias that in fact took place?* Table 9.3 reports this counterfactual experiment while holding all other parameters constant, and maintaining the same overall sectoral rates of total factor productivity growth (at least initially in the late 1880s). The results confirm the arguments presented earlier in this chapter: real wages would have grown more than twice as fast had the post-World War II bias prevailed in the Meiji period.

We are somewhat surprised that the impact on real wages in the counterfactual experiment is not more pronounced. This result casts some doubt on the quantitative importance of the labor-saving bias in industry during the Meiji period on labor absorption rates. Johnston (1970, p. 75) has argued:

Japan's own experience following World War I suggests some of the reasons why the labor absorption problems facing contemporary developing countries are more difficult than those that prevailed during the Meiji era. The slowing down of the rate of growth of non-farm employment in Japan during the 1920's and early 1930's was the result of increasing emphasis on capital-intensive investment by the large-scale modern sector together with circumstances that discouraged the expansion of smaller firms in the semi-modern sector.

Table 9.3 Real Wages in Meiji Japan: "Actual" Labor-Augmenting Bias and "Counterfactual" Capital-Augmenting Bias

Year	Real Wages: w(t)	
	"Actual"	Counterfactual
1887	100.0	100.0
1890	100.6	101.2
1895	101.6	103.5
1900	103.1	106.7
1905	104.6	110.4
1910	107.3	115.7

Note: The "actual" wage series is produced by the model when $\lambda_L = .0194$ and $\lambda_K = .0114$, reported in Table 10.1. The "Counterfactual" wage series is produced by the model when $\lambda_L = .0094$ and $\lambda_K = .0283$.

Johnston's argument can be interpreted to mean that the bias shifted toward greater labor saving after World War I. This position could be debated,[4] but it is the implication that interest us. If the "labor absorption" problems of the interwar Meiji economy can be explained by a change in the bias of technical progress, then it surely follows that labor absorption rates in manufacturing during the pre-World War I period would have also been influenced by the bias. Table 9.4 documents no such influence. The rate of growth of industrial employment would have been very little different had the Meiji economy enjoyed the capital-augmenting bias typical of the post-World War II period. The explanation of rapid rates of labor absorption in manufacturing during the Meiji period must lie elsewhere. Chapters 10 and 11 will offer alternative explanations of the labor absorption performance during Japan's early phases of Modern Economic Growth.

Table 9.4 Industrial Employment Indices in Meiji Japan: "Actual" Labor-Augmenting Bias and "Counterfactual" Capital-Augmenting Bias

Year	Industrial Labor Force: $L_1(t)$	
	"Actual"	"Counterfactual"
1887	15.00	15.00
1890	16.43	16.15
1895	18.74	18.16
1900	21.07	20.41
1905	23.34	22.81
1910	25.68	25.52

10

The Pace of Meiji Industrialization and the Role of Demand

10.1 The Sources of Industrialization

10.1.1. An Overview

Japan's rapid industrialization during the Meiji period is well known. Table 10.1 indicates that the share of industrial output

Table 10.1

Measures of Industrialization in Meiji Japan, 1887-1915

Year	Industrial Output Share	Agricultural Output Share
1887	0.229	0.771
1891	0.249	0.751
1895	0.289	0.711
1899	0.332	0.668
1903	0.334	0.666
1907	0.415	0.585
1911	0.449	0.551
1915	0.493	0.507

Note: Shares in total commodity output in 1934-36 prices. Appendix A, Table A.7.

in total commodity output (1934–36 prices) increases from about 23 percent in 1887 to 50 percent by 1915. Japanese economic historians commonly emphasize the industrialization experience after 1905 and on the eve of the World War I hostilities. True, a large part of the industrial expansion up to 1905 is in "traditional" activities (e.g., silk manufactures) and the bulk of industrial value added is produced in small-scale establishments. Yet these characteristics of early Meiji industrialization do not in any way detract from the measured magnitude of the employment and output shift away from agriculture as early as the mid 1880s. The evidence presented in table 10.1 is not consistent with the thesis that the majority of the "structural transformation" before World War I occurs after the Russo-Japanese War, with the appearance of large-scale manufacturing enterprise-producing Western industrial commodities. Ohkawa and Rosovsky have perhaps been somewhat overzealous in identifying this second phase as the "big spurt" period of industrialization (Ohkawa and Rosovsky 1960, pp. 43–67; Hayami and Ruttan 1971, p. 221). The data suggest instead a consistently rapid industrialization performance beginning with the 1880s. (In chapter 11 we shall focus at length on the unusual fact that *absolute* employment levels in Meiji agriculture begin a decline in the 1880s.)

We do not deny the existence of an *acceleration* in the rate of industrialization after 1903–7. Accelerating rates of industrialization are, of course, to be expected, given the accelerating rates of capital accumulation and output per capita cited in chapter 6. Chapter 7 also showed how the return to peacetime conditions after the Russo-Japanese War contributed still further to the rapid rates of capital formation late in the period. We have argued elsewhere that accelerating rates of industrialization can be expected from dualistic models *even* if the rate of capital accumulation is stable (Kelley, Williamson, and Cheetham 1972*b*, chaps. 3 and 4). Such acceleration is apparent in table 10.1.[1] If the pre-World War I period is divided into two overlapping phases, 1887–1903 and 1899–1915, the increase in the industrial output share is 10.5 percentage points in the first period and 16.1 in the second. Nevertheless, the industrialization performance displayed in table 10.1 documents rapid structural change throughout the period.

The magnitude of the Japanese achievement can best be appreciated by comparison with other nations. Japan was shifting out of agricultural production at a rate of −0.94 percent per annum up to 1915. This rate far exceeds that of the rest of the world economy. Among countries with per capita incomes similar to Meiji Japan, according to a study by Chenery and Taylor, a rate of decline in agriculture's share of about −0.44 percent per annum would have been predicted. Kuznets's cross-sectional sample implies a rate of −0.46 percent per annum.[2] Similar results are forthcoming from Kuznets's time series of nine Western countries from 1850 to 1895:[3] on average, their agricultural output share declines at a rate of −0.52 percent per annum. Clearly, Meiji Japan was undergoing very rapid industrialization by the standards of either the late nineteenth century or the post-World War II developing economies. For roughly the same rate of aggregate per capita income growth, Meiji Japan was industrializing at *twice* the "typical" rate.

How do we explain this unusually rapid pace of industrialization? Economists have long emphasized the role of consumption demand in industrial revolutions and its importance to growth and structural change, but analytical attention to its role has been limited. There appear to be two conflicting views concerning the nature and extent of its influence, and they have their counterparts in Japanese historiography. Support for the view that consumption demand plays an important role in the process of growth and structural change has come mainly from empirical studies which have established the existence of different expenditure and income elasticities for food and nonfood commodities. It has been argued that the presence of these Engel effects not only causes a shift in the industrial origin of production but also induces higher levels of productivity and output (Houthakker 1960; Kuznets 1966; Kelley 1969).

Challenges to the prime role of demand have developed on many fronts. Conventional trade theory, at least under "small country" conditions, concludes that supply factors dominate and that domestic demand only serves to determine passively the volume of trade and plays no role in determining patterns of specialization, the trade mix, and output distribution. Empirical studies on the sources of industrialization have also concluded that supply factors occupy the central role. Chenery (1960), for example, shows that changes in relative factor supplies associated with growth cause systematic shifts in comparative advantage, and that these shifts account for the majority of the observed changes in industrial structure.

The role of demand and supply factors in explaining industrialization can be successfully appraised only in a model in which both elements possess meaningful specification. Our dualistic model of the Meiji economy may furnish one such framework. This chapter utilizes our closed economy model to explore the role of demand in accounting for the unusual rate of industrialization in Meiji Japan.

10.1.2. The Revisionist View of Demand in Japanese Industrialization

The role of demand in Japanese economic development is still being debated. On the one hand, demand has been highlighted as an important factor in a recent hypothesis by Kaneda (1970, pp. 426–27):

> As agricultural production grew slowly . . . people's food consumption habits also changed slowly. There was no pressing and persistent demand for large quantities of imported foods. . . . Nor were there sudden, pressing demands . . . for a radical transformation of agriculture in order to cultivate and raise "preferred" foods. . . . Indeed, the terms of trade between agricultural products and other products seems to have remained more or less stable during the early period. . . . Just as it can be said that a rapid development of agricultural production "contributes" to the development of an entire economy, it can be stated that . . . slow changes in food consumption patterns "contributed" to high rates of savings and "enabled" the Japanese to purchase . . . products of the domestic industrial sector.

Kaneda is suggesting that demand conditions in Meiji Japan were somewhat unique and may account for the equally unusual rapidity of industrialization up to 1915. This interpretation is consistent with evidence presented by Kuznets (1968, p. 223), who has noted the sharp decline in the food share in consumer expenditures from 75 percent in 1879–83 to less than 40 percent in 1934–38. Although Engel effects have always been appreciated by economists, it is the unusual *magnitude* of the decline in the Japanese food expenditure share which is impressive:

> The striking part of the story of Japanese food consumption is that the elasticities estimated, .2 and .4, are rather low at this meager level of per capita income. In recent years "accepted" values of income elasticit[ies] for food have ranged around .6 and .7 for poor countries whose per capita income is roughly comparable to Japan's in the 1920's. [Kaneda 1970, p. 407]

The implication is clear: unusually low demand elasticities for foodstuffs may account for the uncommonly high rate of industrialization up to the interwar period. In Professor Kuznets's words, and in his typically careful analysis:

> If the food proportions in the 1930's . . . , relative to per capita consumption, were moderate in Japan, compared with other industrialized countries, then the very high shares of food in the early periods are all the more intriguing. More careful scrutiny of the estimates . . . would probably provide information germane to the explanation of Japan's economic growth. [Kuznets 1968, p. 231]

The revisionists have taken a very different approach. The most articulate spokesmen have been Chenery, Shishido, and Watanabe (1962). Taking secular movements in commodity price relatives, aggregate output, and primary inputs as given, Chenery and his associates decompose trends in the structure of Japanese output. Utilizing an explicit input-output framework and examining *expost* data, they conclude that

> Although industrialization is usually attributed to changes in demand, more than 75 percent of Japan's industrial growth is traceable to changes in supply conditions. These include substitution of domestic for imported manufactured goods, substitution of manufactured goods for primary products, and other technological changes. [Ibid., p. 129]

No doubt supply conditions are crucial, but the Chenery study does not confront the issue raised by Kaneda, Kuznets, and others: To what extent can demand conditions account for the *unusual* industrialization performance of Japan? Supply conditions play a critical role even in an economy closed to trade, but this hardly excludes a demand influence. Unless we are prepared to accept the "small country" international trade assumption, demand parameters will enter into our accounting of industrialization. The question is: how do they enter and what was their quantitative impact?

10.2. A Fresh Look at Demand in Meiji Growth

Considerable debate has taken place over the measured income elasticity of demand for foods during the Meiji period. The range of estimates, displayed in table 10.2, is wide indeed. Time series estimates (which fail to control for relative price effects)

Table 10.2

Estimates of Income Elasticities for Foodstuffs

Products	Source	Years Covered	Income or Expenditure Elasticity
	Time Series		
Agricultural Food Products Available for Consumption (Nakamura-Noda Estimates)	Kaneda (1970)	1878-1922	0.18
Agricultural Food Products Available for Consumption (Yamada-Noda Estimates)	Kaneda (1970)	1878-1922	0.39
Rice Available for Consumption (Yamada Estimates)	Kaneda (1970)	1878-1922	0.21
Agricultural Food Products	Noda (1956)	1878-1921	0.63
Agricultural Food Products	Noda (1963)	1878-1917	0.59
Starchy Staple Foods	Nakayama (1958)	1878-1922	0.38
Food Products	Shinohara (1972)	1877-1936	0.71
Food Products	Kaneda (1970)	1911-1940	0.35
	Cross Section		
Food Products	Kaneda (1970)	1921	0.49
Food Products	Kaneda (1970)	1926-27	0.39
Food Products	Kaneda (1970)	1931-32	0.35
Food Products	Kaneda (1970)	1935-36	0.33

Sources: With the exception of M. Shinohara, "Personal Consumption Expenditures," p. 8, all estimates are listed in H. Kaneda, "Long-Term Changes in Food Consumption," pp. 404-5 and 413.

range between 0.18 and 0.71. The most recent is by Shinohara whose estimate of 0.71 lies close to those estimated for other less developed economies at per capita income levels similar to Meiji Japan (Houthakker 1957; Clark and Haswell 1964; Kelley 1969). As we indicated in the previous section, Kaneda and others have argued with considerable merit that the elasticity lies between 0.2 and 0.4. The evidence surveyed from both time series and cross section in table 10.2 supports Kaneda's position (Kaneda 1970). Because of the lack of resolution to the debate, we decided (Appendix B) to utilize the "upper" estimate by

Kaneda ($\eta = 0.39$) which is closest to Shinohara's estimates and those of contemporary developing economies. Note, however, that under this assumption our model predicts a somewhat lower rate of industrialization than that implied by the *LTES* data (see chapter 4). While the constant price industrial output share in total commodity output rises by 26.4 percentage points (1887–1915), the model predicts a rise of 21.3 percentage points. Perhaps this disparity can be explained by the relatively high income elasticity of demand for food assumed in the model.

Lower demand elasticities for foodstuffs imply a downward pressure on the relative price of agricultural products and a stimulus to industrial consumer goods' output expansion. Yet Kaneda is apparently appealing to more than this simple comparative static result. He is also emphasizing a *dynamic* effect since "slow changes in food consumption patterns 'contributed' to high rates of savings" (ibid., p. 426). Meiji industrialization would have received a twofold stimulus from the asserted relatively low demand elasticities for foodstuffs. Kaneda's underlying model, which generates these second-order dynamic effects, is not made explicit, however; and thus the mechanism by which the higher savings rates are induced is not immediately obvious. Nevertheless, his predictions are certainly fulfilled in our dualistic model. Given the linear expenditure system postulated in chapter 3, the income elasticity of demand for foodstuffs ($i = 2$) can be written as

$$\eta_{2j}(t) = \frac{\beta_{2j}y(t)w_j(t)}{\beta_{2j}y(t)w_j(t) + [1-\beta_{2j}]\gamma},$$

where j denotes the sector of residence and $y(t)w(t)$ represents household labor earnings. This elasticity is always less than unity since $[1-\beta_{2j}]$ is always positive.[4] A decline in β_{2j} (equivalent to a *rise* in β_{1j}) implies a lower demand elasticity for foodstuffs. Thus, the impact of a "uniquely low" $\eta_{2j}(t)$ for Meiji Japan can be analyzed in the same fashion as an exogenous shift in tastes.

Consider a shift in preference out of foodstuffs and into manufactured consumer goods (e.g., an increase in β_{11} and β_{12}). The increase in β_{1j} leads to a short-run expansion in industrial output and a rise in the price of industrial goods. It also leads to a fall in the wage-rental ratio as a result of the adjustment to the excess demand for industrial goods in which capital is used more intensively than labor compared to the traditional agricultural sector. That is, an increase in β_{1j} would tend to reinforce the observed stability in real wages over time. This shift in tastes toward urban goods tends to diminish labor's share in national income. To the extent that this redistribution of income fosters higher savings rates, then more rapid rates of capital accumulation would be obtained. This, in turn, would foster more rapid rates of industrialization. In summary, *given that Meiji Japan had unusually low demand elasticities for foodstuffs, there is a presumption that these unique demand conditions were in part responsible for the unusually rapid rates of observed industrialization.*

10.3. Consumer Demand and Meiji Industrialization

10.3.1. A Counterfactual

The theoretical impact of demand parameters on growth in the dualistic economy has been explored at length elsewhere (Cheetham, Kelley and Williamson 1972). Our interest here is solely on the likely *magnitude* of these effects in the case of Meiji Japan. Table 10.3 reports the quantitative impact of these effects. This table documents the percentage response of a given variable to a once-over (1 percent) change in demand parameters. These figures should be viewed as structural elasticities. A 1 percent rise in β_{11} involves a change from the assumed value of 0.459 to 0.46359. This marginal change implies only a small

Table 10.3

Elasticities of Key Economic Variables to a Marginal Increase in β_{11} and β_{12}, 1895-1915

Variable	Year 1895	1905	1915
1. Industrial Employment Share	0.940	0.989	1.019
2. Industrial Output Share in Constant Prices	0.478	0.384	0.288
3. Labor's Income Share	-0.259	-0.311	-0.349
4. Aggregate Savings Rate	0.177	0.200	0.217
5. Per Capita Income Growth in Constant Prices	0.122	0.150	0.193

Note: The elasticities are computed by comparing the percentage change in a given variable at a given point in time to a once-and-for-all one percent $d\beta_{11}$ (= $-d\beta_{21}$) and $d\beta_{12}$(= $-d\beta_{22}$). See text.

decline (rise) in the urban household food (nonfood) expenditure elasticity in 1885. Table 10.3 indicates that this parametric change, in conjunction with a similar change in β_{12}, would have raised the urban employment share in 1895 from 0.183 to 0.185. Since Kaneda feels that the true income elasticities for foodstuffs in Japan were approximately one-third to one-half of the conventionally estimated elasticities (ranging between 0.2-0.4 rather than 0.6-0.7), the structural elasticities reported in table 10.3 can be interpreted to represent a potent effect on Meiji Japanese growth and structure. The quality of the income elasticity estimates from historical data being still in doubt, we prefer to focus on the structural elasticities reported in table 10.3 rather than estimate the total impact of a departure of Japan from "normal" demand conditions.

Consider first our indices of economic structure, lines 1 and 2. The industrial employment share and the industrial output share are both sensitive to demand conditions, and their sensitivity is explained primarily by "first-order" comparative static effects. Note that these elasticities do not rise consistently between 1895 and 1915. This result implies a small positive dynamic effect on the Meiji economy. The source of the positive dynamic effect lies with a redistribution of income away from labor (line 3), and a resulting positive impact on savings rates (line 4). But the increased demand for industrial goods tends to raise their relative price (not shown in table 10.3). The rate of capital stock growth is only marginally affected, and thus per capita income growth is *not* significantly changed (line 5), although the impact is positive and increasing.

These findings are only provisional, but they lend support to Professor Kuznets's admonition that "the role of consumption in the mechanism of economic growth is too important to be neglected (Kuznets 1968, p. 197). If our analysis is roughly accurate, the impact of demand is more a comparative static one explaining in part the uniquely rapid industrialization experience of Meiji Japan. The dynamic effects stressed by Kaneda appear to be relatively small.

10.3.2. Summary and Some Qualifications

We conclude that demand conditions *may* have played an important role in Meiji development. This conclusion must be qualified for three reasons. First, the discussion in section 10.2 underscores the tentative aspect of the demand-parameter estimates and, in particular, the estimates of the income elasticity of demand for food. Our conclusion on the role of demand will be most strongly supported if the low income elasticities for food estimated by Kaneda and others are vindicated in future research. This chapter demonstrates the importance of such empirical research. By using an explicit general equilibrium model and posing demand counterfactuals, we have found that much of what is unique about Meiji industrialization may be attributed to demand conditions.

Even this conclusion is subject to a second qualification. If we were to depart from the "closed economy" tradition in analyzing early Japanese development, different results would be forthcoming. In the "small country" model, domestic demand would play no role—domestic demand conditions would only serve to determine the *volume* of trade flows. But this, too, is an unrealistically extreme view. After all, Japan did not satisfy the small-country assumptions but rather faced price-inelastic demands for her traditional exports and price-inelastic supplies for rice imports. An appropriate trade specification could well yield results similar to those predicted in the present chapter. Low income elasticities of demand for food (imports) would have held down the deterioration in Japan's external terms of trade. Whichever foreign trade characterization seems correct, we have the realities of historical inflexibilities in exchange rates to consider. Given the fixed exchange standard, higher income elasticities for food and thus imports would have fostered continual balance of payments crises which, without long-term capital inflows, would surely have inhibited Meiji Japanese expansion. Another way of stating the results of this chapter, then, is that Meiji Japan may have avoided the persistent payments deficits typical of contemporary developing economies since income elasticities of food (import consumption) demand were so low. The potential *quantitative* effect may have been highly significant.

Note that this chapter has been written without reference to "market surplus" or "turning points." They do not play the role reserved for them in the Fei-Ranis-Lewis labor-surplus models. Since capital formation is financed only through profits generated in the industrial sector in the classical model, and since real wages in terms of agricultural goods are assumed stable as well, then the ability of the farm sector to inhibit the rise in food prices by an elastic expansion in marketable surplus becomes crucial. The real wage is not fixed in our dualistic model, nor are industrial profits the only source of savings. Yet a critical key to both our dualistic model and that of the labor-surplus framework is the distribution of income. Demand may play a *potential* role in influencing current output structure, current income distribution, and the future growth performance via the savings effort. On that point, we are in agreement. In empirical fact, however, we find those dynamic effects to be of marginal importance.

A third qualification should be added in conclusion. In chapter 7 we devoted considerable space to documenting the importance of the Japanese military commitment to Meiji growth performance. Although we explored the impact of wartime conditions on capital formation and thus on industrialization in the long run, nowhere did we explore the possible quantitative impact of military expenditures on short-run industrialization experience. Military outlays between 1893 and 1907 were heavily dominated by industrial goods. Surely the importance of government expenditures in aggregate demand should be included in any accounting of rapid Meiji industrialization.

How can we account for the impact of government demand? Our model is not sufficiently detailed to supply an unambiguous answer to this question. However, any future attempt to do so must take account of the evidence presented in chapter 7, which shows an inverse relation between government military and social overhead expenditures. Nevertheless, the analysis contained in this chapter does supply insight into the potential impact of Meiji fiscal policy on the "uniquely" rapid rates of industrialization achieved before 1915. Table 10.3 illustrates that shifts in demand parameters favoring industrial goods (that is, military expenditures) would have had powerful comparative static effects fostering industrialization.

Finally, we return to a theme which runs throughout this book. The gains of Modern Economic Growth in Japan were not slow in trickling down to the common worker. While in chapter 9 we documented stability in real wages during this period of rapid national development, we also showed that real labor earnings rose substantially, albeit at a slower rate than did per capita GNP. Thus the Japanese worker benefited substantially during the development process, but he still received the smaller share of the increasing gains from growth. Contemporary development economists feel that the structure of final demand plays a prominent role in accounting for the adverse distributional and employment conditions associated with development in the post-World War II period. Furthermore, the demand structure is felt to be closely related to government policy. Import substitution policy represents a notable example. A comparable case is presented by the Meiji military commitment discussed in chapter 7. Given the capital-intensive character of industry supplying military goods and given the importance of military expenditures in Meiji final demand after 1894, it should come as no surprise that real wage improvement was suppressed and labor's share diminished. The sensitivity of these distributional variables to final demand parameters has been given a quantitative dimension in table 10.3. The more than doubling of military expenditures in GNP after 1894 is equivalent to a rise in β_{11} and β_{12} in our model from 0.459 to 0.510. The elasticities displayed in table 10.3 refer to changes in β_{11} and β_{12} from 0.459 to only 0.464. It follows that the increased military expenditures after 1894 would have had an impact on real wages and income distribution far in excess of the elasticities displayed in table 10.3. Indeed, we estimate that real wages were reduced some 25 to 30 percent by the effects of wartime expenditures from 1894 to 1905. This is only a crude estimate, but it indicates the importance of Meiji expenditure policy on income distribution and standards of living during this phase of Modern Economic Growth.

11

Agriculture and Meiji Economic Development

11.1 A Revisionist View of Meiji Agricultural Development

11.1.1. Rumbles in the Ricefields: The Data Debate

In chapter 6, we reviewed the debate over aggregate Meiji growth performance. Based on the earlier Ohkawa estimates, the rate of agricultural productivity expansion was "miraculous" indeed. Agricultural production was thought to have expanded at a rate of 2.5 percent per annum, almost three times the rate of population growth. This performance was all the more remarkable since the agricultural labor force was *contracting* during the same period (Nakamura 1966, p. 140). The combination of these two historical events implied a sustained productivity growth performance in agriculture bordering on the astounding: 2.6 percent per annum.[1] Attempts to account for this unusual development performance have relied heavily on productivity improvements through the use of new technologies, seeds, and biochemical developments. Indeed, a reading of the earlier literature gives the impression that Meiji Japan raised agricultural productivity with little resource cost, by the judicial use of "slack" in existing resource utilization and by the contraction of the wide gap between average practice and best practice, a gap generated by the peculiar institutional restrictions of the Tokugawa period.

In 1965, Professor James Nakamura lent his voice to the earlier minority critics, most notably Professor Oshima (Nakamura 1966; Oshima 1953, 1958). Nakamura asserted that official agricultural output statistics were particularly understated in early years, yielding spurious high growth rates. Ohkawa's group was aware of the downward bias embodied in the early Meiji official statistics, but the extent of the bias was not fully understood until the appearance of the new *LTES* estimates reported in Appendix A. We hope that they supply a resolution of the debate.

The quantitative impact of the revision on conventional views of Meiji Japanese agriculture is summarized and defended in an excellent paper by Hayami and Yamada (1970). Their findings are reported in tables 11.1 and 11.2. For the period 1878–1922, output growth rates are reduced from 2.4 to 2.0 percent per annum. The downward revision is even more marked for the period ending in 1902: the rate is diminished from 2.8 to 1.8 percent. Labor productivity and yield growth rates show comparable adjustments. The revised *LTES* data diminish the extent of the Japanese agricultural miracle. Moreover, the revised

Table 11.1

Growth in Agricultural Output and Productivity: Meiji Japan, 1878-1922

Estimate	1878-1882 to 1898-1902	1898-1902 to 1918-1922	1878-1882 to 1918-1922
Production			
LTES Gross	1.8	2.1	2.0
Net	2.0	1.8	1.9
Official Gross	2.8	2.1	2.4
Net	2.7	1.6	2.2
Labor Productivity			
LTES Gross	2.0	2.2	2.1
Net	2.2	1.9	1.9
Official Gross	3.0	2.2	2.5
Net	2.5	1.7	2.3
Yields			
LTES Gross	1.2	1.5	1.4
Net	1.4	1.2	1.3
Official Gross	2.2	1.5	1.8
Net	2.1	1.0	1.7

Source: Y. Hayami and S. Yamada, "Agricultural Productivity at the Beginning of Industrialization," Table 2, p. 110.

Table 11.2

Rice Yields and Man-Land Ratios: Meiji Japan and Contemporary Asia

Observation	Rice yields per unit of acre planted: Paddy (ton/ha.)	Rice yields per unit of acre planted: Brown Rice (koku/tan)	Arable Land per Farm Worker (ha./worker)
Japan, 1878-82			
Official	2.36	1.20	0.326
LTES	2.53	1.29	0.334
Japan, 1918-22			
Official	3.79	1.93	0.433
LTES	3.79	1.93	0.433
Monsoon Asia, 1953-62			
Philippines	1.17	-	1.310
India	1.36	-	1.280
Thailand	1.38	-	0.770
Pakistan	1.44	-	1.720
Burma	1.49	-	1.740
Ceylon	1.57	-	0.910
Indonesia	1.74	-	0.750
Malaya	2.24	-	1.760

Source: Y. Hayami and S. Yamada, "Agricultural Productivity at the Beginning of Industrialization," Table K, p. 108.

figures suggest an acceleration in output and productivity growth which was not apparent in the earlier estimates.

In spite of the reduction in growth rates, an impressive achievement is documented nevertheless. Labor productivity growth rates in agriculture around 2 percent per annum over four decades would (and does) generate envy on the part of planners in contemporary Asia.

In short, these revised *LTES* estimates hardly dispel the view that the Japanese "model" is one of *concurrent* growth in agriculture with the remainder of the economy. The prerequisite thesis, on the other hand, *appears* to be damaged by the revised data.

Since the terms "prerequisite" and "concurrent" growth are used so often by historians of agricultural development, perhaps some discussion of their meaning might be warranted at this point. The prerequisite thesis is based upon Western experience and it argues that "an agricultural revolution and a subsequent rise in agricultural productivity" are necessary prerequisites for the initial spurt of industrialization (Hayami and Yamada 1970, p. 105; Kelley and Williamson 1971, pp. 733 and 771–73). The concurrent growth thesis is viewed by many as a competitor. It asserts that rapid growth in agricultural productivity occurred simultaneously with, but not before, industrialization. There is no reason why these theses need be mutually exclusive. Nevertheless, it is of some interest to inquire whether initial agricultural productivity levels were "high" at the start of the Restoration, and whether the Tokugawa period was one of rapid productivity growth. True, rice yields per hectare in early Meiji Japan were 1.5 to 2 times higher than the levels which prevailed in Monsoon Asia during the 1950s. Yet *labor* productivities in the 1950s in, say, India and Pakistan, were considerably above Meiji Japan in the 1870s: Pakistan was three times higher and India twice as large.[2] Since we certainly would not classify either of these two developing nations as having undergone a "prerequisite" agricultural revolution before World War II, early Meiji Japan might be considered as failing to meet that criterion as well.

But perhaps this interpretation of the prerequisite thesis is much too narrow. Indeed, we shall argue below that the productivity levels prevailing at the time of the Restoration are a very poor index of the contributions of the earlier period to the subsequent Meiji growth.

11.1.2. The Tokugawa Heritage and the Lessons of History

The revised *LTES* data can be viewed as a *confirmation* of the importance of the Tokugawa heritage and the relevance of the prerequisite thesis. At first glance, this statement would appear to be inconsistent with the evidence just reviewed. There we argued that farm labor productivities were no higher in early Meiji Japan than in modern India or Pakistan. But the Tokugawa heritage entailed far more than simply the low average labor productivities prevailing in the 1870s. The revised *LTES* data imply a very high rate of total-factor productivity growth (TFPG) ranging between 1.2 and 1.3 percent per annum up to World War I (Appendixes A and B). How is this impressive TFPG to be explained? Is it related to the Tokugawa inheritance?

The old view of Tokugawa Japan was one of stagnation, implying a sharp break with the Meiji reforms in the 1870s. Nakamura estimates that yields per *tan* probably rose by some 23 percent from the late 17th century.[3] T. C. Smith (1959, pp. 83, 118, 130, and 134) has emphasized the rapid development of rural industrial and commercial activity during the early 19th century. The evidence has led Nakamura and others to attribute a more positive role to Tokugawa performance:

> Much of the groundwork for growth had been laid before modern industrialization began. These included the development of a national transportation and communications system, a national market, banking institutions, and an entrepreneurial spirit; the achievement of national unity and a remarkably high literacy; and the maintenance of independence from foreign domination. [Nakamura 1966, p. 16; see also Ishikawa 1963, pp. 114–22; Bronfenbrener 1961; Patrick 1961; Ogura 1963]

This is an impressive list, but its ingredients are much too vague. Hayami and Yamada have translated these ingredients into a more precise and quantifiable hypothesis. They are able to cacount for the rapid rates of TFPG in agriculture from 1878 to the stagnation in the 1920s by use of a diffusion model. Defining s_t as the actual shift and u_t as the potential shift in the aggregate production function, they describe the diffusion of agricultural technologies by

$$s_{t+1} - s_t = \lambda_t \, (u_t - s_t)$$

where $0 \leq \lambda_t \leq 1$ is the rate of diffusion:

> Over the preceding 300 years of the Tokugawa period, agricultural techniques advanced slowly in raising *u*. As T. Smith has pointed out, by the end of the Tokugawa period several advanced techniques were already practiced in various districts in the nation. But the restraints of the feudal system had suppressed the diffusion of new techniques. . . . Under the feudal system, peasants were bound to the land. . . . Neither were they free to choose what crops to plant, nor to

> choose what varieties of seeds to sow. . . . Though feudal lords were anxious to raise agricultural productivity within their territories, in many cases they prohibited the export of the improved techniques. . . . It is not difficult to imagine how such institutional restraints suppressed λ . . . [diffusion] had been so low that the discrepancy between u and s had widened cumulatively. Abolition of such feudal restraints at the Meiji restoration . . . brought a jump in λ . . . [resulting] in a rapid increase in s. [Hayami and Yamada 1968, pp. 143–44; see also Hayami 1971, pp. 454–60]

This rapid diffusion of new seed varieties after the Restoration was dependent upon two crucial inputs inherited from the Tokugawa period: the high level of farm literacy and the availability of irrigation facilities (Taira 1971; Tang 1963, pp. 27–41 and 91–99).

These Tokugawa bequests, in conjunction with the average- versus best-practice gap in seed varieties, made the Meiji period's "green revolution" rapid even when compared to contemporary standards. The high level of literacy in the 1870s is well known. Perhaps less well known is the social overhead capital in irrigation facilities in the 1870s. In contrast to contemporary Asia, even at the start of the Meiji Restoration almost all of the paddy fields in Japan were irrigated, and the majority of land was in paddy. These irrigation systems were built by communal labor under encouragement of Tokugawa lords. "The fact that no statistics have ever been collected on the irrigated area is consistent with the fact that in Japan 'paddy field' and 'irrigated field' have been regarded as identical. Construction of drainage facilities has been the primary objective in land improvement projects in [Meiji] Japan (Hayami and Ruttan 1971, p. 200).

11.1.3. The New View of Meiji Agricultural Development
The "old" view of Meiji agricultural development is consistent with policy toward agriculture in the 1950s in most developing economies. The emphasis by Ranis (1970; see also Fei and Ranis 1966) and others has been on the land tax revision (1873–76) and the subsequent "squeeze agriculture" policy. In the 1880s "the government shifted to a strategy of agricultural development which emphasized raising yields of traditional food staples—above all, rice" (Hayami 1972, p. 23). This period of

Meiji Noho (Meiji Agricultural Methods) was based on seed improvement and, most importantly, the supply of purchased working and fixed capital inputs to agriculture. The agricultural investment commitment was instrumental in increasing domestic rice supplies. As will be shown (section 11.2.2), about half of the observed rapid labor productivity growth in Meiji agriculture can be "accounted for" by capital formation in agriculture.

This view of agricultural development through the use of key purchased industrial inputs is very different from that embodied in the conventional dualistic models constructed by Lewis (1954), Fei-Ranis (1964), and Jorgenson (1961). It is now the dominant view supported by the writings of Hayami, Ruttan, Schultz, Yamada, and Ohkawa. The old view of Meiji agricultural development was one in which purchased industrial inputs played no notable role in the agricultural sector. Agricultural productivity development was seen as exogenously determined and the industrialization effort stood or fell on the parameters describing population growth and TFPG. The new view emphasizes the *resource cost* of agricultural development, the high "pay-off" to the introduction of purchased industrial inputs[4] (fertilizer, farm machinery, modern irrigation, etc.) in agriculture, and an even greater role for the two-way interdependence of agricultural-industrial development. As a result of this more recent research, we took considerable care in chapter 3 to embed the "new view" of agricultural development in our general equilibrium model of Meiji development.

11.2. Model Predictions and History: Sources of Agricultural Progress

11.2.1. Key Variables in Meiji Agricultural Performance

In chapter 4 we explored the plausibility of our general equilibrium model at length. We suggested broad conformity between the Meiji quantitative record and the predictions generated by the dualistic model. It may be useful at this point to examine the conformity in the agricultural sector in greater detail. We have seen, for example, that the *LTES* data document the following growth rates in agricultural labor productivity (table 2.1, "Gross output"): from 1878/82 to 1898/1902, 2.0 percent; from 1898/1902 to 1918/22, 2.2 percent; and from

1878/82 to 1918/22, 2.1 percent. The model predicts remarkably similar performance and even captures the mild acceleration in growth rates (table 11.7A): from 1887 to 1903, 2.19 percent; from 1899 to 1915, 2.37 percent; and from 1887 to 1915, 2.28 percent. What were the movements in hectare yield, employment, sectoral productivity gaps, and input prices associated with this marked expansion?

Table 11.3 reports yields per hectare for both Meiji Japan

Table 11.3

Yields Per Hectare, 1887-1915

Year	Yields Per Hectare (1887 = 100.0)	
	Model	Japan
1887	100.0	100.0
1888-92	103.5	103.0
1893-97	111.3	103.0
1898-02	119.9	113.1
1903-07	129.8	120.5
1908-12	137.6	128.3
1913-17	148.2	140.4

Source: Five-year averages from S. Yamada and Y. Hayami, "Agriculture," Appendix Table C, p. 26 where 1887 = 100.0 in the average of 1883-87 and 1888-92.

and the model. Yields rise by about 40 percent from 1887 to World War I. They increase at a slightly more rapid rate in the model, and furthermore, cyclic movements appearing in the historical series are not replicated. Nevertheless, the overall empirical correspondence bodes well for our general equilibrium characterization of Meiji development.

Earlier in this book (chapters 9 and 10) we stressed a notable feature of Meiji agricultural development: the "gainfully employed" agricultural workforce declines in absolute numbers from the mid-1880s. This pattern is almost unique in national historical accounts at similar levels of development. For example, "the absolute decline in the number of the agricultural workforce in many European countries is a relatively recent phenomenon which began only in the 1920's" (Umemura 1970, p.

186). The counterfactual analysis in section 3 attempts to identify the causes of this unique aspect of Meiji development. Note that the model almost exactly reproduces the extent of the decline up to World War I.

The model also does well in capturing the oft-noted appearance of an increasing "productivity gap" between Meiji agriculture and the remainder of the commodity-producing economy. Much has been made in Japanese historiography of the labor productivity gap and it has been cited often as evidence of "differential structure" (Watanabe 1968; Ohkawa and Rosovsky 1968). This characteristic of development is pervasive and is often erroneously cited as evidence of a "lagging" or "backward" sector which places a drag on national development. Regional disparities in per capita income and labor productivity frequently increase during Modern Economic Growth as well (Williamson 1965). One can hardly characterize Meiji Japanese agriculture as lagging or stagnant! However, in spite of rapid rates of TFPG and impressive increases in the use of purchased inputs, gaps in productivity appear nonetheless (table 11.4). The moral of the story is that labor productivity gaps are possi-

Table 11.4

Agricultural Labor Force and Labor Productivity Gaps, 1887-1915
(1887 = 100)

Year	Labor Force: L_2		Productivity Gap: $Q_1/L_1 \div Q_2/L_2$	
	Model	Japan	Model	Japan
1887	100.0	100.0	100.0	100.0
1891	99.2	99.2	102.8	94.4
1895	98.4	98.2	106.6	104.1
1899	97.5	98.5	110.7	118.4
1903	96.8	98.1	115.6	111.9
1907	96.1	97.3	120.8	151.1
1911	95.4	97.1	126.3	164.1
1915	94.7	94.5	132.9	166.6

Source: The agricultural labor force and productivity data are taken from Appendix A, Tables A.6 and A.8. The productivity measures are in 1934-36 prices.

ble, indeed inevitable, even in a neoclassical model which postulates no factor market imperfections. Sectoral differences in capital-intensity and production parameters are sufficient to generate the result. Table 11.4 shows that the model faithfully reproduces the increaing labor productivity gap throughout the period. Furthermore, the *extent* of the rise is almost exactly replicated up to 1903. In the subsequent decade, while the model predicts a mild acceleration in the growth of the gap, the *LTES* data document an abrupt change, most of which is centered on 1903–7. This discontinuity, along with other evidence, has lead Ohkawa and Rosovsky to date 1905 as the end of one phase of Japanese development and the start of another. Indeed, we found in chapter 7 that after the Russo-Japanese War, the Meiji government competed less vigorously in the domestic capital market for scarce investment resources to finance military adventurism. This permitted the savings rates in the private sector to return to the secular trend interrupted in the mid-1890s. Yet much of these military outlays were replaced by government capital expenditures on social overhead capital outside of agriculture. One could therefore view the period from the early 1890s to 1905 as one in which all sectors, including agriculture, were starved for investment resources. After 1905, industry is favored while agriculture continues to develop under a "squeeze agriculture" policy. This view is confirmed by the dating of Ohkawa and Rosovsky who suggest a structural change somewhere early in the twentieth century:

> During Phase I [1886–1919] the wage rate and productivity increases in both sectors were more or less parallel until around 1905 whereas differentials widened [thereafter]. . . . We have called this phenomenon the creation of a *differential structure*. . . . In contrast to this, until around the Russo-Japanese War, Phase I is marked by a relatively homogeneous structure which characterizes the initial process of concurrent growth between the traditional and modern sectors. [Ohkawa 1970, p. 32]

Our model with stable parameters fails to reproduce the magnitude of the productivity gap shift. Note that it is not agriculture's performance that produces this result, but a development spurt elsewhere in the economy. This conclusion follows from the evidence reviewed above, documenting a close conformity between

LTES and model movements in agricultural productivity from 1903 to 1915. It is also consistent with our analysis in chapter 7 of wartime expenditures and subsequent peacetime spurts.

The labor-surplus interpretation of development relies heavily on terms of trade movements in analyzing Meiji Japanese growth. For example, Fei and Ranis (1964, chap. 10) argue that the "turning point" can be forestalled and growth inhibited by a rise in the relative price of agricultural commodities. The mechanism is simple enough. Given a fixed institutional wage in terms of agricultural ("wage") goods, a rise in the price of foodstuffs implies an increase in the real wage facing industrial firms. As a result, labor absorption rates in industry diminish, profits are suppressed, capital accumulation curtailed, and the development effort forestalled. In short, a rise in the relative price of farm products signals the breakdown in the economic transformation leading to sustained growth in the labor-surplus models. The Japanese economic historian has placed considerable stress on the relative price of rice in his accounts (see section 11.1.3 above). The consensus seems to be that "whether 'impressive' or not, the rate of expansion of farm output was 'sufficient.' Apart from the rice riots of 1918, there seems to be no evidence that food shortages hampered industrial expansion" (Johnston 1970, p. 59). We disagree. Table 11.5 documents a secular decline (rise) in industrial (agricultural) price relatives from 1887 to 1911. The wartime conditions of 1915, on the eve of the rice riots, fail to fully offset this secular trend.[5] While the model predicts a decline in the relative price of industrial goods from an 1887 base of 100 to 73.3 by 1911, the *LTES* data show the relative price falling to 77.6 in the same year. True, much of the historical decline takes place very early in the period while the model predicts a smooth decline over time. But the evidence unambiguously confirms the model's prediction: in spite of unusually rapid productivity growth in agriculture and an absence of population pressure, the relative price of agricultural products rises over time.[6]

The new view of Meiji Japanese agricultural development does not stress resource slack in accounting for agriculture's performance, but instead emphasizes purchased inputs, external resource demands, and the role of factor input prices in inducing new land-saving technologies. This is consistent with Hayami's and

Table 11.5

Terms of Trade and Key Agricultural Purchased Input Prices, 1887-1915

Year	Terms of Trade: $P(t) = P_1(t)/P_2(t)$ Model	Japan	Year	Purchased Input Prices: Japan Fertilizer: P_F	Machinery: P_M	P_M/P_F
1887	100.0	100.0	1885	100.0	100.0	100.0
1891	96.4	85.4	1890	99.7	97.6	97.9
1895	92.0	81.6	1895	117.2	99.8	85.2
1899	87.5	82.4	1900	141.7	127.7	90.1
1903	82.6	83.3	1905	139.5	139.2	99.8
1907	77.9	87.4	1910	134.5	148.1	110.1
1911	73.3	77.6	1915	134.5	155.0	115.2
1915	68.5	93.3				

Sources: The terms of trade are taken from Appendix A, Table A.1, col. (6), and represent a five-year moving average of the annual observation. The remaining price series are taken from Y. Hayami and V. Ruttan, Agricultural Development, Table C-3, p. 342. Fertilizer prices are from J23 and are five-year averages. Machinery prices are from J21, refer to farm machinery, and are five-year averages.

Ruttan's position that relative input price movements explain much of Meiji agriculture's induced *bias* in technical change, while the relative price of output (compared to inputs) explains much of the *rate*. Hayami and Ruttan (1971, p. 133) make the following prediction on the historical behavior of input prices in Meiji agriculture:

> In Japan, the labor supply has been more elastic than the land supply. With the increased demand for farm products in the course of economic development, the price of the less elastic factor tends to rise relative to the prices of the more elastic factors. Given the differences in supply elasticities . . . [p]rices of agricultural inputs, such as fertilizer and machinery supplied by the nonfarm sector, tended to decline relative to the prices of land and labor.

We have already seen that both the model and history show the farm output price rising relative to industrial goods' prices. Table 11.6 presents further evidence on the movements in relative input prices. The first two columns report "real" land values, V_L, observed and predicted. V_L is determined in the model by

Table 11.6

Land Values and Input Price Ratios, 1887-1915

Year	"Real" Land Values: V_L		V_L/P		V_L/w		w/P	
	Model	Japan	Model	Japan	Model	Japan	Model	Japan
1887	100.0	100.0	100	100	100	100	100	100
1890	103.6	105.5	107	120	103	125	104	96
1895	113.6	110.6	123	140	112	130	111	109
1900	124.6	132.8	142	174	121	141	120	140
1905	140.8	123.3	170	191	134	140	131	158
1910	156.4	146.5	213	315	146	175	145	181
1915	178.0	166.2	260	321	162	143	162	226

Sources: All historical data are derived from Y. Hayami and V. Ruttan, Agricultural Development, Table C-3: Undeflated land values is an arable land price index (J20) which is deflated by an agricultural price index ("all crops," J16) to yield a "real" land value index, V_L, in terms of agricultural goods; P is the relative price of fertilizer (J23 ÷ J16); and w is a farm daily wage index in real terms (J18 ÷ J16). All data are in five-year moving averages.

simply treating land as an asset of infinite life and by assuming expectations regarding future returns to land to be determined solely by current returns. The present value of this stream, V_L, is derived by utilizing the interest rate (rate of return on efficiency capital) and is expressed in terms of agricultural goods.[7] Land values per hectare rise by 78 percent over the three decades in the model while Hayami and Ruttan document an actual rise of 66 percent. The next two columns exhibit a relative rise in land values compared with purchased inputs and farm wage rates. Presumably, in Hayami's and Ruttan's account these two relative input price movements induced the land-saving innovations typical of Meiji agriculture during the period. The last column indicates that the relative price of labor compared to purchased inputs *rises* sharply over the period both in the model and in reality, although Meiji history records a more dramatic increase. The explanation for the more rapid historical rise in w/P can be seen by reference to the last three columns which report historical prices of fertilizer and farm machinery. The price of fertilizer declines more rapidly than does that of farm machinery. Hayami and Ruttan use the former as their index of "purchased input" prices. It should be emphasized that the conventional labor-surplus accounts of Meiji agricultural development rarely focus on this key input price ratio.

In summary, the model appears to replicate well Meiji Japanese agricultural experience in terms of yields, labor productivity, and input price relatives. We are therefore in a position to examine the sources of that remarkable productivity expansion.

11.2.2. The "Sources" of Meiji Agricultural Expansion

The agricultural production function embedded in our model is usefully restated at this point:

$$Q_2(t) = A_2 \{x(t)K_2(t)\}^{\alpha_K} \{y(t)L_2(t)\}^{\alpha_L} R(t)^{\alpha_R}, \quad [3.2]$$

where

$$\alpha_K + \alpha_L + \alpha_R = 1.$$

In addition,

$$x(t) = x(o)e^{\lambda_K t}, \text{ and} \quad [3.17]$$

$$y(t) = y(o)e^{\lambda_L t}. \quad [3.18]$$

TFPG in agriculture, T_2, is simply an average of the rates of factor efficiency augmentation weighted by the relevant factor shares:

$$T_2 = \lambda_K \alpha_K + \lambda_L \alpha_L.$$

Agricultural output and labor productivity can be expressed in terms of growth rates:

$$\frac{\dot{Q}_2}{Q_2} = \alpha_K \left\{ \lambda_K + \frac{\dot{K}_2}{K_2} \right\} + \alpha_L \left\{ \lambda_L + \frac{\dot{L}_2}{L_2} \right\} + \alpha_R \frac{\dot{R}}{R} \text{ or} \quad [11.1]$$

$$\left\{ \frac{\dot{Q}_2}{Q_2} - \frac{\dot{L}_2}{L_2} \right\} = \alpha_K \left\{ \lambda_K + \frac{\dot{K}_2}{K_2} - \frac{\dot{L}_2}{L_2} \right\} + \alpha_L \lambda_L + \alpha_R \left\{ \frac{\dot{R}}{R} - \frac{\dot{L}_2}{L_2} \right\}. \quad [11.2]$$

Expression [11.2] provides a convenient representation of labor productivity changes as "decomposed into" or "accounted by" the contributions of capital, labor, and land. Indeed, Hayami and Ruttan (1971, chap. 5) find it more useful to examine the sources of labor productivity growth by using equation [11.2] rather than estimating the residual directly. In their analysis $\left\{\lambda_K + \frac{\dot{K}_2}{K_2} - \frac{\dot{L}_2}{L_2}\right\}$ is interpreted to represent the rate of growth in "technical inputs" purchased from the industrial sector per farm worker; λ_L the rate of expansion in human capital "broadly conceived to include the education, skill, knowledge, and capacity" (ibid., p. 87) embodied in the farm workforce; and $\left\{\frac{\dot{R}}{R} - \frac{\dot{L}_2}{L_2}\right\}$ the growth per worker in resource endowments including "internal capital accumulation in the form of land reclamation and development, livestock inventories" (ibid., p. 86), and the like. In accounting for the agricultural labor productivity differences between India and the United States, they find 32 percent attributable to resource endowments, 24 percent to technical inputs, and 44 percent to human capital. Table 11.7 presents a comparable decomposition of our model applied to Meiji agriculture. Over the period 1887–1915, 10.7 percent of labor productivity growth is attributable to resource endowment growth, 43.6 percent to technical inputs, and 45.7 percent to human capital. This result is consistent with the qualitative histories reported in sections 11.2 and 11.3. The implied growth rate in technical inputs per farm worker are 4.6 percent and 5.3 percent in the periods 1887–1903 and 1899–1915, respectively. The interdependent growth between the two sectors is apparent in this accounting. Almost half of the average labor productivity growth is explained by the accumulation of purchased inputs from the industrial sector. As we have seen, these inputs are declining rapidly in price. To turn the labor-surplus model on its head, agricultural development is critically related to conditions in the industrial sector. Yet, one can take this "high pay-off" approach too far, since we also note that λ_L accounts for an equal share in the average labor productivity expansion. Moreover, in chapter 9 we argued that λ_L, at least for the period up to 1910, reflects increased labor utilization in addition to education or skill improvement. Indeed, Hayami and Ruttan are careful to include "capacity" in their definition of human capital per

Table 11.7

Sources of Growth in the Kelley-Williamson Model of Meiji Japanese Agriculture, 1887-1915

11.7A. Input and Output per Worker Growth

Period	Growth Rates in Model			
	Productivity per Worker: $\dot{Q}_2/Q_2 - \dot{L}_2/L_2$	Technical Inputs per Worker: $\lambda_K + \frac{\dot{K}_2}{K_2} - \frac{\dot{L}_2}{L_2}$	Human Capital per Worker: λ_L	Resource Endowment per Worker: $\frac{\dot{R}}{R} - \frac{\dot{L}_2}{L_2}$
1887-1903	2.19	4.62	1.94	0.75
1899-1915	2.37	5.31	1.94	0.90
1887-1915	2.28	4.95	1.94	0.85

11.7B. Sources of Growth in Output per Worker

Period	Percent of Output per Worker Growth in Model			
	Technical Inputs: $\alpha_K\left[\lambda_K + \frac{\dot{K}_2}{K_2} - \frac{\dot{L}_2}{L_2}\right]$	Human Capital: $\alpha_L\left[\lambda_L\right]$	Resource Endowment $\alpha_R\left[\frac{\dot{R}}{R} - \frac{\dot{L}_2}{L_2}\right]$	TFPG: $\alpha_K\left[\lambda_K\right] + \alpha_L\left[\lambda_L\right]$
1887-1903	.906 (42.5)	1.017 (47.7)	.210 (9.8)	1.24 (58.2)
1899-1915	1.041 (45.1)	1.017 (44.0)	.252 (10.9)	1.24 (53.7)
1887-1915	.970 (43.6)	1.017 (45.7)	.238 (10.7)	1.24 (55.7)

Note: In panel B, the numbers in parentheses express the percentage of average labor productivity growth. The first three columns should add up (ignoring rounding errors) to 100 percent. TFPG, total-factor productivity growth in agriculture, is presented as an independent measure, not to be added to the other three columns.

worker. Labor slack appears to play an important role in our narrative. Resource endowment growth accounts for little of the productivity expansion, a result which conforms to conventional descriptions of natural resource constraints on Japanese agriculture.

11.3. Some Lessons from Meiji History: Counterfactual Analysis

11.3.1. Three Key Counterfactuals

There is much that is unusual in Meiji agriculture's experience. Certainly the performance of traditional agriculture is uncommon whether judged by the absolute decline in the farm labor force, by the high rates of industrialization (chapter 10), or by the relatively rapid rise in the price of land compared to other purchased and traditional farm inputs. In addition, the exogenous conditions under which agricultural output performance was achieved are somewhat unique. Japan faced a more inelastic supply of land than is typical of many contemporary less-developed economies. She also developed without the burden of population pressure. Finally, the rate of TFPG in agriculture was unusually high and this impressive rate may be related to the underutilized technical potential bequeathed as a Tokugawa legacy. These conditions in Meiji agriculture sound much like those of developing nineteenth-century Western economies which have been cited as evidence supporting the irrelevance of Western historical experience for contemporary developing economies.[8] This raises an important issue. In Professor Nakamura's words: "If the preconditions and conditions of the Japanese experience were substantially different from those of a present developing nation, a detailed comparative study and much ingenuity will be required to extract lessons from Japan's experience" (Nakamura 1966, p. 20). We shall attempt to extract some of those lessons of history not through the methodology of comparative analysis, but rather by use of the counterfactual. How and in what degree was Japanese agricultural performance related to the low rates of population and labor force growth? How and in what degree was this performance influenced by land constraints? How and in what degree was her performance determined by TFPG? And finally, are these three unusual circumstances sufficiently important quantitatively, either individually or in concert, to reduce substantially the relevance of the "Japanese model" of agriculture for today's developing countries?

With reference to our general equilibrium model of dualistic development, the counterfactual has two distinct advantages over the *expost* sources-of-growth accounting performed in section 11.2.2. First, the sources-of-growth approach decomposes *ex ante* performance without the use of an underlying model of development. As such, it postulates complete independence between growth rates in each of the inputs as well as TFPG. In fact, interdependence is more plausible. Second, the approach treats agriculture in isolation. There is considerable evidence, both in theory and in fact, that agriculture was dependent upon conditions outside the sector, and vice versa. A full general equilibrium model is required to reveal this interdependence and to confront the "concurrent growth" thesis. In effect, this section is designed to respond to the type of challenge raised by Hayami and Ruttan:

> We accept as fundamental that growth in agricultural output is . . . essential to the development process and that the contribution of agricultural growth to the development process is positively related to the rate of productivity growth in the agricultural sector. . . . *We look to others to provide an understanding of the conditions under which these opportunities for over-all growth are fully realized.* [Hayami and Ruttan 1971, p. 4; italics added]

11.3.2. The Impact of Total-Factor Productivity Growth in Agriculture

Statements like the following can be found throughout the literature on Meiji economic development:

> Technical change represents an essential element in the growth of agricultural production and productivity from the very beginning of the development process. [Hayami and Ruttan 1971, p. 26]

> Agricultural surpluses had to exist. It is through technological progress that the surpluses have been generated. On this account, technological progress in agriculture has been a key to Japan's general development. [Hayami and Yamada 1968, p. 135]

We now propose to put some quantitative flesh on these bare bones. In particular, we ask: If the rate of total-factor productivity expansion in agriculture had been lower, by how much would Meiji economic growth have been reduced? To answer this question it is first necessary to specify a useful historical counterfactual.

Between 1910 and 1920, the rate of TFPG in Japanese agriculture begins a sharp decline. The rate from 1883/87 to 1908/12 was about 1.24 percent per annum; the rate from 1913/17 to 1933/37 was 0.73 percent per annum.[9] In conjunction with the 15 percent ad valorem tariff imposed on rice during the Russo-Japanese War, the retardation in productivity growth is said to have generated a "population-food problem" which eventually resulted in the 1918 Kome Sodo (Rice Riot). Hayami and

Ruttan (1971, pp. 221–28) attempt to explain the declining rate of growth in rice yields and production during the interwar period by appealing to the rate of growth in a seed improvement index and to the increased import of colonial rice from Korea and Taiwan. Their success in applying a counterfactual to the interwar period suggests an equally relevant counterfactual experiment for the pre-World War I period: *How would the pre-1915 Meiji economy have been influenced if the rate of total-factor productivity growth had been that prevailing during the 1920s and 1930s rather than the much higher rate achieved in the earlier decades?*[10]

First, let us examine agriculture's performance under these counterfactual conditions. The reduction in agriculture's TFPG which we impose on the early Meiji economy is 0.51 percent per annum; that is, from 1.24 to 0.73 percent, the actual retardation observed after the 1910s. Table 11.8A documents the impact

Table 11.8A

The Impact of Agricultural TFPG on Meiji Agriculture's Performance

Variable and Period	"Actual"	Counterfactual: Interwar TFPG in Agriculture
Productivity per Farm Worker		
Growth: $\frac{\dot{Q}_2}{Q_2} - \frac{\dot{L}_2}{L_2}$		
1887–1903	2.19	1.40
1899–1915	2.37	1.54
1887–1915	2.28	1.48

of TFPG on farm labor productivity: from 1887 to 1915, labor productivity growth would have been reduced by 0.60 percent. In contrast with the conventional sources-of-growth accounting undertaken in section 11.2, our counterfactual experiment now shows that labor productivity growth in agriculture would have been diminished by more than the reduction in TFPG. The explanation, of course, is that achievable national savings rates and thus rates of capital accumulation would have been suppressed. The estimated diminution in the Meiji savings rate is documented in table 11.9A.

Although the reader may have anticipated this result, he may be surprised by the low magnitudes involved. Farm labor productivity growth is reduced by only 0.10 percent over and above the TFPG reduction. This implies a small reduction in capital accumulation in agriculture in response to an enormous decline in agricultural TFPG in the counterfactual. There are two offsetting influences which produce this joint effect. First, the economywide rate of capital accumulation is diminished. Second, and critical to the outcome, the relative price of purchased inputs declines more rapidly in the counterfactual economy, and agriculture is more successful than industry in substituting capital for labor. The net result is only a minor diminution in capital-labor ratio growth in agriculture. Thus, agricultural labor productivity expansion is reduced by only slightly more than the reduction in TFPG.

Table 11.8B displays three key variables crucial in judging

Table 11.8B

The Impact of Agricultural TFPG on Meiji Agriculture's Performance

Year	Agricultural Labor Force: L_2		Productivity Gap: $Q_1/L_1 \div Q_2/L_2$		Terms of Trade: $P = P_1/P_2$	
	"Actual"	Counterfactual: Interwar TFPG in Agriculture	"Actual"	Counterfactual: Interwar TFPG in Agriculture	"Actual"	Counterfactual Interwar TFPG in Agriculture
1887	100.0	100.0	100.0	100.0	100.0	100.0
1891	99.2	99.6	102.8	106.8	96.4	91.7
1895	98.4	99.3	106.6	114.7	92.0	83.5
1899	97.5	98.9	110.7	123.0	87.5	76.1
1903	96.8	98.6	115.6	132.5	82.6	69.0
1907	96.1	98.1	120.8	142.5	77.9	62.6
1911	95.4	97.5	126.3	153.0	73.3	56.8
1915	94.7	97.1	132.9	165.0	68.5	51.3

agriculture's performance. The rate of employment shift out of agriculture would have been somewhat lower under the interwar TFPG conditions. Yet, the *absolute* decline in the Meiji agricultural labor force would still have taken place. This unique aspect of Meiji development cannot be explained by the high rates of TFPG actually achieved during the period. We must search for other explanations of this unusual aspect of early Japanese growth. Perhaps even more striking is the impact on the sectoral productivity gap and the terms of trade. The literature on the Japanese economy during the interwar period has explained the joint appearance of productivity gaps and upward pressure on rice prices by appealing to the retardation in domestic agriculture's rate of TFPG. Table 11.8B confirms that analysis. The productivity gap would have been doubly severe and the rise in the relative price of farm products far more dramatic had the interwar experience with agricultural TFPG appeared in the 1880s.

We turn now to the economywide impact of the counterfactual rates of TFPG (table 11.9A). Predictably, expansion rates

Table 11.9A

The Impact of Agricultural TFPG on Meiji Economy-wide Performance

Year	GNP (Constant Prices) per Worker		Real Wage Earnings		Aggregate Savings Rate	
	"Actual"	Counterfactual: Interwar TFPG in Agriculture	"Actual"	Counterfactual: Interwar TFPG in Agriculture	"Actual"	Counterfactual Interwar TFPG in Agriculture
1887	100.0	100.0	100.0	100.0	.122	.122
1891	111.0	107.6	108.8	105.6	.124	.123
1895	123.7	116.1	118.5	111.5	.125	.123
1899	138.5	126.2	129.4	118.0	.126	.124
1903	155.8	137.7	141.4	125.0	.127	.125
1907	176.2	151.3	155.2	132.8	.128	.125
1911	200.5	167.4	170.9	141.6	.129	.125
1915	229.0	185.9	188.2	150.8	.130	.125

of both real GNP and real wage earnings per worker are significantly reduced in the counterfactual regime. The *relative* impact on these two series might not have been anticipated, however. Real wage earnings are less seriously affected, resulting in a notable influence on savings rates. The savings rate in the counterfactual regime is almost stable while it underwent a mild secular rise in the "actual" model. A favorite explanation for the modest secular rise in the Meiji savings rate had always been agricultural productivity growth. We find quantitative support for this hypothesis. Furthermore, given the retardation in agriculture's TFPG during the interwar period, this analysis suggests that the sharp acceleration in the national savings rate after 1910 is all the more remarkable. Finally, these results shed more light on the decade prior to 1905. Coupled with the arguments in chapter 7, they underscore the critical role of governmental activity in inhibiting Meiji growth through its military requirements and its investment in relatively unproductive wartime activities.

Finally, how did the unusually rapid rate of TFPG in Meiji agriculture affect the economy's experience with structural change? In chapter 10 we noted that Meiji Japan underwent a rate of industrialization almost twice as rapid as either nineteenth-century or twentieth-century developing economies. Can the unusually rapid rate of agricultural TFPG account for some part of that performance? Our counterfactual experiment calls for a rejection of that hypothesis. True, the industrial employment share would have been lower in 1915 (table 11.9B), but

Table 11.9B

The Impact of Agricultural TFPG on Meiji Economy-wide Performance

Year	Industrial Employment Share		Industrial Output Share (Constant Prices)	
	"Actual"	Counterfactual: Interwar TFPG in Agriculture	"Actual"	Counterfactual: Interwar TFPG in Agriculture
1887	.150	.150	.244	.244
1891	.167	.163	.274	.276
1895	.183	.175	.304	.313
1899	.199	.188	.334	.350
1903	.214	.200	.365	.390
1907	.229	.213	.396	.433
1911	.244	.226	.427	.475
1915	.258	.239	.457	.519

Note: Cols. (3) and (4) are in 1915 prices. Col. (4) has been rebased at 1887 = .244 to facilitate comparisons between the actual and counterfactual experience.

not by much, given the magnitude of the decline in TFPG imposed on the counterfactual economy. In any case, *the industrial output share would have been higher under the more moderate rates of TFPG in agriculture!* This result should prove to be somewhat sobering to those who feel that Meiji Japan's rapid rate of industrialization can be explained in large part by her dynamic technological achievements in agriculture. Indeed, *it follows that the acceleration in industrialization rates during the period following the 1910s may be explained by the retardation in agriculture's technological performance.* This result is in sharp contrast with the conventional closed dualistic models in which rising agricultural TFPG is a crucial stimulus to industrialization since it postpones the "turning point" and insures a persistence of labor slack.

11.3.3. The Impact of Population Growth

In chapter 8 we explored the impact of demographic factors on Meiji Japanese growth. The present section returns to this issue and considers its effect on agriculture's performance.

It bears repeating that surprisingly few analysts of Meiji economic development have cited the unique demographic conditions in their analysis of Japanese economic history. Nakamura (1966, p. 20), Johnston (1966, pp. 65–75), and Umemura (1970, pp. 175–97) are not among them. For example, Umemura (1970, p. 183) has explicitly noted that

> The annual rate of growth of the Japanese population in the latter part of the 19th century averaged 0.8 percent, which is almost equal to that of . . . England and Wales in the latter part of the 18th century. . . . We may conclude that the course of demographic evolution in Japan has corresponded with that of Britain with a time lag of a little more than a century. . . . As far as the rate of growth of the population is concerned, Japan possessed no special advantages for accumulating a reserve army of labor.

Our main concern in this section is to isolate the role of population growth by posing the same counterfactual raised in chapter 8: *If Meiji Japan had experienced the contemporary population explosions—with labor force growth rates three times those observed historically—what would have been the impact on employment in agriculture, the relative price of foodstuffs, experience with labor productivity growth, sectoral productivity gaps, and the growth of purchased inputs per farm worker?*[11] Perhaps at the same time we can shed light on two hypotheses which have appeared in the literature. Umemura (1970, p. 186) has suggested that "the rate of increase of employment in the non-agricultural sector in Japan appeared to be quite independent of the growth rate of the labor supply as a whole." Johnston (1970, p. 70) has concluded that had Meiji Japan been burdened with the contemporary population explosion, then "considerably more than 70 years would have been required [from 1885] for Japan to reach the turning point when its farm labor force began to register an appreciable decline in absolute size."

Table 11.10A shows that while the growth in farm labor productivity would indeed have been restrained by the presence of contemporary population pressure, the magnitude of the diminution is small. A key source of the drag of population on agricultural development lies in the behavior of technical inputs per farm worker. These would have been some 1.3 percent lower under the higher population growth rates. Yet technical progress clearly played a far greater role in contributing to the Meiji agricultural "miracle" than did the presence of low population pressure. A comparison between tables 11.10A and 11.8A yields ample support for this conclusion. While contemporary population pressure would have reduced farm productivity growth by only 0.17 percentage points the more modest TFPG of the interwar period would have reduced the growth rate by 0.80 percentage points, almost five times as much. As a conse-

Table 11.10A

The Impact of Labor Force Expansion on Meiji Agriculture's Performance

Variable and Period	"Actual"	Counterfactual: Contemporary Population Pressure
Productivity per Farm Worker Growth: $\dot{Q}_2/Q_2 - \dot{L}_2/L_2$		
1887-1903	2.19	1.92
1899-1915	2.37	2.02
1887-1915	2.28	2.11
Technical Inputs per Farm Worker Growth: $\lambda_k + \frac{\dot{K}_2}{K_2} - \frac{\dot{L}_2}{L_2}$		
1887-1903	4.62	3.33
1899-1915	5.31	4.02
1887-1915	4.95	3.67

quence, the productivity gap is no different (table 11.10B) in the counterfactual regime of population pressure. Nor is the secular rise in food prices much altered. The latter result is especially interesting given the attention that development economists have devoted to population growth as a source of upward pressure on the relative price of farm products.

Table 11.10B

The Impact of Labor Force Expansion on Meiji Agriculture's Performance

Year	Agricultural Labor Force L_2		Productivity Gap: $Q_1/L_1 \div Q_2/L_2$		Terms of Trade: $P = P_1/P_2$	
	"Actual"	Counterfactual: Contemporary Population Pressure	"Actual"	Counterfactual: Contemporary Population Pressure	"Actual"	Counterfactual Contemporary Population Pressure
1887	100.0	100.0	100.0	100.0	100.0	100.0
1891	99.2	101.8	102.8	102.8	96.4	96.6
1895	98.4	103.5	106.6	106.5	92.0	92.5
1899	97.5	105.3	110.7	110.6	87.5	88.3
1903	96.8	107.2	115.6	115.4	82.6	83.6
1907	96.1	109.0	120.8	120.6	77.9	79.1
1911	95.4	110.9	126.3	126.1	73.3	74.6
1915	94.7	112.9	132.9	132.7	68.5	69.9

One thing is clear. Our "population pressure" counterfactual has uncovered one possible explanation for Meiji Japan's unique experience with agricultural employment. Had Meiji Japan been confronted with contemporary population pressure, the rate of employment shift out of agriculture would have been sufficiently retarded to eliminate the absolute decline in the gainfully employed on the farm. We can reject Umemura's hypothesis in favor of Johnston's. Meiji Japan's unique experience with farm employment can be largely explained by her unusual demographic experience.

11.3.4. The Impact of Inelastic Land Supply

The classical doctrine of natural resource scarcity has crept into some neo-Malthusian accounts of the modern challenge of agricultural development. The doctrine asserts "that natural resources are scarce, that the scarcity increases with the progress of time, and that resource scarcity threatens to impair levels of living and economic growth" (Hayami and Ruttan 1971, p. 30). The doctrine appears to suggest that densely populated contemporary developing economies are condemned "to continued stagnation and the agricultural workers in such countries to low levels of productivity" (ibid., p. 86). Japan would certainly seem to be an outstanding counterexample. Hectarage in paddy expanded by as little as 10 percent between 1880 and 1920 (Appendix A, table A.4). It is only because the farm labor force declined by almost 6 percent over the same period (table 11.4) that the land-resource endowment per farm worker grew at an annual rate of 0.85 percent between 1887 and 1915 (table 11.7). Even so, based on a sources-of-growth accounting, this expansion in resource endowment per farm worker contributed to only 10 percent of the marked rise in average farm labor productivity in the pre-World War I period. How important are these resource constraints in accounting for Meiji Japan's unusual growth performance when our counterfactual analysis is applied to our general equilibrium model of Meiji development? Many Japanese economic historians seem to feel that the "limited supply of virgin land" is sufficient to explain the stability or decline in the agricultural work force (Umemura 1970, p. 186). Others have argued that "the supply of land services has been much more elastic than implied by the static view of land" (Hayami and Ruttan 1971, pp. 30–31; Boserup 1965; Barnett and Morse 1963, pp. 101–47). The utilization of a given hectarage can, after all, be augmented by crop frequency, increasing complementary inputs, reducing the share of uncultivated land, and so on. In fact, this is exactly the form which the "Meiji Japanese model" of agricultural development takes.

The issue, then, is to what extent Meiji development was retarded by land scarcity. The accumulation of complementary purchased inputs in agriculture represents real opportunities foregone elsewhere. Yet if aggregate growth performance was diminished by inelasticity in land supply, did this same inelasticity foster a "uniquely" rapid rate of industrialization? If land supply had been more elastic in Meiji Japan, would we have observed a less rapid rate of accumulation of purchased inputs from industry but a comparable rate of labor productivity growth? These are some of the questions which the present section attempts to answer. To do so, we pose the following counterfactual: *What would have been Meiji Japan's agricultural performance had she been blessed with land expansion rates typical of contemporary Philippines—roughly 2.2 percent per annum between 1947 and 1965?*[12]

We turn first to table 11.11A, where the impact of land con-

Table 11 .11A

The Impact of Land Constraints on Meiji Agriculture's Performance

Variable and Period	"Actual"	Counterfactual: Elastic Land Supply
Productivity per Farm Worker Growth: $\frac{\dot{Q}_2}{Q_2} - \frac{\dot{L}_2}{L_2}$		
1887-1903	2.19	2.63
1899-1915	2.37	2.79
1887-1915	2.28	2.73
Resource Endowment per Farm Worker Growth: $\frac{\dot{R}}{R} - \frac{\dot{L}_2}{L_2}$		
1887-1903	0.75	2.48
1899-1915	0.90	2.44
1887-1915	0.85	2.46

straints on Meiji labor productivity performance is documented. The counterfactual economy with elastic land supply has resource endowments per farm worker growing at three times the rate which actually took place. The model predicts that productivity growth would have been raised by some 0.45 percentage points under these counterfactual conditions. Meiji agricultural performance appears all the more impressive given the land constraints which the economy faced. Note the impact which the more elastic land supply would have had on employment, however. Many economic historians feel that inelastic land supplies explain Meiji Japan's uniquely rapid rates of structural change. In fact, had the land supply been more elastic, the farm labor force would have declined more rapidly, not less (table 11.11B). As a result, the industrial employment share in 1915 would have been higher, not lower (table 11.12A). The explanation for this rather striking result is simple and illustrates

Table 11.11B

The Impact of Land Constraints on Meiji Agriculture's Performance

Year	Agricultural Labor Force L_2		Productivity Gap: $Q_1/L_1 \div Q_2/L_2$		Terms of Trade: $P = P_1/P_2$	
	"Actual"	Counterfactual: Elastic Land Supply	"Actual"	Counterfactual: Elastic Land Supply	"Actual"	Counterfactual: Elastic Land Supply
1887	100.0	100.0	100.0	100.0	100.0	100.0
1891	99.2	98.8	102.8	100.5	96.4	98.8
1895	98.4	97.8	106.6	101.6	92.0	96.9
1899	97.5	96.7	110.7	103.2	87.5	94.3
1903	96.8	95.8	115.6	105.4	82.6	91.1
1907	96.1	94.8	120.8	108.1	77.9	87.5
1911	95.4	94.0	126.3	111.4	73.3	83.6
1915	94.7	93.3	132.9	115.2	68.5	79.5

the advantage of general equilibrium history. With a more elastic land supply, the rate of capital accumulation would have been fostered, the growth in the economywide capital-labor ratio raised, and industrialization stimulated (see chapter 6). A simple comparative static analysis would miss this important interaction entirely.

Table 11.12A

The Impact of Land Constraints on Meiji Economy-wide Performance

Year	Industrial Employment Share		Industrial (constant price) Output Share	
	"Actual"	Counterfactual: Elastic Land Supply	"Actual"	Counterfactual: Elastic Land Supply
1887	.150	.150	.244	.244
1891	.167	.170	.274	.271
1895	.183	.188	.304	.299
1899	.199	.206	.334	.326
1903	.214	.223	.365	.351
1907	.229	.239	.396	.376
1911	.244	.255	.427	.401
1915	.258	.269	.457	.425

Note: Cols. (3) and (4) are in 1915 prices. Col. (4) has been rebased at 1887 = .244 to facilitate comparisons between the actual and counterfactual experience.

The remaining results documented in tables 11.11B and table 11.12B can be summarized briefly. Elastic land supply would have produced even more stable movements in the sectoral productivity gap, but a deterioration in agriculture's relative labor productivity would have taken place nonetheless, since capital inputs would have been in even more elastic supply and industry was not constrained by limited land availability. The relative price of agricultural goods would still have risen, a result produced in every counterfactual experiment performed in this chapter. Finally, both GNP per capita and real wage earnings would have grown far more rapidly, as in fact they did after the 1910s when agriculture diminished in relative importance and inelastic land supply diminished as a constraint on aggregate growth.

Table 11.12B

The Impact of Land Constraints on Meiji Economy-wide Performance

Year	GNP (Constant Price) per worker		Real Wage Earnings	
	"Actual"	Counterfactual: Elastic Land Supply	"Actual"	Counterfactual: Elastic Land Supply
1887	100.0	100.0	100.0	100.0
1891	111.0	112.8	108.8	110.6
1895	123.7	127.7	118.5	122.6
1899	138.5	145.1	129.4	136.1
1903	155.8	165.5	141.4	151.5
1907	176.2	189.4	155.2	169.0
1911	200.5	217.7	170.9	188.8
1915	229.0	251.0	188.2	211.2

11.3.5. Summary: Is Meiji Japan an "Atypical" Case of Agricultural Development?

The counterfactual analysis in the preceding pages has provided some additional insight into the sources of agricultural development and into the impact of that development on the remainder of the Meiji economy during Modern Economic Growth. We have examined in turn the contributions of TFPG, demographic factors, and land constraints to this performance. It might be useful at this point to explore how these conditions in combination influenced the course of Meiji development. Throughout this chapter we have argued that each of these conditions was somewhat unique compared to most of contemporary Asia. All developing economies currently face population pressure far more severe than did Meiji Japan at a comparable stage of development. Most developing economies currently face a more elastic land supply than did Japan. Finally, even with the recent advent of the "green revolution," few currently developing countries have been able to achieve rates of agricultural TFPG approaching those of Meiji Japan. This rapid rate of TFPG in Meiji Japan clearly was influenced by the "prerequisite" irrigation system inherited from the Tokugawa period, an inheritance few contemporary Asian economies received from colonial rule. Presumably, if we controlled for all three of these factors simultaneously, the constraints of Meiji agricultural development would approximate those in contemporary developing Asia. What would modern Japanese economic growth have been like under these joint constraints? Would Japanese agricultural performance have been quite ordinary? Would Japanese agriculture begin to look more like contemporary agriculture in underdeveloped Asia? Would the "Japanese model" be reduced to a highly *atypical* case of agricultural development, undeserving of the special attention which economists have lavished upon it?

In section 11.2.2 and table 11.7 we noted that Meiji Japanese agricultural performance was considerably different from that of contemporary developing societies. Hayami and Ruttan decomposed farm labor productivity and found that intercountry differences could be attributed to technical inputs, human capital, and resource endowments in almost equal proportions. In Meiji Japan, on the other hand, technical inputs played a more important role while resource endowment growth made only a marginal contribution. The "joint counterfactual" reported in table 11.13 makes Meiji Japan look far more ordinary since these three sources of farm productivity growth make a more equal contribution. Furthermore, the farm productivity rates are drastically reduced. From 1887 to 1915, Meiji agricultural productivity grew at 2.28 percent per annum. Had the farm sector faced the same demographic, technological, and land supply conditions currently prevailing in developing Asia, her farm productivity growth rate in the counterfactual regime would

Table 11.13

Sources of Meiji Agricultural Growth in the Joint Counterfactual Economy

11.13A Input and Output per Worker Growth

Period	Counterfactual Growth Rates			
	Productivity per Worker: $\dot{Q}_2/Q_2 - \dot{L}_2/L_2$	Technical Inputs per Worker: $\lambda_K + \dot{K}_2/K_2 - \dot{L}_2/L_2$	Human Capital per Worker: λ_L	Resource Endowment per Worker $\dot{R}/R - \dot{L}_2/L_2$
1887-1903	1.57	3.16	0.89	1.72
1899-1915	1.69	3.72	0.89	1.75
1887-1915	1.63	3.42	0.89	1.74

11.13B Sources of Growth in Output per Worker

Period	Percent of Output per Worker in Counterfactual			
	Technical Inputs: $\alpha_K\left[\lambda_K + \frac{\dot{K}_2}{K_2} - \frac{\dot{L}_2}{L_2}\right]$	Human Capital: $\alpha_L\left[\lambda_L\right]$	Resource Endowment: $\alpha_R\left[\dot{R}/R - \dot{L}_2/L_2\right]$	TFPG: $\alpha_K\left[\lambda_K\right] + \alpha_L\left[\lambda_L\right]$
1887-1903	0.62 (39)	0.47 (30)	0.48 (31)	0.73 (46)
1899-1915	0.73 (43)	0.47 (28)	0.49 (29)	0.73 (43)
1887-1915	0.67 (41)	0.47 (29)	0.49 (30)	0.73 (45)

Note: See notes to Table 11.7.

have been 1.63 percent (table 11.13). The 1887–1903 rate would have been even lower: 1.57 percent. The Japanese model of agricultural development begins to appear quite ordinary in this counterfactual accounting.

Furthermore, an absolute decline in the farm labor force would have disappeared under these counterfactual conditions (table 11.14). The farm labor force would have increased by almost 14 percent up to 1915 rather than declined by around 6 percent. Moreover, dualism in sectoral productivity gaps would have been more pronounced and would have approached those of contemporary Asia, since the gap between agriculture and industry would have risen by 43 rather than 33 percent. Finally, the terms of trade would have undergone a more pronounced secular decline under contemporary conditions. While the relative price of industrial goods declines by 31 percent in the actual model, it would have declined by 39 percent in the contemporary counterfactual world.

Table 11.14

Meiji Agriculture's Performance in the Joint Counterfactual Economy

Year	Agricultural Labor Force: L_2		Productivity Gap: $Q_1/L_1 \div Q_2/L_2$		Terms of Trade: $P = P_1/P_2$	
	"Actual"	Joint Counterfactual	"Actual"	Joint Counterfactual	"Actual"	Joint Counterfactual
1887	100.0	100.0	100.0	100.0	100.0	100.0
1891	99.2	101.9	102.8	104.2	96.4	94.3
1895	98.4	103.9	106.6	109.1	92.0	88.6
1899	97.5	105.8	110.7	114.4	87.5	82.8
1903	96.8	107.8	115.6	120.5	82.6	77.1
1907	96.1	109.7	120.8	127.1	77.9	71.6
1911	95.4	111.7	126.3	134.4	73.3	66.2
1915	94.7	113.7	132.9	142.5	68.5	61.0

Note that the rate of industrialization (table 11.15A) is also reduced in the joint counterfactual. But perhaps most interesting is the impact on GNP per worker (constant price) growth rates (table 11.15B). We already documented in section 11.1 that GNP per worker growth rates in Meiji Japan were lower than those achieved in contemporary Asia during the 1950s and 1960s. We find now that the Meiji performance would have been even less impressive had she been burdened with the demographic

Table 11.15A

The Impact of Agriculture on Meiji Economy-wide Performance in the Joint Counterfactual

Year	Industrial Employment Share		Industrial (Constant Price) Output Share	
	"Actual"	Joint Counterfactual	"Actual"	Joint Counterfactual
1887	.150	.150	.244	.244
1891	.167	.163	.274	.272
1895	.183	.176	.304	.301
1899	.199	.189	.334	.332
1903	.214	.203	.365	.363
1907	.229	.216	.396	.397
1911	.244	.229	.427	.431
1915	.258	.242	.457	.465

Table 11.15B

The Impact of Agriculture on Meiji Economy-wide Performance in the Joint Counterfactual

Year	GNP (Constant Price) per Worker		Real Wage Earnings		Aggregate (Constant Price) Savings Rate	
	"Actual"	Joint Counterfactual	"Actual"	Joint Counterfactual	"Actual"	Joint Counterfactual
1887	100.0	100.0	100.0	100.0	.093	.093
1891	111.0	108.1	108.8	106.2	.098	.098
1895	123.7	117.3	118.5	112.9	.103	.105
1899	138.5	127.9	129.4	120.3	.108	.112
1903	155.8	140.2	141.4	128.4	.114	.118
1907	176.2	154.3	155.2	137.2	.119	.125
1911	200.5	170.6	170.9	146.8	.124	.131
1915	229.0	189.6	188.2	157.3	.130	.139

and technological conditions of contemporary Asia. GNP per worker in 1915 would have been some 17 percent lower than that in fact achieved.

It appears that much of what is unique about Meiji agricultural development is the initial conditions over which the Meiji government had little control. To cite Meiji Japan as a "lesson of history" may be hazardous without appropriate qualifications regarding the unusually advantageous conditions confronting Japanese agriculture in the 1870s and 1880s.

12

Trade as an Engine of Growth

12.1 Theorizing about History

Part 3 of this book contains interpretative rather than descriptive history. The economic history written there relies heavily on an analytical framework which broadly accords with the quantitative record. Nevertheless, competing historical models are likely to produce future Meiji economic histories in conflict with ours. We certainly hope that this book will encourage such efforts as well as reinforce current attempts to improve the scope and quality of the data.

To illustrate one such direction which future cliometric research on Japan might take, the present chapter confronts the foreign trade issue. In contrast with chapters 6 through 11, no firm quantitative conclusions will emerge from the following pages regarding the role of trade in early Japanese Modern Economic Growth. While the book could well have been written without this chapter, we feel this chapter usefully highlights the methodological position embodied in our research. Given the novelty of our approach to analyzing Japanese economic development, it is possibly appropriate that this study conclude not only in pointing direction for future research, but also in articulating a methodological approach which we feel yields high returns.

12.2 The Size and Direction of Trade: The Export Data

One of Simon Kuznets's prerequisites for Modern Economic Growth is an increasing national involvement in world trade. There appears to be little doubt that after 1885 Japan conforms to that characterization. Following a long period of relative economic isolation, Japan began an impressive march into the world economy, almost without interruption, up to World War I.

Table 12.1 documents the magnitude of the performance. Exports as a share in GNP rise from a negligible level in 1885, 3.9 percent, to 13.2 percent in 1919, just three decades later. The secular rise in the import share is equally impressive, from 5.6 percent in 1885 to 16.7 percent in 1919. The import share exhibits greater short-run instability. The 1898, 1905, and 1906 figures reflect the unusually high levels of military-related imports.

Table 12.1

The Share of Trade in GNP, 1885-1919

Year	Share in GNP	
	Exports	Imports
1885	.039	.056
1886	.041	.052
1898	.062	.168
1899	.140	.140
1905	.100	.327
1906	.106	.220
1919	.132	.167

Source: K. Ohkawa and H. Rosovsky, "A Century of Japanese Economic Growth," Table 2, p. 90.

The composition of trade changes markedly over these three decades. In 1881, raw silk and tea accounted for 57 percent of Japan's exports while 53 percent of her imports were textiles (Baba and Tatemoto 1968, table 6–4, p. 170). As industrialization proceeded, a larger share of Japanese imports were in the form of capital goods, intermediate (raw material) inputs, and foodstuffs. Exports, on the other hand, continued to be dominated by light manufactures of consumption goods, and a shift out of traditional silk exports into cotton textiles. The data in Appendix A (table A.10) indicate the magnitude of this shift in trade composition. Manufactures as a share in exports increases from 45.6 to 71.7 percent between 1885/89 and 1910/14. Imports of raw materials as a share in the total rise from 9.7 to 36.8 percent over the same period while manufactures fall from 57.5 to 34.7 percent. Furthermore, Japan shifts from a net exporter of rice in the early 1890s. The net import of rice in 1895 was 49,000 million tons while the figure is 406,000 million in 1915. Increasingly over the period, Meiji Japan became more dependent on the importation of rice in satisfying her domestic consumption requirements (Hayami and Ruttan 1971, table 10–1, p. 220).

This *expost* evidence is well known. How is it to be interpreted?

12.3. An Open Dualistic Economy

12.3.1. The Small-Country Specification

Although the closed-economy assumption has a long tradition in Japanese economic history, critics have little difficulty in collecting evidence to support an opposing position. The data reviewed in the previous section shows that Meiji Japan relied heavily on imported primary products and was a net rice importer very early in her phase of Modern Economic Growth. In addition, the exports of simple industrial consumption goods have received prominence in historical accounts of Meiji development. Indeed, Japanese exports have often been viewed as the "engine of growth." But it is one thing to be critical of the closed-economy assumption, and quite another to offer a plausible substitute. There are two related issues involved. First, to what extent did foreign trade alleviate key bottlenecks in Meiji growth? Do limited short-run supply elasticities impose an important restriction on structural transformation in a closed economy? To what extent did the foreign supply of importables and the foreign demand for exportables facilitate that transformation? Was the price elasticity of demand for textile exports very low in foreign markets? Was the price elasticity of supply from neighboring rice suppliers also very low? If so, would an *accurately* modeled open economy produce a very different interpretation of Meiji historical development from that coming from the closed dualistic economy contained in preceding pages of this book? Second, what is an accurate characterization of those elasticities? The historical literature is surprisingly mute on this crucial issue.

Conventional trade theory, for the most part, takes a very special case of "openness," a case which may in fact be less realistic than the closed-economy assumption. The textbooks refer to this special case as the "small-country assumption." The assumption has attained popularity for a poor reason: it makes simple the subsequent analysis of trade problems. The small-country trade model treats relative commodity prices as determined exogenously. It assumes that the price elasticity of export demand and the price elasticity of import supply are infinite. The small country cannot influence its terms of trade but rather takes the terms of trade as a datum, a relative price which is determined by world market conditions over which it has no influence. The justification for this approach is simply that the country is sufficiently small so that an expansion of the supply of exportables to the rest of the world or an expansion of demand for importables from the rest of the world has only a marginal impact on prices.

The comparative statics can be readily described by references to figures 12.1 and 12.2. In the closed economy (figure 12.1), there is no trade and $P(t)$, the terms of trade, is determined endogenously by the joint interaction of demand and

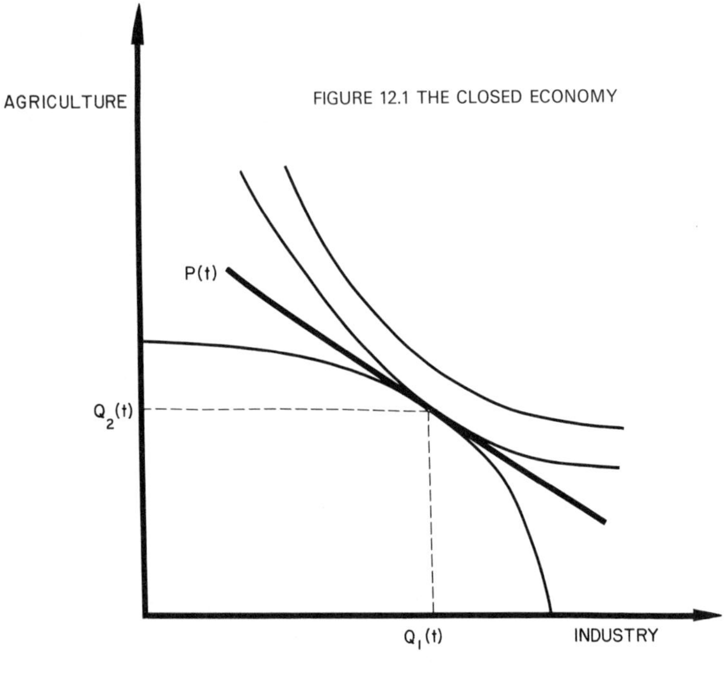

FIGURE 12.1 THE CLOSED ECONOMY

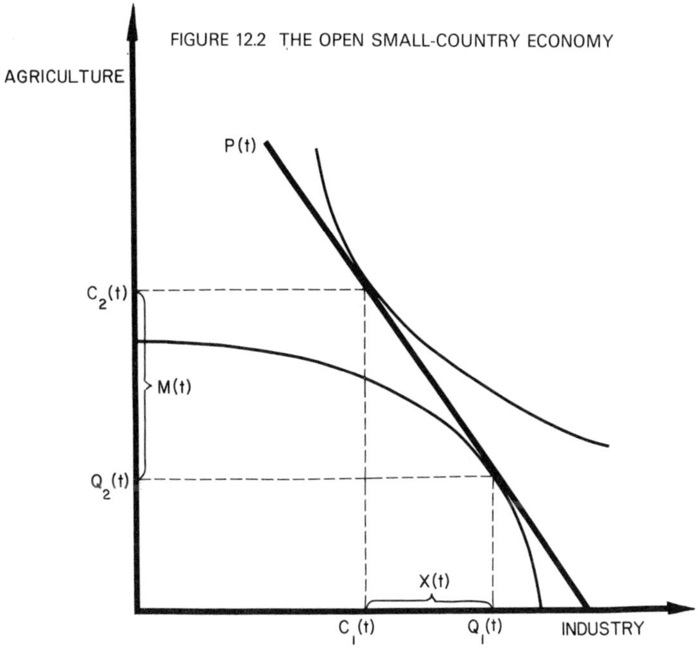

supply conditions in a general equilibrium setting. This is a simplified version of the closed static dualistic economy developed in chapter 3. In the open small-country case (figure 12.2), $P(t)$ is determined exogenously by world market conditions over which the country has no influence. Given that terms of trade, which may vary year to year, the production and consumption decision can be made independently. The volume of trade is determined residually. Given $P(t)$, the production and consumption of industrial goods are established and industrial exports are determined as a surplus "vented" onto the world market: $X(t) = Q_1(t) - C_1(t)$. Imports are treated similarly. The theory only insists that the trade balance be zero. No balance of payments disequilibrium is allowed in the model and, in the absence of capital flows, import and export values must be equated.

The conventional small-country assumptions could be readily

incorporated into our dualistic model presented in chapter 3. We need only add two variables, quantum imports, $M(t)$, and quantum exports, $X(t)$, and two equations. This can be formally expressed as

$$Q_1(t) = D_{11}(t) + D_{12}(t) + C_1(t) + I(t) + X(t), \qquad [3.15a]$$
$$Q_2(t) = D_{21}(t) + D_{22}(t) + C_2(t) - M(t), \qquad [3.16a]$$
$$M(t) = P(t)\,X(t), \qquad [3.22]$$
$$P(t) = \bar{P}(t). \qquad [3.23]$$

The first two equations simply rewrite the market clearing statements to include trade in agricultural and industrial goods. The third equation sets the trade balance equal to zero, and the last equation has the terms of trade given exogenously by world market conditions.[1]

Why wasn't this form of the dualistic model used in analyzing Meiji history? We shall argue below that the small-country version is far less realistic than our closed-economy version. The key issue in Meiji economic history is not whether our analytical framework should or should not be opened to trade. Rather, the key issue should be: What influence did Meiji Japan have over the terms of trade? Were price elasticities sufficiently low in her world markets such that the terms of trade were determined fundamentally by conditions endogenous to the Japanese economy? In section 12.4 we shall review qualitative evidence which suggests that the price-inelastic characterization is far more accurate. But in the absence of explicit quantitative evidence on the issue, we would certainly be advised to ask: What difference would it make?

12.3.2. Growth Analysis under Small-Country Assumptions

Let us examine these two extreme theoretical characterizations of the Meiji dualistic economy: the open small-country model and the closed model. In what way would the analysis of the previous chapters be revised under the open small-country assumptions?

Consider first the topic of chapter 10. There it was shown that the uniquely rapid rate of industrialization in the Meiji economy can be explained in large part by the equally unusual domestic demand conditions prevailing during the period. The income elasticity of demand for traditional products in general, and foodstuffs in particular, was very low, and it was shown that these demand characteristics could largely account for the rapid rate of industrialization up to 1915. The small-country model would have reached a very different conclusion. By reference to figure 12.2, the unusual domestic demand conditions in Japan would have only acted to suppress import demand for foodstuffs and would have reduced the volume of trade, not the structure of production. Since the growth of the dualistic economy, open or closed, is conditioned by the structure of the economy and supply factors (income distribution, overall rates of TFPG as a weighted average of sectoral rates, and so forth), demand would serve only to influence passively the volume of trade. It would not influence the structure of production nor the rate of industrialization. These two interpretations of the role of demand are obviously very different: which is the more appropriate characterization of Meiji development? To what extent did Meiji demand conditions influence the terms of trade and thus the structure of production?

Consider a key issue raised in chapter 9. It was argued that the labor-augmenting bias of technical change helps explain the observed stability in real wages up to 1915. This conclusion was confirmed by a counterfactual experiment. In table 9.3 the movements in real wages predicted by the closed dualistic model were compared with those which would have been forthcoming had the capital-augmenting bias typical of the post-World War II period prevailed in the Meiji period. Real wages would have risen more rapidly in the counterfactual world. Yet we noted nonetheless that the secular increase in real wages was somewhat lower in the counterfactual than expected. The explanation is to be found with terms-of-trade movements. The capital-augmenting bias implies a much more rapid relative rate of productivity growth in industry and a much sharper decline in the relative price of industrial goods as a result. The more pronounced upward pressure of agricultural goods' prices would have suppressed the rise in real wages. The same counterfactual examined in the open small-country model would have predicted a much more dramatic rise in real wages since the terms of trade, by assumption, would not have been influenced. Which is the more appropriate interpretation of Meiji Japanese growth?

Consider the analysis of natural resource constraints on Meiji growth contained in chapter 11. There we posed the following counterfactual: How would Japan have developed under a more elastic land supply? One surprising answer was that farm employment would have diminished at a more rapid rate than was in fact the case. A partial explanation for that result was simply that the relative price of agricultural goods would have risen at a far lower rate under elastic land supply conditions. At the more abundant land stock levels, this implied a relative contraction in output expansion rates, thus releasing labor at a more rapid pace. Had the relative price of foodstuffs remained unaltered as in the small-country case, the gainfully employed in agriculture would have declined at a much slower pace in the counterfactual world of elastic land supplies. Which of these historical interpretations of Meiji agricultural performance is closer to the truth?

Finally, consider once more the analysis of capital formation in the Meiji economy contained in chapters 6 and 7. Equation [6.1] decomposed capital accumulation rates into

$$\frac{\dot{K}(t)}{K(t)} = [1 - \alpha_L(t)]\, \bar{s} \frac{1}{P(t)} \left\{ \frac{K(t)}{G(t)} \right\}^{-1} - \delta.$$

Investment spurts in the Meiji economy might be interpreted as government-induced increases in $\bar{s}$. Chapter 7 devoted considerable attention to an empirical estimate of the impact of these savings rate changes on capital accumulation and thus on output growth rates. No doubt the association is positive in both the closed dualistic and the open small-country model. Yet, the size of the impact may vary considerably. In the closed dualistic model, the rise in $\bar{s}$ represents an upward shift in the investment demand schedule. This parametric change induces two offsetting influences. First, $\alpha_L(t)$ declines. That is, as industrial goods production rises to fulfill the increased demand for investment goods, this shift in industrial structure tends to suppress labor's share since industrial goods production is less labor-intensive. The resulting impact on capital accumulation rates is magnified since the economywide savings rate is raised by more than the initial rise in $\bar{s}$. Second, $P(t)$ rises. The relative price of industrial (capital) goods increases in response to excess demands and this price rise tends to dissipate the impact of the increased savings parameter. In short, some portion of increased savings is eaten up by the increased cost of capital goods. It is not obvious a priori which of these two effects should dominate in a given closed-economy model. What is obvious, however, is that the small-country model would ignore *both* effects. The change in demand would have no effect on the production mix and thus no effect on income distribution. In addition, it would have no effect on $P(t)$ since the relative price of capital goods would be determined exclusively by world market conditions. Which of these simple characteristics is closer to historical truth? We assert that it is the closed model.

12.3.3. Critique of the Small-Country Approach to Meiji History

Although the small-country assumption is a common one in trade theory and analysis, it is not embraced by most development economists. On the contrary, since the appearance of Nurkse's forceful arguments relating to the sharp differences between nineteenth- and twentieth-century conditions in primary product markets (Nurkse 1959), foreign exchange constraints on economic growth have become the cornerstone of theorizing and planning in contemporary developing economies (McKinnon 1964; Chenery and Strout 1966; Maizels 1968; Raj and Sen 1961). The key to this literature, of course, is a recognition of low price elasticities in foreign export markets for primary products. This empirical insight has motivated some economists to consider seriously the possibility of "immiserizing growth" where export earnings *fall* with an expansion of quantum exports to the world market and the subsequent decline in world prices given inelastic demand conditions (Bhagwati 1958). Growth under limited import capacity has, as a result, found its counterpart in theorizing under closed-economy conditions (Domar 1957; Mahalanobis 1952; Harris 1972). This book has followed that tradition; so too have many historians of Meiji Japan.

What we attempt to show below is that trade cannot be assigned a prime role in Meiji growth—as "export-led" or as an "engine of growth"—without serious attention to the foreign trade specification. Surely prices were never determined exogenously in world markets, independent of Japanese home supply and demand conditions. A more appropriate specification appears to be one of price-inelastic conditions abroad, both for exports and imports.

12.4. The Trade Specification Problem in Partial Equilibrium

Thus far we have confessed that nowhere in our closed-economy model do we account for the rapid *expost* rise in exports and imports as a share in GNP, especially from the mid-1890s to the end of World War I. A critical analytical issue, however, is the extent to which the performance reflects "export-led" growth induced by world market conditions external to the Japanese economy, and to what extent it reflects the forces of home supply. The answer would yield the appropriate specification for the determinants of relative commodity prices in Meiji Japan over time. Certainly the evidence of sharply declining relative prices of exports up to 1915 suggests support for the supply-oriented view of Meiji industrialization experience. We have already seen in chapter 4 that our closed-economy model reproduces closely the historical movements in the terms of trade. This indirect evidence suggests that our closed dualistic economy captures the essential elements of Japanese growth during the period. The next step is to improve on this first approximation. The agenda for future revisions can best be seen in simple partial equilibrium.

Figure 12.3 presents one potential description of Japanese exports, say textiles, at one point in time. In the left-hand panel, Japanese home consumption for textiles, D_T, and home supply, S_T, are described. The excess supply is "vented" onto the world market as textile exports, ES_T, in the right-hand panel. Given the excess demand function for textiles in world markets, ED_T, an equilibrium price for home and foreign textiles, P^*_T, can be determined. (For expository convenience we ignore transport costs, tariffs, and other protectionist devices in this example.) The small-country assumption would take ED_T as perfectly elastic, so that changes in either home supply or demand would have no effect on P^*_T, but only on the surplus vented, X^*_T. The impact of shifts in ES_T over time on P^*_T and X^*_T depend critically on the elasticity of ED_T and its shift over time. We observe a decline in the relative price of exports (especially textile exports) from

FIGURE 12.3

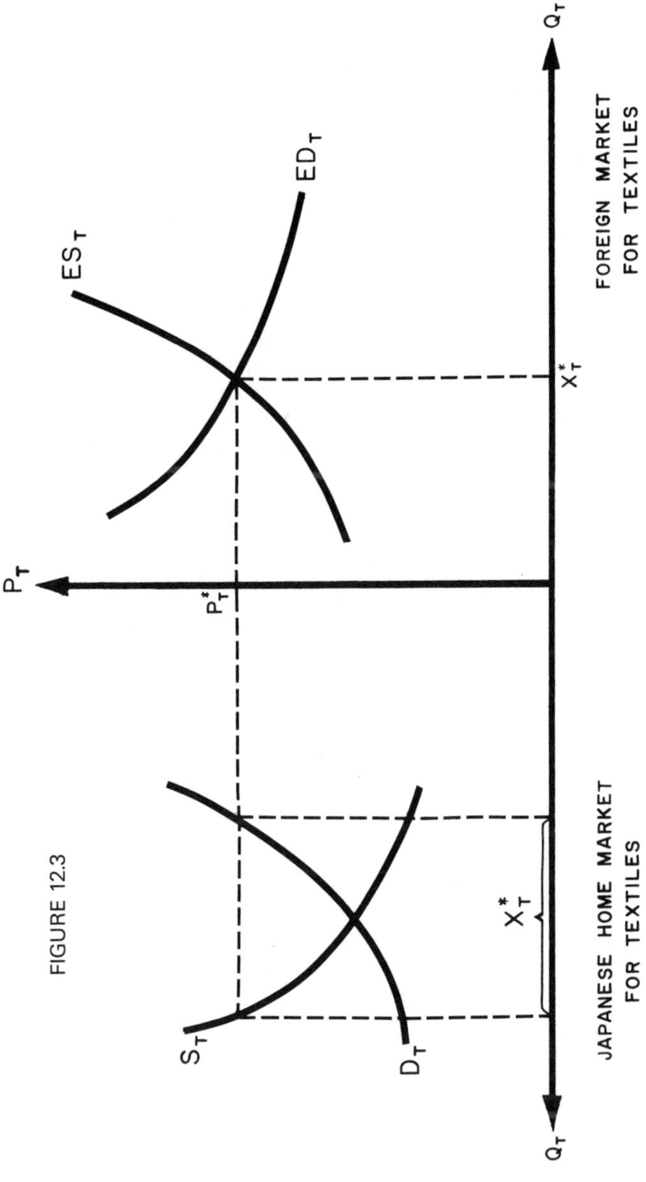
P_T
P^*_T
ES_T
ED_T
S_T
D_T
X^*_T
X^*_T
Q_T
Q_T
JAPANESE HOME MARKET FOR TEXTILES
FOREIGN MARKET FOR TEXTILES

1885 to 1915, and an even more dramatic rise in quantities exported (especially textiles) as in figure 12.4. There are three historical interpretations of these *expost* equilibrium observations. Figure 12.4A captures the historical trends by assuming a *stable* but price-elastic ED_T. The observed expansion would be entirely attributed to domestic supply factors. This would appear to be the position taken in a recent paper by Shionoya and Yamazawa (1972, p. 5):

> The role of export demand as a stimulus to industrial growth is generally stressed and little regard is paid to the fact that exports are in turn accounted for by supply factors associated with domestic industrial growth. . . . The export growth of cotton textiles and other labor-intensive light manufactures, which accounted for a major part of Japanese exports at least until World War II, was not benefitted from favorable foreign demand. . . . It is mainly attributed to a decline in the relative export prices of Japanese products compared with foreign products and a consequent increase in the share of Japanese exports in the world market.

An alternative interpretation is presented in figure 12.4B. Here, Japanese exports expand in spite of increasingly unfavorable world market conditions. Had world market conditions remained unchanged at $P_{T,85}$, exports would have expanded even more rapidly. In this interpretation, trade is hardly an "engine of growth," but rather a "brake on growth." The rate of industrialization would be forestalled in this account. This appears to be the position taken by Shinohara (1972*a*) who views trade movements between 1874 and 1940 as exogenously determined.[9] Figure 12.4C yields an intermediate position which also appears to be consistent with the historical evidence. This position is the one taken by Baba and Tatemoto (1968, p. 182): "Japanese exports of textiles found a growing demand in the world market. In addition, its competitive strength in exports enabled Japan to increase its share in the world market."

Since we have argued that the sources of Meiji industrialization cannot be fully understood by an examination of *expost* data alone, it might prove useful at this point to explore alternative counterfactuals in terms of these three divergent views of Meiji Japan. First, consider the impact of increased capital formation rates. The creation of additional industrial capacity in 1885 would have had the following effects: (1) in figure 12.4C,

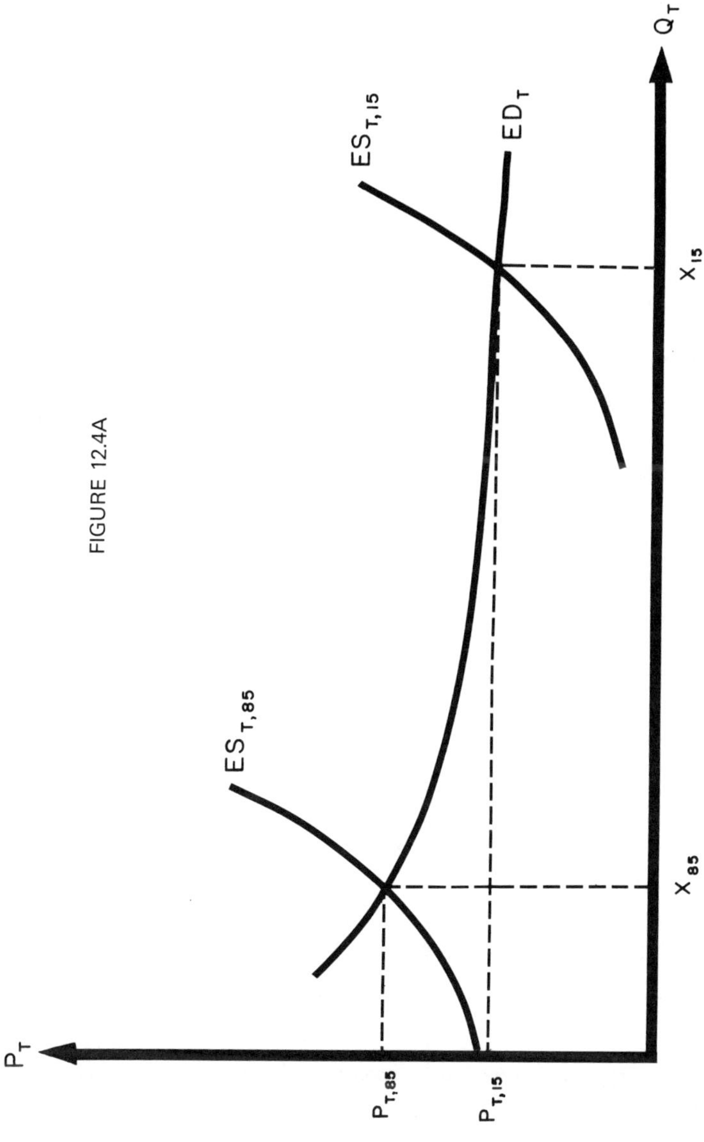

FIGURE 12.4A

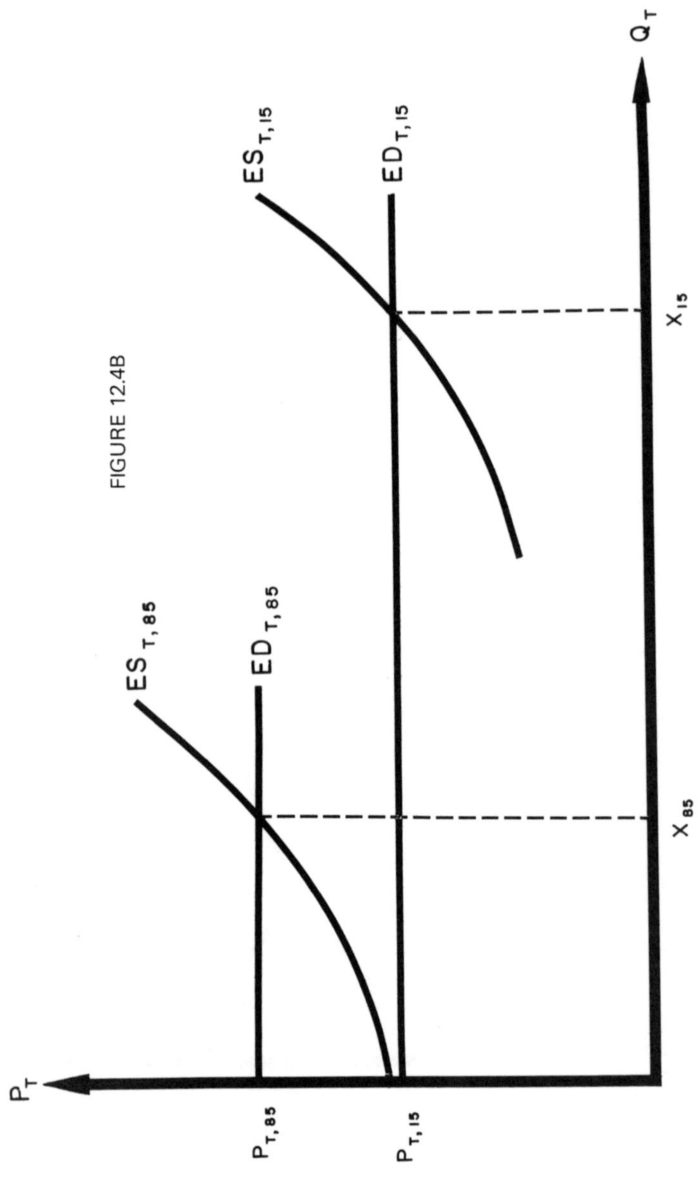

FIGURE 12.4B

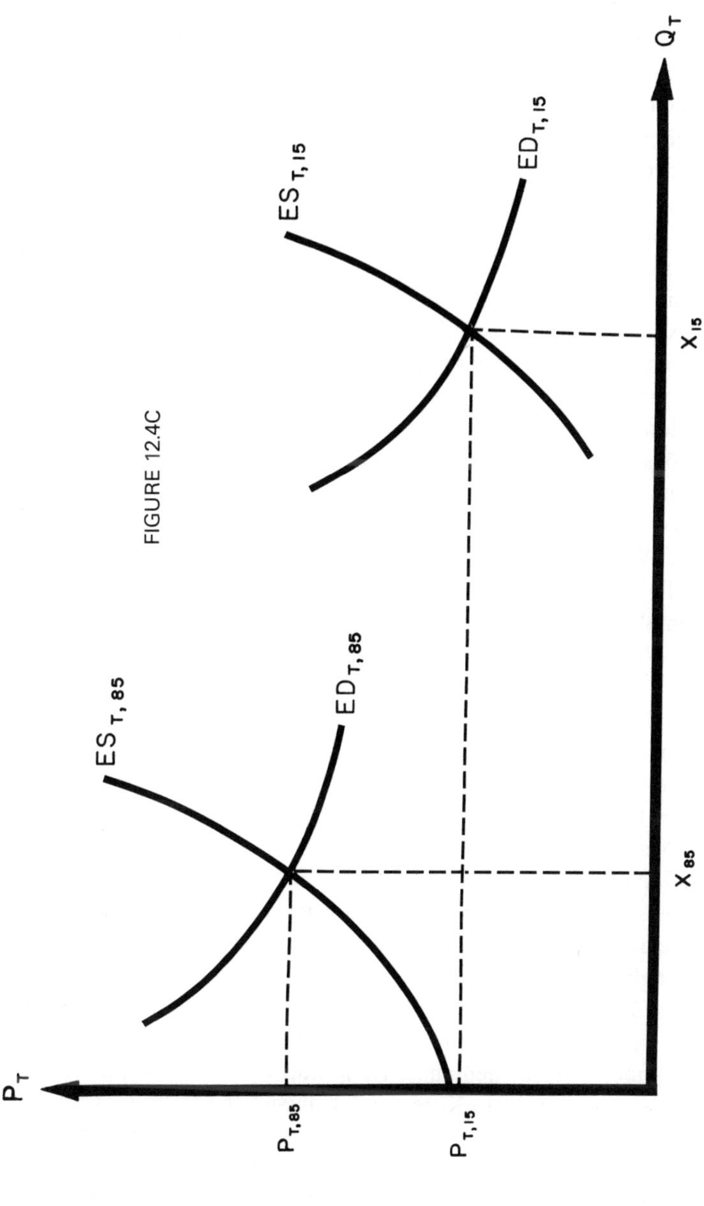

FIGURE 12.4C

very little expansion in output (or exports) would have been forthcoming, but rather the relative price of industrial goods would have declined markedly; (2) in figure 12.4B, an impressive expansion in industrial output (and exports) would have taken place with stable prices; (3) figure 12.4A would have predicted mixed effects on exports, output, and prices. Second, consider the impact of an increased home demand for industrial products induced either by military activity, by a change in tastes, or by a change in the distribution of income away from rural households: (1) figure 12.4B would predict a reduction in exports, but with stable prices, and industrial output would remain unaffected; (2) figure 12.4A would suggest a rise in P_T, an expansion in industrial output, but a contraction in exports; (3) figure 12.4C would predict a more marked rise in P_T, a more pronounced expansion in industrial output, but a marginal contraction in exports. Obviously, knowledge of the price elasticities describing ED_T are crucial before Japanese economic historians can untangle the "lessons of history."

Nor does the problem of trade specification cease with exports. What is the appropriate historical description of excess supplies of primary products in Japan's trading partners and colonial areas from which her key imports came? This is not to deny that Japan's imports were mixed. Appendix table A.19 shows the following: between 1890/94 and 1915/19, foodstuffs decrease as a share in total imports from 23 to 15 percent, raw materials increase from 19 to 37 percent, manufactures decrease from 54 to 35 percent, while services make up the residual. Let us focus on primary products in general, and rice in particular. Net rice imports to Japan rise from 49,000 million tons in 1895 to 406,000 million tons in 1915.[2] The majority of these net imports came from Korea and Taiwan. We have also seen that the relative price of rice tends to rise over the period 1890–1915, although not nearly as rapidly as the expansion in imports. Figure 12.5 displays these observations in a fashion comparable to figure 12.4, but now the "foreign" market for rice is composed of Japanese excess demands, ED_R, and the excess supply function abroad (that is, in Korea and Taiwan), ES_R. Only two cases are considered in figure 12.5, and once more it is clear that the elasticity of ES_R and ED_R will be crucial in any analysis of Meiji Japan. The first case, labeled $ES_{R,t}$, takes the foreign ex-

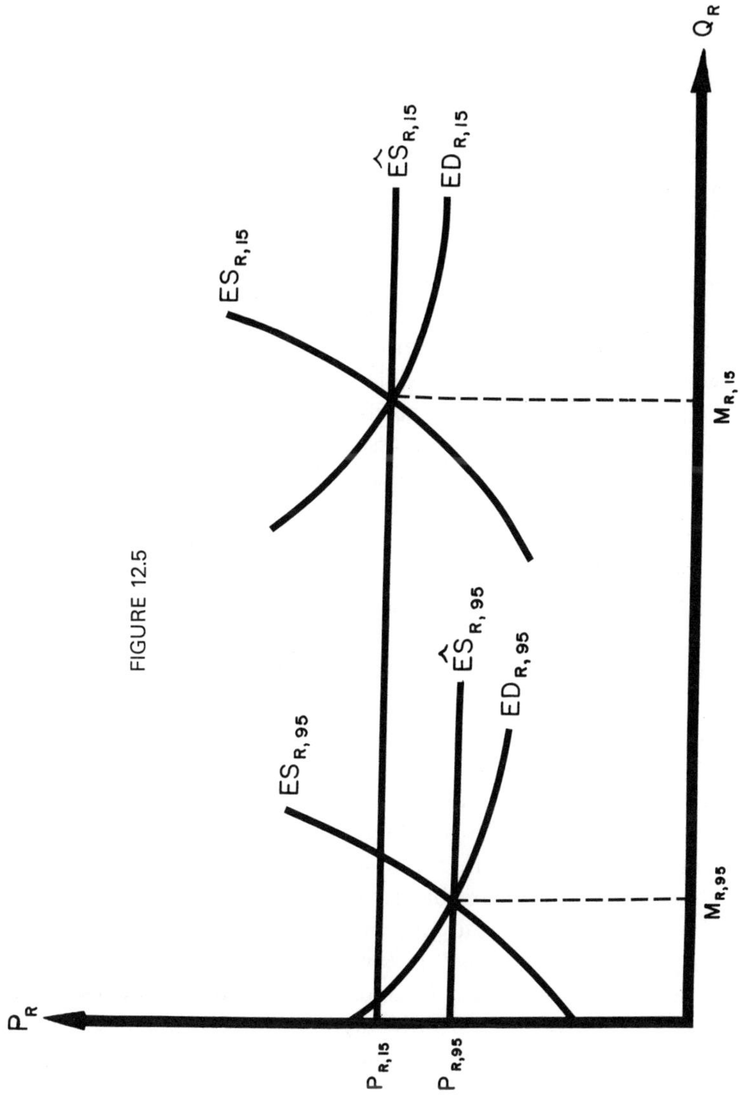
P_R
Q_R
$ES_{R,15}$
$\hat{ES}_{R,15}$
$ED_{R,15}$
$ES_{R,95}$
$\hat{ES}_{R,95}$
$ED_{R,95}$
$M_{R,15}$
$M_{R,95}$
$P_{R,15}$
$P_{R,95}$

FIGURE 12.5

cess supply function as relatively inelastic, reflecting what we assume to be high short-run inelasticities of demand and supply in Korea and Taiwan. These are allowed to shift to the right over time, reflecting the transfer of technology and agricultural resources to those colonial areas over the two decades (Hayami 1972, 1971). In this case, a counterfactual experiment involving, say, more elastic land supplies in Japan, or a relative shift out of rice consumption associated with increasingly regressive Meiji taxation, would predict an abrupt decline in rice prices but only a marginal contraction in net imports and home consumption. The second position is that adopted by Hayami and Ruttan (1971, pp. 230–37) in their counterfactual experiment applied to the interwar period: rice prices are given exogenously so that $\widehat{ES}_{R,t}$ is treated as perfectly elastic. In this case, imports would contract markedly while home consumption would remain unchanged. Which specification is more appropriate to Meiji Japan? Obviously, the assumed short-run price elasticities will make a great deal of difference to the "lessons of history" learned by such analyses.

What evidence do wc have? In spite of the great importance to be attached to the estimates, we have almost none. A sample of the evidence is displayed in table 12.2. These results seem to corroborate the position that Japanese world trade conditions before the late 1930s were characterized by very low price elasticities. To be sure, these estimates are only crude guidelines. A substantial econometric literature has developed since the 1940s which suggests that import and export price elasticities estimated from time series data have an inherent downward bias (Orcutt 1950; Leamer and Stern 1970, pp. 7–55). Indeed, the only cases in which the regression estimates like those reported in table 12.2 are reasonably accurate seem to be "when countries are relatively small and also [in the case of exports] when demand is relatively stable" (Leamer and Stern 1970, p. 34). Stability in export demand is hardly consistent with the Japanese "trade as an engine of growth" literature, and the relative "smallness" assumption is, unfortunately, precisely the point upon which these elasticity estimates are supposed to shed light! Indeed, it is not the elasticity of import demand which is crucial but the elasticity of excess supply of importables, and the research reported in table 12.2 uniformly assumes perfectly elastic excess

Table 12.2

Estimated Price Elasticities of Demand
For Meiji Imports and Exports

Author	Period	Exports	Imports
Baba and Tatemoto [1968]	1879-1896	+0.882	-0.586
Baba and Tatemoto [1968]	1897-1913	-0.858	-1.144
Shionoya and Yamazawa [1972]	1905-1914	-1.370	na
Shionoya and Yamazawa [1972]	1921-1931	-1.150	na
Shionoya and Yamazawa [1972]	1905-1938	na	-1.285
Odaka and Ishiwata [1972]	1906-1938	+0.096	na

Sources: M. Baba and M. Tatemoto, "Foreign Trade and Economic Growth in Japan: 1858-1937," pp. 174 and 178; Y. Shionoya and I. Yamazawa, "Industrial Growth and Foreign Trade in Pre-War Japan," pp. 17 and 23, where imports include only manufactures and raw material imports have a price elasticity of demand equal to zero; K. Odaka and S. Ishiwata, "Effective Demand and Cyclical Growth of the Japanese Economy: 1906-1938," pp. 23-24.

supply functions. Thus, we are left with these ambiguous estimates which, nevertheless, argue for the inelastic specification. What little evidence we do have on the issue appears to confirm the relevance of our closed-economy assumptions where commodity price relatives are determined endogenously and where demand and supply conditions play a critical role. The burden of proof would appear to lie at the doorstep of those who reject a closed-economy assumption.

12.5. Trade as an Engine of Japanese Growth?

> If the Japanese economy flew like a wild bird from an opened cage after the opening of the country, it is not unreasonable to expect Japan's foreign trade to have been one of the propelling engines. [Baba and Tatemoto 1968, p. 162]

> Exports did not lead economic growth in Japan, but provided close support. [Kindleberger 1962, p. 206]

> The impact of foreign trade on growth is then indeterminate over a wide range. Trade can stimulate growth, when the demand is right abroad and the supply is right at home. It can inhibit it when the demand is wrong abroad and the supply is wrong at home. In the two intermediate cases, we do not know. [Ibid., p. 211]

Statements such as these are hardly very useful in evaluating trade as an engine of Japanese growth. Since Japan has conventionally been viewed as a classic example of the beneficial effects of trade on growth, the stakes appear to be high. It also seems clear that in seeking an answer to this question we must discard the favorite experiment of the trade theorist: it is not very useful to calculate the gains from trade by comparing a Japanese economy first closed and then opened to trade under small-country assumptions (see, for example, Corden 1971). Nor is it very useful to pursue qualitative analysis and to rely on a "vent for surplus" taxonomy (Caves 1971). There was no surplus to be vented onto the world economy in the Japanese case in the sense that resources were underutilized. Clearly, Meiji Japanese trade performance was determined by the joint interaction of domestic conditions and exogenous shifts in foreign market conditions.

It seems to us that the export-led adherents have been asking the wrong counterfactual. In our judgment, the appropriate counterfactual that any "new" economic history of Japan should ask is the following: *given foreign excess supply and demand elasticities for Japanese importables and exportables, how did shifts in those functions over time influence the growth and structural change of the Japanese economy?* No doubt the quantitative analysis may be difficult, but the arguments given above suggest how we might proceed.

Consider once again the simple partial equilibrium characterization of textiles in figure 12.3. If we could successfully identify the shifts in ED_T over time, 1887–1915, then we could ask any number of counterfactuals which would isolate the role of trade. We could allow ED_T to grow at a constant but low rate over time; or at a high rate over time; or impose stability on it. In addition, given an estimate of the temporal shift in ED_T, we could then recompute all the counterfactual experiments performed in this book to see to what extent the closed-economy assumption generates erroneous lessons of history. The difficult step, of course, is the initial estimate of $ED_T(t)$. The following notation will prove helpful:[3]

S_T: Japanese textile supply
D_T: Japanese textile demand

P_T: price of textiles
ED_T: excess demand for textiles in the rest of the world
ES_T: Japanese excess textile supply
η: elasticity of home textile supply
γ: elasticity of home textile demand
α: elasticity of foreign excess demand function for textiles.

Using this notation, let

$$S_T(t) = A(t)\,P_T(t)^{\eta},$$
$$D_T(t) = C(t)\,P_T(t)^{\gamma},$$
$$ED_T(t) = B(t)\,P_T(t)^{\alpha},$$
$$ED_T^*(t) = ES_T^*(t) = S_T^*(t) - D_T^*(t),$$

where the "*" refers to market clearing values. From this system of equations, we can derive an expression for $B(t)$:

$$B(t) = \frac{A(t)P_T^*(t)^{\eta} - C(t)P_T^*(t)^{\gamma}}{P_T^*(t)^{\alpha}}.$$

$P_T^*(t)$, $S_T^*(t)$ and $D_T^*(t)$ can all be documented directly from the historical data, and approximations of η and γ presumably could be readily derived from Meiji evidence. It follows that the shifts in Japanese textile demand and supply over time can be identified by

$$A(t) = \frac{S_T^*(t)}{P_T^*(t)^{\eta}},$$

and

$$C(t) = \frac{D_T^*(t)}{P_T^*(t)^{\gamma}}.$$

Given an estimate of α, the price elasticity of the foreign excess demand function for textiles, a historical series for $B(t)$ could be identified. The $B(t)$ series would represent the changing exogenous world market conditions facing the Meiji economy 1887–1915. Indeed, *it is an index of export-led growth.* Alternative series on $B(t)$ could be generated under various assumptions regarding α. In any case, having estimated the historical shifts in $B(t)$ it is but a simple matter to answer relevant counterfactuals like: How would Japan have grown if $B(t)$ had remained constant over these three decades? Similar calculations could be performed for imports.

12.6. The Agenda

It may seem ironic that we have elected to conclude this study of a closed model of Meiji Japan by pointing out ways in which an open-economy rendition *could* influence the results. Yet at this point, the chapter's message must be abundantly clear. Not only have we shown that the development of an open model must await further econometric analyses of Japanese trade, but more important, it is *not* obvious whether an open-economy model of Meiji Japan *would* notably affect the major findings of this study. True, it is a simple enough matter to document a rising share of exports and imports in Meiji development. But in virtually every chapter of part 3 of this book, we have also shown that quantitatively impressive *expost* data trends, or dramatic parametric shifts, do not represent sufficient evidence to demonstrate that the economy was, in some sense, importantly influenced by the observed trend or parametric change in question. Indeed, our most typical finding has been that there are numerous linkages in a general equilibrium model of economic development which, when fully revealed and quantified, provide both reinforcing and offsetting influences with respect to a particular economic force which may have been considered "important" on the basis of a priori analysis.

Consider again briefly the role of population change. Very few economists would even question the hypothesis that a tripling of population growth rates would have dramatically reduced output per capita performance in early Meiji development. Yet, as shown in chapter 8, the reduction is far less than might have been expected. There are offsetting influences which come into play in a general equilibrium model. They are sufficiently important that simple comparative static analysis provides relatively few guidelines in assessing the quantitative role of population in the economy. So too with trade—indeed, with almost any other specification one might add to our basic paradigm. A tripling of exports may or may not have had a major impact on the pace and structure of Japanese development during the Meiji period. Depending on the precise nature of the trade specification and the quantitative estimates of the supply and demand elasticities, simple comparative statics may lead significant, moderate, or even insignificant impacts of trade. Trade may be responding merely to basic endogenously determined forces, or it may represent a fundamental determining influence on Japanese development. *Expost* data and a priori analysis is not sufficient to form a conclusive judgment on these matters.

This observation provides a fitting conclusion to our study since it speaks to the underlying theme of the research. One judges economic models both by their predictive capacity and by their ability to come to grips with important problems. Our model, founded on postulates documented as empirically relevant to early Japanese development, appears to offer a reasonable description of the Meiji historical record. Moreover, the problems it confronts constitute a large set of the primary issues raised by development economists, growth theorists, and economic historians over the two or three decades prior to 1970: the role of demand in development, the sources of industrialization, the impact of population growth, the influence of government fiscal policy, the nature of take-offs, the strategic role of agriculture, and so forth. Admittedly, our objectives must of necessity be limited. Several aspects of development have not been modeled and may represent a useful agenda for future research. Foreign trade, fiscal policy, factor market imperfections, the service sector, and embodied technical change are just some of these. Revisions of our dualistic model by others may well provide additional insights into the problems we have confronted, and into problems our paradigm was not designed to analyze. However, short of providing such formal specifications, short of parameterizing these within a general equilibrium framework, and short of comparing the resulting forecasts with those of our model, with others, and with history, little further progress is likely to be made in assessing the "importance" of those elements which represent modifications of our paradigm. Equally true, the methodology developed in this study demonstrates that no claims for unique validity of our interpretation of Meiji Japanese development can be made. Any history of this type "will today be no more than a parable agreed upon"

(Abramovitz and David 1971, p. 1). Ours offers a reasonable norm against which further model improvements can be made. We would encourage others to engage in this endeavor. Only then may we expect to edge closer to the truth and uncover the lessons of Meiji history.

Appendix A

The Historical Data

A.1. Prices: Table A.1

A.1.1. Sources to Table A.1

$P_A(t)$, col. (1): Ohkawa et al., *Estimates of Long-term Economic Statistics of Japan since 1868* (hereafter *LTES*), vol. 8, table 10, col. (4), p. 165. This is an annual all-commodity index of agricultural products, 1934–36 = 100. The index excludes cocoons, livestock, and poultry products.

$P_I(t)$, col. (2): Ibid., table 15, col. (1), p. 192. This is an annual production price index for manufacturing, 1934–36 = 100. The index excludes mining products.

$P_K(t)$, col. (3): Ibid., table 1, col. (3), p. 134. This is an annual index of investment goods prices in expenditure terms; 1934–36 = 100. The index includes construction costs of all structures; producers durable equipment, machinery, and tools; and ships.

$P_X(t)$, col. (4): Ibid., table 18, col. (1), p. 212. This is an annual export price index, 1934–36 = 100.

$P_M(t)$, col. (5): Ibid., table 18, col. (2), p. 212. This is an annual import price index, 1934–36 = 100.

$P_I(t)/P_A(t)$, col. (6): col. (2) ÷ col. (1) and 1887 = 100.

$P_K(t)/P_A(t)$, col. (7): col. (3) ÷ col. (1) and 1887 = 100.

$P_X(t)/P_M(t)$, col. (8): col. (4) ÷ col. (5) and 1887 = 100.

A.1.2. Discussion of Table A.1

For the most part the Japanese historical data are of high quality. Furthermore, they conform well to the needs of our analysis. They are all based on commodity output (with exception of the construction component in P_K), and both P_A and P_I correspond almost exactly to the agricultural and industrial commodity output series presented below in table A.6.

Table A.1 - Prices

Year	$P_A(t)$ (1)	$P_I(t)$ (2)	$P_K(t)$ (3)	$P_X(t)$ (4)	$P_M(t)$ (5)	$\frac{P_I(t)}{P_A(t)}$ (6)	$\frac{P_K(t)}{P_A(t)}$ (7)	$\frac{P_X(t)}{P_M(t)}$ (8)
1880	38.50	45.90	28.90	70.90	38.50	74.30	50.50	93.66
1881	40.90	55.60	30.20	71.40	40.40	84.72	49.67	89.88
1882	34.20	50.40	29.90	70.30	40.60	91.84	58.81	88.06
1883	25.40	39.90	31.90	63.60	37.00	97.90	84.49	87.42
1884	22.10	35.60	32.20	62.90	35.30	100.39	98.02	90.62
1885	25.90	34.40	31.20	62.50	35.40	82.77	81.04	89.79
1886	23.70	33.30	31.40	71.10	36.10	87.56	89.13	100.16
1887	22.00	35.30	32.70	69.80	35.50	100.00	100.00	100.00
1888	21.10	35.40	35.70	64.50	34.70	104.56	113.83	94.53
1889	24.50	36.60	35.90	71.30	37.50	93.10	98.58	96.70
1890	32.90	38.00	35.10	73.40	38.00	71.98	71.77	98.23
1891	28.70	35.70	33.60	71.50	35.60	77.52	78.76	102.14
1892	29.40	37.10	35.00	74.20	35.30	78.64	80.09	106.90
1893	30.10	38.30	35.10	79.50	36.30	79.30	78.45	111.38
1894	34.30	40.20	37.50	83.40	38.80	73.04	73.55	109.32
1895	34.40	43.30	42.40	90.40	39.50	78.44	82.92	116.39
1896	37.00	45.80	45.00	86.80	42.10	77.14	81.82	104.86
1897	44.70	52.40	51.00	92.90	45.90	73.05	76.76	102.93
1898	52.70	56.30	51.00	101.30	47.00	66.58	66.00	109.61
1899	45.30	58.70	52.90	108.50	50.70	80.75	78.56	108.84
1900	47.40	61.90	55.60	94.20	60.00	81.38	78.91	79.85
1901	44.80	59.90	54.50	91.70	58.80	83.32	81.84	79.31
1902	48.80	59.30	51.60	104.10	56.60	75.73	71.13	93.54
1903	55.40	62.30	52.40	110.70	56.90	70.08	63.63	98.94
1904	53.60	65.90	53.30	107.40	61.80	76.62	66.90	88.38
1905	54.40	72.40	56.70	115.90	61.70	82.94	70.12	95.53
1906	57.70	74.80	59.30	122.00	62.30	80.79	69.14	99.59
1907	63.80	81.00	65.00	136.90	66.30	79.12	68.54	105.01
1908	60.90	77.30	61.20	115.10	63.60	79.10	67.61	92.04
1909	54.30	74.70	57.00	109.50	60.60	85.73	70.62	91.90
1910	55.30	75.00	57.40	101.20	69.00	84.52	69.83	74.59
1911	68.00	78.10	58.30	102.80	63.40	71.58	57.68	82.46
1912	79.30	81.40	63.70	103.80	70.90	63.97	54.04	74.46
1913	78.80	79.80	63.50	107.40	70.00	63.11	54.21	78.03
1914	56.50	76.30	60.80	103.50	71.60	84.16	72.39	73.51
1915	53.30	80.60	64.90	98.50	63.40	94.24	81.92	79.01
1916	60.50	100.50	80.20	127.80	84.60	103.52	89.18	76.83
1917	85.50	129.40	107.20	153.90	106.20	94.32	84.35	73.70
1918	132.70	160.80	133.90	181.20	143.60	75.52	67.88	64.17
1919	182.00	186.00	139.40	244.20	159.30	63.69	51.53	77.96

A.2. WAGES AND EARNINGS: Table A.2

A.2.1. Sources to Table A.2

$w_A(t)$, col. (1): *LTES,* vol. 8, table 25, col. (34), p. 245. This is a male laborer daily wage series for agriculture (in sen), current prices.

$w_c(t)$, col. (2): Ibid., table 25, col. (30), p. 245. This is a daily wage figure for common labor (in sen), current prices.

$w_m(t)$, col. (3): Ibid., table 25, col. (1), p. 243. This is a male wage rate in manufacturing (in sen), current prices.

$w_m^*(t)$, col. (4): Tussing, "The Labor Force in Meiji Economic Growth," table 5, p. 211. This is a real daily wage index (1885/87 = 100) for female workers in Yamanashi Prefecture silk-reeling factories. The deflator is a local cost-of-living index.

$w_m^*(t)y(t)$, col. (5): Ibid., table 12, p. 217. This is an annual earnings index in real terms for female (Yamanashi Prefecture) silk-reeling workers. The deflator is a local cost-of-living index.

$w_A(t)/P_A(t)$, col. (6): col. (1) $\div$ col. (1), table A.1 where 1887 = 100. A real wage index for agriculture.

$w_c(t)/P_A(t)$, col. (7): col. (2) $\div$ col. (1), table A.1 where 1887 = 100. A real wage index for common labor.

$w_m(t)/P_A(t)$, col. (8): col. (3) $\div$ col. (1), table A.1 where 1887 = 100. A real wage index for manufacturing.

A.2.2. Discussion of Table A.2

The three *LTES* wage series correspond well with the efficiency wage variables defined in the model, after, of course, deflating by $P_A(t)$. They are specific to sex and occupation, and are daily rates. The annual wage earnings data reported in the *LTES* are less useful for our purposes. We therefore rely on Tussing's manufacturing wage and earnings data reported in table A.2, cols. (4) and (5). These data are specific to silk reeling in one prefecture, Yamanashi. It appears to be reasonably representative of Japanese manufacturing as a whole. Cols. (1) through (3) are in current prices while cols. (4) through (8) are in constant prices.

A.3. NOMINAL AND REAL INTEREST RATES: Table A.3

A.3.1. Sources to Table A.3

$i_1(t)$, col. (1): Bank of Japan, *Hundred-Year Statistics of the Japanese Economy,* table 111, pp. 260–61. This is a nominal

Table A.2 - Wages and Earnings

Year	$w_A(t)$ (1)	$w_c(t)$ (2)	$w_m(t)$ (3)	Period	$w^*_m(t)$ (4)	$w^*_m(t)y(t)$ (5)
1880	22.00	21.00	24.00	1885-87	100	2.54
1881						
1882	22.00	22.00	27.00	1888-92	102	2.79
1883	19.00	19.00	25.00			
1884	16.00	18.00	20.00	1893-97	122	3.31
1885	15.00	16.00	22.00			
1886	14.00	15.00	20.00	1898-02	108	3.24
1887	15.00	16.00	21.00			
1888	-	-	21.00	1903-07	109	3.38
1889	-	-	20.00			
1890	-	-	19.00	1908-11	113	4.46
1891	-	-	22.00			
1892	17.00	18.00	24.00			
1893	-	-	24.00			
1894	18.00	21.00	24.00			
1895	19.00	22.00	25.00			
1896	22.00	26.00	28.00			
1897	26.00	29.00	33.00			
1898	29.00	33.00	36.00			
1899	27.00	34.00	40.00			
1900	31.00	37.00	41.00			
1901	33.00	39.00	42.00			
1902	32.00	39.00	44.00			
1903	32.00	40.00	44.00			
1904	31.00	40.00	45.00			
1905	31.00	41.00	46.00			
1906	39.00	42.00	49.00			
1907	39.00	49.00	56.00			
1908	41.00	53.00	59.00			
1909	41.00	52.00	60.00			
1910	41.00	53.00	60.00			
1911	44.00	56.00	62.00			
1912	44.00	58.00	63.00			
1913	48.00	59.00	65.00			
1914	49.00	56.00	65.00			
1915	46.00	55.00	64.00			
1916	48.00	57.00	67.00			
1917	54.00	70.00	77.00			
1918	74.00	96.00	99.00			
1919	120.00	143.00	144.00			

Table A.2 - Wages and Earnings
(continued)

Year	$\frac{w_A(t)}{P_A(t)}$ (6)	$\frac{w_c(t)}{P_A(t)}$ (7)	$\frac{w_m(t)}{P_A(t)}$ (8)
1880	83.81	75.00	65.30
1881	78.89	70.59	64.03
1882	94.34	88.45	82.70
1883	109.71	102.85	103.11
1884	106.18	111.99	94.80
1885	84.94	84.94	88.98
1886	86.63	87.02	88.40
1887	100.00	100.00	100.00
1888	104.26	104.26	104.26
1889	89.79	89.79	85.52
1890	71.32	71.04	60.50
1891	81.76	81.44	80.30
1892	84.80	84.18	85.52
1893	82.83	91.36	83.53
1894	76.96	84.18	73.30
1895	81.00	87.93	76.13
1896	87.20	96.62	79.27
1897	85.30	89.20	77.34
1898	80.70	86.10	71.56
1899	87.41	103.20	92.50
1900	95.92	107.33	90.61
1901	108.03	119.69	98.21
1902	96.17	109.88	94.45
1903	84.71	99.27	83.20
1904	84.82	102.61	87.95
1905	83.57	103.63	88.58
1906	99.13	100.08	88.96
1907	89.65	105.60	91.95
1908	98.74	119.66	101.49
1909	110.74	131.67	115.75
1910	108.74	131.78	113.66
1911	94.90	113.23	95.51
1912	81.37	100.56	83.22
1913	89.34	102.95	86.41
1914	127.19	136.28	120.52
1915	126.57	141.88	125.79
1916	116.36	129.54	116.01
1917	92.63	112.57	94.34
1918	81.78	99.47	78.15
1919	96.70	108.03	82.88

Table A.3 - Nominal and Real Interest Rates

Year	$i_1(t)$ (1)	$i_2(t)$ (2)	$i_3(t)$ (3)	$r_1(t)$ (4)	$r_2(t)$ (5)	$r_3(t)$ (6)
1882	13.87	7.62	9.49	12.8	6.6	8.5
1887	12.70	4.70	5.48	14.7	6.5	7.1
1892	12.05	4.30	5.84	15.5	7.5	9.1
1897	11.64	5.89	7.30	3.9	-1.4	-0.1
1902	11.86	6.93	6.21	11.6	6.6	5.9
1907	11.68	5.41	6.57	7.1	1.1	1.8
1912	12.78	5.30	5.48	8.1	0.9	1.1
1916	10.59	4.27	5.84	9.0	2.7	4.3

discount rate (highest) quoted in Tokyo, converted to an annual rate.

$i_2(t)$, col. (2): Ibid., table 111, pp. 262–63. This is a nominal rate on time deposits in Tokyo converted to an annual rate.

$i_3(t)$, col. (3): Ibid., table 111, pp. 260–61. This is the discount rate on commercial bills by the Bank of Japan (lowest) converted to an annual rate.

$r_1(t)$, col. (4): Derived from

$$r_1(t) = \frac{i_1(t) - \dot{p}(t)}{1 + \dot{p}(t)}$$

where $\dot{p}(t)$ is the average rate of annual price inflation for the preceding three years. Prices refer to a general consumer price index from *LTES,* vol. 8, table 2, col. 1, p. 135.

$r_2(t)$, col. (5): Derived from $i_2(t)$ applying $\dot{p}(t)$ as in $r_1(t)$.

$r_3(t)$, col. (6): Derived from $i_3(t)$ applying $\dot{p}(t)$ as in $r_1(t)$.

A.3.2. Discussion of Table A.3

In cols. (4) through (6), the nominal rate is adjusted in an attempt to reflect better the real rate of interest. The adjustment for price inflation is approximate and assumes that the rate of current price change is known with perfect certainty. The resulting real rates are useful as rough measures of trends in the real cost of finance and thus, presumably, trends in the real net rates of return.

A.4. AGRICULTURAL LAND STOCK: Table A.4

A.4.1. Sources to Table A.4

$R_p(t)$, col. (1): Yamada and Hayami, "Agriculture," Appendix table B, p. 25. This is a four-year average of paddy field acreage, in units of 1,000 hectares.

Table A.4 - Agricultural Land Stock

Period	$R_p(t)$ (1)	$R_u(t)$ (2)	$R(t)$ (3)
1878-82	2,790	1,945	4,735
1883-87	2,825	1,996	4,821
1888-92	2,857	2,067	4,924
1893-97	2,875	2,158	5,033
1898-02	2,904	2,289	5,193
1903-07	2,936	2,371	5,307
1908-12	3,006	2,568	5,574
1913-17	3,073	2,711	5,784
1918-22	3,133	2,850	5,983

$R_u(t)$, col. (2): Ibid., Appendix table B, p. 25. This is a four-year average of upland field acreage in units of 1,000 hectares.

$R(t)$, col. (3): Sum of cols. (1) and (2).

A.4.2. Discussion of Table A.4

Note that the growth in irrigated paddy appears to be quite low throughout this period. Indeed, the share of total arable land in paddy actually falls from 58.6 to 53.1 percent from 1883/87 to 1913/17. The quality of land inputs as judged by the percentage of irrigated hectarage does not increase over the period. This characteristic of land expansion will be discussed in detail in section A.5.2 below.

A.5. CAPITAL STOCK: Table A.5

A.5.1. Sources to Table A.5

$K_I^G(t)$, col. (1): *LTES,* table 57, pp. 246–49. Gross capital stock in nonprimary sectors, excluding residential structures. All of the capital stock data presented in table A.5 are in millions

Table A.5 - Capital Stock

Year	$K_I^G(t)$ (1)	$K_A^G(t)$ (2)	$K^G(t)$ (3)	$K_I^N(t)$ (4)	$K_A^N(t)$ (5)	$K^N(t)$ (6)
1887	2,673	3,835	6,508	1,790	1,918	3,708
1891	3,252	3,837	7,089	2,183	1,914	4,097
1895	4,069	3,846	7,915	2,750	1,922	4,672
1899	5,100	3,874	8,974	3,493	1,940	5,433
1903	6,131	3,909	10,040	4,200	1,957	6,157
1907	7,618	3,979	11,597	5,252	1,995	7,247
1911	9,865	3,981	13,846	6,801	2,046	8,847
1915	12,509	4,163	16,672	8,616	2,088	10,704

Table A.5a - Land Values

Year	V_p	V_{up}	V_p/V_{up}
1890	60	21	2.86
1899	126	47	2.68
1904	133	49	2.71
1909	(203)	(79)	2.57
1914	250	91	2.75
1919	653	271	2.41
Average	238	93	2.66

Source for Table A.5a: Estimates of Long-Term Economic Statistics, Vol. 9, Table 34, p. 220, cols. (9) and (10); in current yen per tan. V_p denotes paddy, and V_{up} upland.

of yen, 1934–36 prices. Each series represents a seven-year moving average centered on the indicated dates. The aggregate gross stock excludes residential structures, livestock, and plants.

$K_A^G(t)$, col. (2): col. (3) minus col. (1). Gross capital stock in primary (agricultural) sector, excluding residential structures, livestock, and plants.

$K^G(t)$, col. (3): *LTES,* vol. 3, table 55, pp. 240–43.

$K_I^N(t)$, col. (4): Ibid., table 57, pp. 246–49. Capital stock net of depreciation in nonprimary sectors.

$K_A^N(t)$, col. (5): col. (6) minus col. (4). Capital stock net of depreciation in primary (agricultural) sector.

$K^N(t)$, col. (6): Ibid., table 55, pp. 240–43. Capital stock net of depreciation.

A.5.2. Discussion of Table A.5

The capital stock data are, like that of most economies, of questionable quality. We know, for example, that the net capital stock figures are but rough approximations (see Clark, "Investment and Net Stock of Fixed Capital"). As a result, the gross stock figures are used throughout this book. This is consistent with Ohkawa et al., who wrote: "we believe that gross stock measurement (net of retirement) is in general less arbitrary than net stock measurement and the gross stock series excluding residential buildings is intended to be the major one for measuring production capacity" (*LTES,* vol. 3, p. 134).

The capital stock series in agriculture is especially questionable since it excludes investment in land improvements, I_L. Indirect evidence on the extent of this downward bias can be readily derived. The *LTES* reports prices of upland and paddy field hectarage beginning in 1890. These prices represent capitalized land values. The difference between these prices may therefore be attributed to improvements, the most important component of which is irrigation. Let

V_p = value of paddy (per unit)
V_{up} = value of upland (per unit).

Then

$$V_p = V_{up} + I_L/R_p;$$

the capital stock in improvements can be expressed as

$$I_L = (V_p - V_{up})\, R_p$$

where R_p is paddy hectarage found in table A.4. Table A.5a gives V_p and V_{up} per *tan* in current yen 1890–1919. The ratio of these two prices is relatively stable, ranging between 2.41 and 2.86 with a mean of 2.66.

The R_p data given in table A.4 are in 1,000 hectares. The following conversion for 1890 is used:

16.27 *tan* = 1 hectare.

From this, it follows that

V_p[per hectare] = (16.27) (60 yen) = 976.2 yen

in 1890 (current prices). Furthermore,

I_L(per hectare) = 634.53 yen.

Since 2,857,000 hectares were in paddy in 1888–92, it follows that

I_L = (634.53 yen) (2.857 million hectares) = 1,813 million yen.

Compare this with the gross capital stock in agriculture, excluding I_L: for example, $K_A^G(t)$ in 1888–92 was 3,782 million yen (1934–36 prices). This figure must be converted to current (1890) prices. Using the "All Commodity" price indexes (*LTES*, vol. 8, table 2, col. (1), p. 135), for 1889–92 K_A^G = 1,273 million yen (in 1890 prices). In summary, these rough calculations indicate that the "true" capital stock in agriculture, at least in 1890, was 2.42 times the reported figure.

A.6. Employment and Population: Table A.6

A.6.1. Sources to Table A.6

$L_I(t)$, col. (1): K. Ohkawa, "Intersectoral Differences in Product per Worker," table 2.B; all figures are in thousands and

Table A.6 - Employment and Population

Year	$L_I(t)$ (1)	$L_A(t)$ (2)	$L(t)$ (3)	$L_S(t)$ (4)	$L^*(t)$ (5)	$N(t)$ (6)
1887	2,909	16,533	19,442	3,161	22,603	38,703
1891	3,416	16,394	19,810	3,421	23,231	40,251
1895	3,775	16,337	20,112	3,672	23,784	41,557
1899	4,063	16,291	20,354	3,942	24,296	43,404
1903	4,304	16,214	20,518	4,269	24,787	45,546
1907	4,468	16,089	20,557	4,675	25,232	47,416
1911	4,728	16,051	20,779	4,955	25,734	49,852
1915	5,414	15,617	21,031	5,436	26,467	52,752

represent seven-year moving averages centered on the indicated years. This series constitutes the industrial labor force, gainfully employed, where industry includes manufacturing, mining, transportation, communications, public utilities, and construction.

$L_A(t)$, col. (2): Ibid., table 2.B. The agricultural labor force, gainfully employed, includes forestry and fisheries; seven-year moving average.

$L(t)$, col. (3): Sum of cols. (1) and (2).

$L_S(t)$, col. (4): Ibid., table 2.B. Gainfully employed in all other industries: for example, services.

$L^*(t)$, col. (5): Sum of cols. (3) and (4).

$N(t)$, col. (6): Total population from *Hundred-Year Statistics of the Japanese Economy,* tables 1, 12; seven-year moving average.

A.6.2. Discussion of Table A.6

$L(t)$ in table A.6 refers to the gainfully employed in commodity-producing sectors of the economy. This commodity/labor-force orientation is utilized in the text of this book since the Japanese output and employment measures for services are sufficiently crude to be of dubious value. Note also that the labor force series refers to the gainfully employed. Labor utilization rates (man hours per year) are essential to an understanding of Meiji development. Unfortunately, to our knowledge no such estimates exist.

A.7. OUTPUT: Table A.7

A.7.1. Sources to Table A.7

All output data are in millions of yen in 1934–36 prices. The observations represent seven-year moving averages with the exception of 1903 (three-year average) and 1907 (five-year average).

$Q_I(t)$, col. (1): Ohkawa, "National Product and Expenditure, 1885–1969," Appendix table 2, p. 28. Output of manufacturing, mining, construction, transportation, communications, and public utilities.

$Q_A(t)$, col. (2): Ibid., Appendix table 2, p. 28. Output of agriculture and forestry.

$Q(t)$, col. (3): Sum of cols. (1) and (2). Output of commodity-producing sectors.

Table A.7 - Output

Year	$Q_I(t)$ (1)	$Q_A(t)$ (2)	$Q(t)$ (3)
1887	453	1,526	1,979
1891	546	1,644	2,190
1895	710	1,750	2,460
1899	929	1,865	2,794
1903	1,021	2,038	3,059
1907	1,360	1,921	3,281
1911	1,728	2,118	3,846
1915	2,276	2,336	4,612

A.7.2. Discussion of Table A.7

The income and product series for Meiji Japan have undergone extensive revision and improvement over the two decades prior to 1970. The main weakness remaining is the output and income estimates for the service sector. Given the tentative character of the service sector estimates, we have elected to focus exclusively on commodity-producing activity. The "gross national product" figure given in col. (3) excludes services as a result.

A.8. Labor Productivity and per Capita Output: Table A.8

A.8.1. Sources to Table A.8

Table A.8 - Labor Productivity and Per Capita Output

Year	$Q_I(t)/L_I(t)$ (1)	$Q_A(t)/L_A(t)$ (2)	$Q(t)/L(t)$ (3)	$Q(t)/N(t)$ (4)
1887	155.7	92.3	101.8	51.1
1891	159.8	100.3	110.6	54.4
1895	188.1	107.1	122.3	59.2
1899	228.6	114.5	137.3	64.4
1903	237.2	125.7	149.1	67.2
1907	304.4	119.4	159.6	69.2
1911	365.5	132.0	185.1	77.1
1915	420.4	149.6	219.3	87.4

All measures are in 1934–36 yen.

$Q_I(t)/L_I(t)$, col. (1): Table A.7, col. (1) ÷ table A.6, col. (1). Average labor productivity in industry.

$Q_A(t)/L_A(t)$, col. (2): Table A.7, col. (2) ÷ table A.6, col. (2). Average labor productivity in agriculture.

$Q(t)/L(t)$, col. (3): Table A.7, col. (3) ÷ table A.6, col. (3). Average labor productivity in the commodity-producing sector.

$Q(t)/N(t)$, col. (4): Table A.7, col. (3) ÷ table A.6, col. (6). Per capita commodity output.

A.9. CAPITAL FORMATION STATISTICS: Table A.9

A.9.1. Sources to Table A.9

Unadjusted $s^*(t)$, col. (1): Ohkawa, "National Product and Expenditure, 1885–1969," table 2, p. 11. Share of private gross domestic capital formation in gross domestic product. These figures are based on current prices and the annual observations are centered on seven-year moving averages.

Table A.9 - Capital Formation Statistics

Year	Unadjusted $s^*(t)$ (1)	Adjusted $s^*(t)$ (2)	Year	$\frac{\delta K^N(t)}{I(t)+\delta K^N(t)}$ (3)
1887	0.134	0.122	1891	0.389
1897	0.169	0.141	1896	0.463
1904	0.148	0.123	1901	0.532
1913	0.168	0.148	1906	0.436
1919	0.199	0.166	1911	0.383

Adjusted $s^*(t)$, col. (2): col. (1) adjusted for military expenditures. Rosovsky has supplied estimates of military durable expenditures as a percentage of gross domestic capital formation. See Rosovsky, *Capital Formation in Japan, 1868–1940,* p. 9.

$\delta K^N(t)/[I(t) + \delta K^N(t)]$, col. (3): The share of depreciation in gross domestic capital formation. The estimates can be found in ibid., p. 10.

A.9.2. Discussion of Table A.9

There has been extensive debate over the savings rate in Meiji Japan. It is of some interest to note that the Ohkawa adjusted series reported in table A.9 and utilized in the text is similar to Rosovsky's 1961 estimates. It should also be emphasized that to date the *LTES* capital stock data have not been reconciled with these capital formation rates.

A.10. FOREIGN TRADE: Table A.10

A.10.1. Sources to Table A.10

$X(t)$, col. (1): Ohkawa, "National Product and Expenditure,

Table A.10 - Foreign Trade

Year	X(t) (1)	M(t) (2)
1887	91	178
1891	121	257
1895	163	458
1899	245	575
1903	345	753
1907	444	960
1911	622	1,088
1915	1,102	1,290
1919	1,288	1,692

Period	$x_m(t)$ (3)	$x_o(t)$ (4)	$x_s(t)$ (5)	$m_m(t)$ (6)	$m_r(t)$ (7)	$m_f(t)$ (8)	$m_s(t)$ (9)
1855-89	.456	.453	.091	.575	.097	.260	.068
1890-94	.598	.318	.084	.540	.189	.226	.045
1895-99	.637	.266	.097	.493	.233	.244	.030
1900-04	.665	.212	.123	.461	.275	.136	.128
1905-09	.665	.166	.169	.432	.243	.102	.223
1910-14	.717	.167	.116	.372	.332	.142	.154
1915-19	.625	.109	.266	.347	.368	.154	.131

1885–1969," Appendix table 1, p. 27. Exports in millions of yen in 1934–36 prices.

$M(t)$, col. (2): Ibid. Imports in millions of yen in 1934–36 prices.

$x_m(t)$, $x_o(t)$ and $x_s(t)$, cols. (3) through (5): Shares of manufactured products, other commodities, and services in total exports. $m_m(t)$, $m_r(t)$, $m_f(t)$, and $m_s(t)$, cols. (6) through (9). Shares of manufactured products, raw materials, foodstuffs, and services in total imports. Shionoya and Yamazawa, "Industrial Growth and Foreign Trade in Pre-War Japan," table 3, p. 7.

Appendix B

Parameters and Initial Conditions

B.1. Introduction

The estimation of parameters and initial conditions for a general equilibrium model of the type considered here is compounded by two problems. First, even though our model is relatively efficient in the sense that it economizes on parameters and variables, it still generates a demand for historical data which at present exceeds the available stock. This problem becomes particularly acute given the requirements of production, consumption, and demographic information by sector. Second, most of the available historical information has been compiled by researchers who for the most part have worked independently of one another and have often employed quite different accounting concepts and sources of primary information. The estimates provided are thus not always consistent with one another. In spite of these difficulties, the estimates discussed below, based on the most recent revisions of the historical data, provide acceptable representations of the long-term historical record. These estimates are certainly of higher quality than is the case for the record of almost any other country at such an early stage in the development process.

Our general procedure has been to search the historical record to identify parameters and initial conditions relevant to the requirements of the model. This search typically yields insufficient data to estimate all the parameters and to establish initial conditions. However, with the imposition of additional constraints on the model, and coupled with the requirement that in the initial period the model must be in equilibrium, the few remaining unknown parameters and initial conditions can be derived residually as being consistent with both the model structure and the available data on Japan.

The following parameters have been "estimated" for Japan: σ_2, λ_K, λ_L, n, δ, β_{ij}, s, π_i, α_{L2}, α_{K2}, α_{R2}, and Φ. Wherever possible each is estimated for the year 1887, the first year for which we have revised estimates of Japanese output and labor force. Additionally, the following initial conditions are available or can be derived from the historical statistics: PK/Y; $L_1/L = u$; $PQ_1/(PQ_1 + Q_2) = v$; α_{L1}, α_{K1}, and s^*. With these parameters and initial conditions, consistent estimates of the remaining parameters (A_i, ξ) and initial conditions (ω, k, P) are derived. The algorithm employed to solve for the unknown parameters and initial conditions is presented in the next section. Sections B.3 and B.4 discuss the estimates of parameters and initial conditions, respectively. We conclude with a summary of the parameters, initial conditions, and key statistics employed in the simulation of Japanese economic history.

B.2. An Estimation Algorithm

The algorithm used to develop the estimates of the unknown parameters and initial conditions yields estimates consistent with several imposed initial conditions drawn from Japanese experience, with several parameters estimated directly with Japanese data, and with the assumption that the model is in equilibrium in the initial simulation period. Based on Japanese historical series (see section B.4), the following initial conditions have been established: u, v, PK/Y, s^*, α_{Ki}, α_{Li}, and α_{R2}. Estimates of key parameters used in the calculation of the initial-period equilibrium solution are developed from several sources (see section B.3), yielding σ_1 and the β_{ij}'s.

The unknowns remaining in the model are the A_i's in the sectoral production functions, the wage-rental ratio ω, the terms of trade P, the minimum subsistence parameter γ, the distribution parameter in the CES production function, ξ, and the sectoral distribution of capital, K_1/K_2. These can be derived residually given the assumption of equilibrium in the initial period. A question may arise regarding the justification for deriving the initial sectoral distribution of capital rather than obtaining this statistic directly from the Japanese historical record. The sectoral distribution of capital must be permitted to float to provide a degree of freedom resulting from our inability to estimate directly from Japanese sources the subsistence parameter in the Stone-Geary expenditure system or the intercepts in the production functions. The derived sectoral distribution of capital will therefore depart somewhat from the "observed" share in 1887, although given the relatively unreliable estimates of the agricultural capital stock (see Appendix A), we do not consider this departure of the model estimates from the historical record to be a liability.

Consider the estimation algorithm in greater detail. By definition and after setting $xK_i = K_i$ and $yL_i = L_i$ in the first period, $\frac{rK_1}{wL_1} = \frac{\alpha_{K1}}{\alpha_{L1}}$ and $\frac{rK_2}{wL_2} = \frac{\alpha_{K2}}{\alpha_{L2}}$. The wage-rental ratio is defined as $\omega = \frac{w}{r}$, so that $\frac{k_1}{\omega} = \frac{\alpha_{K1}}{\alpha_{L1}}$ and $\frac{k_2}{\omega} = \frac{\alpha_{K2}}{\alpha_{L2}}$. Hence, $k_1/k_2 = (\alpha_{K1}/\alpha_{L1})/(\alpha_{K2}/\alpha_{L2})$, which is independent of ω. We can arbitrarily define the economywide stocks of capital and labor to be:

$$K \equiv K_1 + K_2 = 100,$$
$$L \equiv L_1 + L_2 = 100.$$

Furthermore, the economywide capital-labor ratio is a weighted sum of the sectoral k's: $k = k_1 u + k_2(1-u)$, which yields k_1 and k_2, given u and k. Substituting k_2 into $\frac{k_2}{\omega} = \frac{\alpha_{K2}}{\alpha_{L2}}$ yields ω since we already know α_{K2} and α_{L2}. Given k_1/k_2, the ratio α_{K1}/α_{L1} is also determined. Furthermore, since $\alpha_{K1} + \alpha_{L1} = 1$, it follows that α_{K1} and α_{L1} can be computed.

The CES production specification in industry is $Q_1 = A_1 [\xi K^g + (1-\xi)L^g]^{\frac{1}{g}}$, where $x = y = 1$, and $g = [\sigma_1 - 1]/\sigma_1$, so an alternative specification for ω can be derived:

$$\omega = \frac{w}{r} = \left(\frac{1-\xi}{\xi}\right)k_1^{1-g},$$

which simply equates the wage-rental ratio to the ratio of factor marginal products. These factor marginal productivities are:

$$w = \frac{1-\xi}{A_1{}^g} q_1{}^{-g+1}$$
$$r = \frac{\xi}{A_1{}^g}(q_1/k_1)^{-g+1},$$

where q_1 is the average labor productivity. We know the 1887 economywide capital-output ratio to be 1.87. Letting $Y = 100$, and recalling that $K = 100$, then $P = 1.87$. For notation simplicity, let

$$A_i Q_i^* = Q_i,$$

so that

$$vY = Q_1 P = A_1 Q_1^* P,$$
$$(1-v)Y = Q_2 = A_2 Q_2^*.$$

Since all terms in Q_i^* are now known, A_1 and A_2 can be readily computed.

Finally, to derive the minimum subsistence bundle γ, we express the 1887 historically observed industrial output share in terms of the demand for industrial goods. Namely, the share of income going to industrial goods is

$$v = [(D_{11} + D_{12})P + C_1 P + IP]/Y.$$

We have in the initial period $Y/L = 100/100 = 1$. Expanding the above expression for v we get:

$$\frac{D_{11}}{Y} = \beta_{11}\left[\frac{L_1}{L}\Pi_L - \gamma\frac{L_1}{Y}\right] = \beta_{11}\,[u\Pi_L - \gamma u],$$
$$\frac{D_{12}}{Y} = \beta_{12}\left[\frac{L_2}{L}\Pi_L - \gamma\frac{L_2}{Y}\right] = \beta_{12}[(1-u)\Pi_L - \gamma(1-u)],$$
$$\frac{CP}{Y} = \beta_{11}\left[(1-s)\Pi_{KR} - \gamma\frac{\phi L}{Y}\right] = \beta_{11}[(1-s)\Pi_{KR} - \gamma\phi],$$
$$\frac{IP}{Y} = s\,\Pi_{KR},$$

where Π_{KR} is the combined share of land and capital $(rK + \tau R)/Y$ (τ is the land rent), and Π_L is labor's share wL/Y. Finally:

$$v = [\beta_{11}u + (1-u)\beta_{12}]\,\Pi_L + [s + (1-s)\beta_{11}\Pi_{KR}]$$
$$- \gamma[u\beta_{11} + (1-u)\beta_{12} - \beta_{11}\phi],$$

which can be solved for γ.

B.3. Parameters

Substitution elasticities (σ_i). Two key hypotheses relating to dualism are employed in this study: technological dualism—differential rates of technical progress by sector—and production dualism, as captured in the parameters of the sectoral production functions. In chapter 3 we provided considerable evidence to suggest that a Cobb-Douglas specification appears appropriate for Japanese agriculture. This is consistent not only with the assumption made by many researchers on Japanese growth, but with a direct estimate of the elasticity of substitution for the period we are considering. The qualitative literature on Meiji Japan argues that the elasticity of substitution in industry is less than unity but precise estimates are unavailable. Contemporary Asian evidence is used to fill this gap. The econometric results by Sicat (1968) and Williamson (1971*b*) on the production conditions in Philippine industry lend some support to the assumption that the elasticity of factor substitution is less than unity in at least one Asian country. For a larger sample of countries, these results have been confirmed by Chetty's extensive empirical survey (Chetty 1969). On the basis of these findings we have elected to employ an elasticity of factor substitution in industry of 0.8.

The depreciation rate (δ). We have no reliable evidence upon which to base an estimate of the depreciation rate. Estimates vary enormously for Japan, ranging from Rosovsky's figure of 0.46 to a range between .150 and .200 used by Fei and Ranis in their compilation of Japanese industrial capital (Rosovsky 1961, p. 10; Fei and Ranis 1964, p. 147). The most recent net capital stock figures have been compiled by Colin Clark (1972), who assumes a depreciation rate of 11.8 percent for equipment and 2.0 percent for nonresidential structures. Given the distribution of the capital stock between nonresidential structures and equipment in 1887, the aggregate depreciation rate implied by Clark's assumptions is 2.6 percent, a figure even lower than that used by either Rosovsky or Fei-Ranis.

Our procedure for computing the Japanese depreciation rate is to derive a consistent estimate of the depreciation parameter based on the share of replacement to gross investment provided by Rosovsky's series of Japanese capital formation. Define that share as

$$\frac{\delta K(t)}{I(t)} = D(t) \text{ so that } \delta = \frac{D(t)I(t)}{K(t)}$$

where $I(t)$ is gross domestic capital formation and $\delta K(t) = [GDCF(t) - NDCF(t)]$. From Rosovsky we know that $D(1887)$

is around .389. Using the *expost* identity $S(0) = P(0)I(0)$, it must follow that $\delta = [D(0)I(0)]/K(0) = [.389\ S(0)]/P(0)K(0)$. Given the initial period values of $s(1887) = .122$ and $P(1887)K(1887)/GNP(1887) = 1.87$ derived from the *LTES* data, a consistent value for the depreciation parameter can be estimated. The resulting δ is .025. While this figure may appear to be implausibly low, it is almost identical to the one used by Clark. Furthermore, it is consistent with the evidence that the early Meiji capital stock was dominated by structures rather than equipment. Given the extremely wide variability in the "estimates" of the parameter offered by scholars of Japanese economic history, we have elected to place a relatively heavy weight on the extent to which the parameter is consistent with the extensively researched macro data series.

Factor shares (α_{Li}, α_{Ki}, α_{R2}). Factor shares in the total cost of agricultural production are available in a recent study by Yamada and Hayami (1972, p. 6), yielding $\alpha_{L2} = .524$, $\alpha_{K2} = .196$, and $\alpha_{R2} = .280$. These refer to the period 1885–89. The labor share includes male and female wages. Table B.1 indicates

Table B.1

	$\alpha_{L2}(t)$	$\alpha_{K2}(t)$
1885-89	.524	.196
1888-92	.507	.192
1893-97	.510	.178
1898-02	.526	.168
1903-07	.512	.183
1908-12	.510	.192

the remarkable stability in these factor shares over time. This is consistent with our Cobb-Douglas specification.

Factor shares for industry are unavailable for the Meiji period. Yoshihara (1972, p. 9), however, provides an estimate for manufacturing for the interwar period: the share of wages in gross value added (1934–36) is 0.314. Given a CES specification in industry where $\sigma_I < 1$, a labor share in 1887 which is considerably less than 0.30 does not seem implausible. In fact, the solution algorithm produces $\alpha_{LI} \cong 0.20$ and $\xi \cong .855$ in the CES production function

$$Q_1(t) = A_1\left\{\xi[x(t)K_1(t)]^{\frac{\sigma_1-1}{\sigma_1}} + (1-\xi)\,[y(t)L(t)]^{\frac{\sigma_1-1}{\sigma_1}}\right\}^{\sigma_1/\sigma_1-1}.$$

The rate and bias of technical change (λ_i). Given the paucity of independent estimates of the bias and rate of technical change by sector during the Meiji period, we have resorted to the derivation of a set of technical change parameters consistent with our model's structure while drawing on the limited evidence available on Japanese TFPG after the early 1880s. The dualistic model has

$$R_1(t) = \lambda_L\alpha_{L1}(t) + \lambda_K\alpha_{K1}(t) \qquad [B.1]$$
$$R_2 = \lambda_L\alpha_{L2} + \lambda_K\alpha_{K2} + \lambda_R\alpha_{R2} \qquad [B.2]$$

where α_{Li}, α_{Ki}, and α_{R2} are the income shares of labor, capital, and land in sector i. The $R_i(t)$ are the overall rates of TFPG by sector. R_2 is constant given the Cobb-Douglas specification in agriculture. The rates of augmentation through technical change to labor, capital, and land are, respectively, λ_L, λ_K, and λ_R.

In Appendix A we showed that λ_R must have been close to zero during the Meiji period. The Yamada and Hayami study also provides information relating to the rate of augmentation of the land stock. Since a primary means by which this factor is augmented through most of this period is through the development of irrigation facilities, a rough index of the growth of this form of land-improved capital can be obtained by examining the share of paddy field land as a percentage of the total rice hectarage under cultivation. There appears to be no increase in this percentage over the period 1885–1915; indeed, there is a slight decline (Yamada and Hayami 1972, p. 25). Other forms of land improvement may have partially or wholly offset this decline. As a first approximation, however, we will assume that the rate of overall efficiency improvement to the land stock is zero, although, as noted in chapter 5, the *physical* stock of land is assumed to grow through this period at a rate consistent with the Japanese historical record.

The recent study by Yamada and Hayami provides an index of total productivity growth in agriculture. Over the period 1883/

87–1908/12, they estimate $R_2 = .0124$ (calculated from Yamada and Hayami 1972, p. 26). With this estimate, and coupled with the above information on factor shares by sector in 1887, expressions [B.1] and [B.2] can be solved explicitly in terms of alternative pairs of R_1 and (λ_K, λ_L). Although we do not have any information on the overall rate of technical change in industry for the early Meiji period, we do have estimates for the interwar period. Yoshihara (1972, p. 9) estimates $.014 \leqq R_1 \leqq .016$ for the period 1906–36 (for an excellent survey also see Yoshihara 1969*b*). Since there is evidence of trend acceleration in rates of TFPG during the first four decades of the twentieth century, the lower value of $R_1 \cong .014$ seems most appropriate for the 1880s. This implies $\lambda_L = .0194$ and $\lambda_K = .0114$. These parameter values are utilized in the simulation and they accurately capture our commitment to a labor-augmenting-bias view of Meiji Japanese history.

Workforce growth rate (n). Our model makes no distinction between the rates of population growth and workforce growth. For Japan over the period 1887–1915, the compound rates of growth of population and growth of the gainfully employed in commodity-producing sectors are, respectively, 1.02 percent and .29 percent (Ohkawa 1972*a*, table 2). We have taken $n = .0029$. This definition of gainfully employed corresponds to our output series, and encompasses those working in the commodity-producing sectors, together with workers in transportation, communications, public utilities, and construction. The service sector, which is excluded from our output series, grew relatively rapidly during this period. Had services been included, the gainfully employed would have grown at a rate of .56 percent.

The savings rate (s^*). Ohkawa has recently provided a revised estimate of the proportion of gross national expenditure (*GNE*) devoted to capital formation (*CF*). In 1887 $CF/GNE = .134$. This estimate includes military expenditures. It is therefore appropriate to reduce the series by the proportion of spending on military activities. Rosovsky (1961, p. 15) provides such an adjustment factor. When applied to the Ohkawa figures, the 1887 savings and investment rate exclusive of military activity is .122.

The savings parameter (s). Given the economywide average savings rate s^*, and utilizing the identity from our model that

$s^* = s\alpha_K$, it is possible to derive a consistent estimate of the savings parameter s using the figure for the nonlabor share in the initial time period, $\alpha_K(1887)$. This yields a savings parameter s of 0.209694.

The parameters in the Stone-Geary linear expenditure system (β_{ij}). A major constraint in estimating the parameters of the Stone-Geary linear expenditure system for Japan during the Meiji period is the lack of data on sectoral food and total expenditures. The general procedure we have used to construct the Stone-Geary slope (β_{ij}) estimates is to develop a framework that employs as much relevant Japanese data as possible, while introducing assumptions consistent with qualitative Japanese economic history wherever quantitative information is missing.

Two key equations in the Stone-Geary system describe expenditure elasticities:

$$\eta_1 = \beta_1 p_1 \quad [B.3]$$
$$\eta_2 = \beta_2 p_2 \quad [B.4]$$

where η_i are the sectoral food expenditure elasticities, β_i the slope estimates of the Stone-Geary system, and p_i the proportion of each sector's total expenditure on food, E_i^f/E_i. Since independent estimates of the parameters and variables in equations [B.3] and [B.4] are not available, it is necessary to derive them by utilizing alternative estimates of variables and parameters relevant to Meiji Japan expenditure patterns. The following definitions shall prove helpful in this effort.

$$\eta_1/\eta_2 = a \quad [B.5]$$
$$p_1/p_2 = b \quad [B.6]$$
$$\eta = p_1^*\eta_1 + p_2^*\eta_2 \quad [B.7]$$
$$p_1^* = E_1^f/(E_1^f + E_2^f) \quad [B.8]$$
$$p_2^* = E_2^f/(E_1^f + E_2^f) \quad [B.9]$$
$$p^* = (E_1^f + E_2^f)/(E_1 + E_2) \quad [B.10]$$
$$E_1 + E_2 = c \quad [B.11]$$
$$p_1 = E_1^f/E_1 \quad [B.12]$$
$$p_2 = E_2^f/E_2 \quad [B.13]$$
$$E_1/E = d. \quad [B.14]$$

Historical information is available for the following statistics:

η = the total expenditure elasticity on food,
a = the ratio of the sectoral expenditure elasticities on food,
b = the ratio of the proportion of food expenditure in each sector's total budget,
p^* = the economywide proportion of total expenditure on food,
c = total consumption expenditure,
d = the proportion of total expenditure by rural residents;

while historical information is not directly available for

η_i, the sectoral expenditure elasticities on food,
β_i, the sectoral slope estimates in the Stone-Geary expenditure system,
p_i, the share of each sector's total expenditure on food,
p_i^*, each sector's proportion of the economywide food expenditures,
E_i, the total sectoral consumption expenditure, and
E_i^f, the sectoral expenditure on food.

Kaneda provides an estimate of the income elasticity for food corresponding to the Yamada series of agricultural output. This estimate, $\eta = .39$, is based on a time series study of the period 1878–1922 (Kaneda 1970, p. 7). Using the 1887 Shinohara figure of .65 as the proportion of total Japanese expenditure on food, the economywide estimate of the β coefficient in the Stone-Geary expenditure system is .60.

While these aggregate expenditure elasticities are of interest, the model requires information on sectoral expenditure patterns. For this we utilize an estimate of the ratio of food expenditure elasticities by sector. Using four separate postwar budget studies, Kaneda (1970, p. 22) finds the urban/rural ratio of food elasticities to be .91, .86, .90, and .83. In currently ongoing work for the Philippines, Kelley and Williamson have identified a 1965 ratio of .83. For purposes of the present study, the ratio is taken to be .85.

The economywide proportion of total expenditure on food ($p^* = .650$) in 1887 is available directly from Shinohara's estimates, as is the value of total expenditures (c = 3,811,050 thousand yen) (Shinohara 1967, p. 138).

We do not possess direct Japanese data on the proportion of each sector's total expenditure devoted to food. In low-income economies, where both sectors are relatively near subsistence, this ratio may be expected to be high and approximately the same in each sector. This is confirmed by an examination of data from Philippine budget studies where, over the four low-income groupings comprising 76 percent of the country's population in 1965, the ratio of the urban to the rural sector's average expenditure of food is .99, .96, .98, and .97. We have taken the value of b to be .97.

Finally, Japanese data on the ratio of sectoral expenditure in the total is also not available. Yet considerable information does exist on national income produced by sector. Ohkawa (1972*b*, p. 11) estimates that 32.8 percent of total national income originated in the secondary sector in 1887. The use of income generated by sector as a proxy for total expenditures implicitly assumes that the average savings rate is the same for all sectors. There are very little historical data to confirm or refute this hypothesis. The available data lend some support to the proposition. Budget data on rural and urban households in 1926 show the average savings rates to be 9.6 and 10.0 percent, respectively.[1] Similar results were found for the 1930s.

In summary, we have employed the following assumptions in deriving estimates of the β_i's in the Stone-Geary expenditure system for Japan in 1885:

Variable or Parameter	
η	.39
a	.85
b	.97
c	3811050
d	.325
p^*	.65

Solving equations [B.3] through [B.14], the resulting estimates of the sectoral parameters are $\beta_{21} = .541$ and $\beta_{22} = .477$. The corresponding parameters for nonagricultural products are $\beta_{11} = .459$ and $\beta_{12} = .523$.

B.4. Initial Conditions

Sectoral labor and output distribution (u,v). The estimates of the sectoral distribution of labor and output in 1887 employ consistent definitions and refer to output and employment in manufacturing, agriculture, transportation, communications, public utilities, and construction.[2] The resulting output and employment shares are .320 and .150, respectively. (For a discussion of the rationale of the goods-production emphasis, see Appendix A).

Capital-output ratio; capital-labor ratios. The capital stock series utilized in this study is net of depreciation, and excludes residential structures and livestock. The capital-output ratio, 1.87, is compiled in 1934/36 prices and uses definitions of capital stock and output as described above. The figure 1.87 probably represents an underestimate of the capital-output ratio given the underestimation of the size of the capital stock, and notably, the exclusion of land improvements in agriculture (see Appendix A).

B.5. Summary Statement of Parameter Values and Initial Conditions

Parameters

Production functions	$A_1 = .334$
	$A_2 = .309$
	$\sigma_1 = .800$
	$\xi = .855$
Technical change	$\lambda_K = .0114$
	$\lambda_L = .0194$
Labor supply	$n = .0029$
Capital depreciation	$\delta = .025$
Laborer's commodity demand	$\beta_{11} = .459$
	$\beta_{12} = .523$
	$\beta_{21} = .541$
	$\beta_{22} = .477$
	$\gamma = .427$

Capitalists' commodity demand	$s = .210$
	$\Pi_1 = \beta_{11} = .459$
	$\Pi_2 = \beta_{21} = .541$
	$\Phi = .200$

Initial Conditions

Factor efficiency units	$\mathbf{x}(0) = y(0) = 1.000$
Factor stocks	$K(0) = 100.000$
	$K_1(0) = 65.861$
	$K_2(0) = 34.139$
	$L(0) = 100.000$
	$L_1(0) = 15.000$
	$L_2(0) = 85.000$
Terms of trade	$P(0) = 1.870$
Output	$Q_1(0) = 17.112$
	$P(0)Q_1(0) = 32.000$
	$Q_2(0) = 68.000$

Initial Conditions on Key Statistics

Urbanization level	$u(0) = .150$	
Industrialization level	$v(0) = .320$	
Gross savings rate	$s^*(0) = .122$	
Sectoral factor shares	$\alpha_{1L} = .197$	$\alpha_{2L} = .524$
	$\alpha_{1K} = .803$	$\alpha_{2K} = .196$
		$\alpha_{2R} = .280$
Aggregate factor shares	$\alpha_L(0) = .419$	
	$\alpha_K(0) = .390$	
	$\alpha_R(0) = .190$	
Capital-labor ratios	$k_1(0) = \hat{k}_1(0) = 4.391$	
	$k_2(0) = \hat{k}_2(0) = .402$	
	$k(0) = \hat{k}(0) = 1.000$	
Capital-output ratio	$P(0)K_2(0)/[P(0)Q_1(0) + Q_2(0)] = 1.87$	
Economywide labor force growth	$n = .0029$	

Appendix C
Simulation Results

The simulation generates observations for each "period." Given the parameter values employed in the analysis, a simulation period corresponds to a calendar year. For convenience in using the model, the simulation period observations are labeled for the calendar year to which they apply. The results are presented for those years for which the key Japanese data are available. All series relating to output and capital stock are presented in constant 1915 prices.

Year	Unaugmented Factor Stocks: Capital Total	Capital Indus-trial	Capital Agri-cultural	Labor	Land	Efficiency Ratio x/y
1887	100.000	65.861	34.139	100.000	4821.0	1.000
1891	117.018	80.074	36.944	101.165	4946.0	.969
1895	137.285	96.795	40.490	102.344	5033.0	.939
1899	161.531	116.778	44.753	103.536	5161.0	.910
1903	190.649	140.647	50.002	104.742	5261.0	.882
1907	225.744	169.458	56.287	105.963	5414.0	.854
1911	268.153	204.310	63.843	107.197	5616.0	.828
1915	319.537	246.444	73.093	108.446	5784.0	.802

Year	Output	Output per Laborer		
		Total	Industrial	Agricultural
1887	89.917	.899	1.461	.800
1891	101.014	.999	1.636	.871
1895	113.804	1.112	1.845	.948
1899	128.974	1.246	2.092	1.035
1903	146.688	1.400	2.388	1.131
1907	167.887	1.584	2.738	1.241
1911	193.277	1.803	3.154	1.367
1915	223.259	2.059	3.652	1.505

Year	Terms of Trade	Factor Prices and Earnings				
		Wage/ Effic-iency Unit	Wage Earnings per Laborer	Rents/ Effic-iency Unit	Inter-est Rate	Rents/ Physical Unit
1887	1.870	.419	.419	.390	.390	.004
1891	1.802	.423	.456	.372	.389	.004
1895	1.720	.426	.497	.350	.383	.004
1899	1.636	.431	.542	.328	.376	.005
1903	1.545	.436	.593	.304	.365	.005
1907	1.457	.443	.650	.281	.353	.005
1911	1.371	.452	.716	.259	.340	.006
1915	1.281	.461	.789	.237	.325	.006

Year	Ratios: Urbanization	Industrial Output Share	Savings Rate: Current	Savings Rate: Constant	Factor Shares in GNP: Labor	Factor Shares in GNP: Capital	Factor Shares in GNP: Land
1887	.150	.320	.122	.093	.419	.390	.190
1891	.167	.346	.124	.098	.411	.406	.183
1895	.183	.369	.125	.103	.404	.419	.177
1899	.199	.391	.126	.108	.399	.431	.171
1903	.214	.410	.127	.114	.394	.441	.165
1907	.229	.427	.128	.119	.389	.450	.160
1911	.244	.443	.129	.124	.386	.458	.156
1915	.258	.457	.130	.130	.383	.465	.152

Year	Efficiency Capital/Labor Ratio: Total	Industrial	Agricultural	Unaugmented Capital/Output Ratio: Total	Industrial	Agricultural
1887	1.000	4.391	.402	1.424	3.849	.486
1891	1.121	4.592	.425	1.489	3.711	.468
1895	1.259	4.849	.455	1.545	3.585	.456
1899	1.419	5.156	.491	1.604	3.469	.444
1903	1.605	5.527	.536	1.665	3.362	.437
1907	1.820	5.961	.589	1.722	3.264	.429
1911	2.071	6.469	.652	1.777	3.174	.423
1915	2.363	7.069	.728	1.833	3.091	.419

Year	Growth Rates: Output	Output per Capita	Capital Stock
1887	3.037	2.739	3.986
1891	2.984	2.686	4.047
1895	3.135	2.837	4.121
1899	3.250	2.951	4.199
1903	3.338	3.039	4.283
1907	3.550	3.251	4.367
1911	3.628	3.329	4.450
1915	3.714	3.414	4.511

Notes

For full bibliographic details see Bibliography.

Chapter 1. Meiji Japan and Modern Economic Growth

1. A portion of this section is based on the discussion in Kelley and Williamson, "Simple Parables of Japanese Economic Progress," pp. 1, 11–12.

Chapter 2. The Lessons of History

1. This section is an abridgement of materials found in Kelley, Williamson, and Cheetham, *Dualistic Economic Development,* pp. 145–48.

Chapter 3. A Model of Meiji Japanese Growth

1. This is true, for example, in the above cited works by Lewis, Fei and Ranis, and Jorgenson.

2. A portion of this section is based on Kelley, Williamson, and Cheetham, *Dualistic Economic Development,* chap. 2. The model is extensively revised, however, to conform to the special characteristics of the Meiji economy.

3. Gerschenkron, "Economic Backwardness in Historical Perspective." Gerschenkron's model is elaborated to fit the Japanese case in Ohkawa and Rosovsky, "The Indigenous Components in the Modern Japanese Economy."

4. Hayami and Ruttan, *Agricultural Development,* chaps. 6–10; idem, "Factor Prices and Technical Change in Agricultural Development"; Hayami and Yamada, "Agricultural Productivity at the Beginning of Industrialization"; Akino and Hayami, "Sources of Agricultural Growth in Japan." Hayami and Ruttan ("Agricultural Productivity Differences among Countries," p. 908) also make a very strong case along these lines for contemporary developing economies. Indeed "[i]nitially a substantial component of industrial capacity must be designed to provide . . . inputs for the agricultural sector."

5. Akino and Hayami, "Sources of Agricultural Growth in Japan," pp. 3–4. Similar results can be found in Hayami and Ruttan, "Agricultural Productivity Differences among Countries," pp. 908–10.

6. It would be inappropriate to include land's output elasticity in the expression for R_2 since, even though our model assumes that the *stock* of land expands exogenously over time, land is not augmented through *efficiency* change; $\lambda_R = 0$.

7. Williamson, "Capital Accumulation, Labor Saving, and Labor Absorption: A New Look at Some Contemporary Asian Experience," pp. 9–17. Ohkawa and Rosovsky conclude that the expansion after 1905 was due to a movement away from traditional sectors and toward the more modern sectors where more capital-intensive techniques were being utilized. (Ohkawa and Rosovsky, "A Century of Japanese Economic Growth").

8. Ohkawa and Rosovsky, "Postwar Japanese Growth," pp. 17–19; Watanabe, "Industrialization, Technological Progress, and Dual Structure," pp. 122–34. We are aware of the assertions by Japanese economic historians that recruitment costs absorbed most of the short-run labor market adjustment during periods of especially pronounced disproportional growth in sectoral labor demand. This argument does not negate our characterization of efficient labor market operation.

9. A portion of the following review is taken from Kelley, Williamson, and Cheetham, *Dualistic Economic Development,* pp. 38–40.

10. Lewis, "Development with Unlimited Supplies of Labour," pp. 139–92 and Fei and Ranis, *Labor Surplus Economy,* chap. 2. A continuing controversy has surrounded the empirical and theoretical implications of the assumption. For recent studies, see Wellisz, "Dual Economies, Disguised Unemployment, and the Unlimited Supply of Labour" and Hansen, "Employment and Wages in Rural Egypt."

11. These include Houthakker's indirect addilog system, Stone's linear expenditure system, and the double logarithmic system developed by Theil and Barten. Houthakker, "The Influence of Prices and Income on Household Expenditures"; Theil, "The Information Approach to Demand Analysis"; idem, *Economics and Information Theory;* and Barten, "Consumer Demand Functions under Conditions of Almost Additive Preferences." Stone, "Linear Expenditure Systems and Demand Analysis."

12. Kaneda, "Long-Term Changes in Food Consumption Patterns in Japan"; Ohkawa, "Personal Consumption in Dualistic Growth." This result is also highlighted by Kuznets in his *Modern Economic Growth: Rate, Structure and Spread,* pp. 271–74, and idem, "Trends in the Level and Structure of Consumption."

13. The general form of the Stone-Geary demand system is

$$\frac{D_{1j}(t)}{L_j(t)} = \frac{\beta_{1j}}{P_1(t)} y(t)\, w_j(t) + [1 - \beta_{1j}]\,\gamma_1 - \beta_{1j}\gamma_2 \frac{P_2(t)}{P_1(t)},$$

$$\frac{D_{2j}(t)}{L_j(t)} = \frac{\beta_{2j}}{P_2(t)} y(t)\, w_j(t) + [1 - \beta_{2j}]\,\gamma_2 - \beta_{2j}\gamma_1 \frac{P_1(t)}{P_2(t)}.$$

However, assuming $\gamma_1 = 0$, $\gamma_2 = \gamma$, and $P_2 = 1$ (agricultural output is the numeraire), the formulation collapses to the demand system reported in the text.

14. From 1920 to 1942 Ohkawa finds a decrease in both the economywide and in the industrial sector's labor share (Ohkawa, "Changes in National Income Distribution by Factor Share in Japan").

15. Some of what follows is based on Kelley and Williamson, "Writing History Backwards," pp. 757–58.

16. Forced consumption by the daimyo was implemented by the practice of alternate attendance (sankin kotai) where the Tokugawa Shogunate required the daimyo to spend time in court, leaving his wife and children behind as permanent hostages. The low savings potential of the samurai is explained by his relative poverty. "The extent of samurai poverty may be judged from the great number of middle and lower class samurai who turned to farming or other occupations in order to subsist or pay off their debts, despite their abhorrence of employment which was associated with commoners" (Nakamura, *Agricultural Production,* p. 158).

CHAPTER 4. THEORY AND THE QUANTITATIVE HISTORICAL RECORD

1. This general position was also taken by Abramovitz and David, "Towards Historically Relevant Parables of Growth," p. 1.

2. The most telling evidence to support this observation lies in the extensive data debate on the rate of Japanese agricultural production in the Meiji period. For almost a decade it was considered that the extremely rapid rate of Japanese agricultural growth, a historical "fact," was the focal point of Japanese economic progress. Recent estimates, however, have greatly reduced the importance of agricultural output growth and, as a result, have substantially attenuated or made obsolete much of the economic-historical analysis used to explain the previously determined empirical "fact." A detailed survey of this literature can be found in Kelley, Williamson, and Cheetham, *Dualistic Economic Development,* pp. 134–42, and Kelley and Williamson, "Writing History Backwards," pp. 731–35.

3. A close examination of the estimation methods employed in constructing historical series for various countries will reveal that the use of theory to *generate* historical estimates is not uncommon. A notable contribution to this methodology as applied to the American historical literature is provided by Fogel, *Railroads and American Economic Growth,* pp. 166–206.

4. Kelley and Williamson, "Simple Parables of Japanese Economic Progress"; Minami and Ono, "Economic Growth with Dual Structure." Fei and Ranis, *Labor Surplus Economy* should be added to this list, but their model is never utilized for quantitative analysis.

5. Recall from chapter 3 that if we assume that the minimum subsistence demands for necessary consumption are met, our paradigm describes a continuously growing economy. There are no "traps" within which the economy will stagnate.

6. As noted in Appendix B and chapter 6, the present study focuses on Japanese commodity output. The available estimates on the output of the service industries are still sufficiently tentative that their inclusion in our analysis would be premature.

Chapter 5. The "New" Economic History and Counterfactual Analysis

1. A detailed analysis can be found in Kelley, Williamson, and Cheetham, *Dualistic Economic Development;* idem, "Biased Technological Progress and Labor Force Growth in a Dualistic Economy."

2. One example can be found in Hayami and Ruttan, *Agricultural Development,* pp. 221–28, where they explore the impact of trade and technology on rice production and prices after 1920.

3. In addition to Fogel's research see the following partial listing: Conrad and Meyer, *The Economics of Slavery;* Fishlow, *American Railroads and the Transformation of the Ante-Bellum Economy;* David, "The Mechanization of Reaping in the Ante-Bellum Midwest"; P. Temin, *Iron and Steel in Nineteenth-Century America.*

4. To our knowledge the only exceptions are Kelley and Williamson, "Writing History Backwards"; idem, "Modelling Economic Development and General Equilibrium Histories"; Williamson, *Late Nineteenth Century American Development;* and Temin, "General-Equilibrium Models in Economic History."

5. The mathematical analysis underlying this discussion can be found in Kelley, Williamson, and Cheetham, *Dualistic Economic Development,* chap. 3, pp. 89–94.

Chapter 6. Aggregate Growth Performance: Trend Acceleration and Miracles?

1. The following pages in this section are taken primarily from Kelley, Williamson, and Cheetham, *Dualistic Economic Development,* pp. 133–38.

2. Much of this paragraph is based on an excellent summary in Hayami and Yamada, "Agricultural Productivity at the Beginning of Industrialization," pp. 106–12.

3. Nakamura, "Growth of Japanese Agriculture, 1875–1970"; idem, *Agricultural Production;* Oshima, "Survey of Various Long-Term Estimates of Japanese National Income"; idem, Review of *The Growth Rate of the Japanese Economy since 1878* by Kazushi Ohkawa and associates; idem, "Meiji Fiscal Policy and Agricultural Progress." A comprehensive review of the unresolved issues relating to Japanese economic history resulting from the early controversy over the growth of agricultural output is compiled by Sinha, "Unresolved Issues in Japan's Early Economic Development." On the basis of an extensive examination of the qualitative evidence, together with a study of population caloric requirements and foreign trade data, Sinha concludes: "whether or not Nakamura's estimates of a 1 percent rate of growth is nearer the truth is highly conjectural,

but if the circumstantial evidence is assigned some weight, it would seem that his margin of error is not excessive" (p. 119). An important analytic result of the Ohkawa estimates is that agriculture provided sufficient food and savings out of "surplus" production to permit rapid expansion in the secondary-tertiary sector. In an examination of food imports and tax receipts, Sinha concludes: "however fast the sector grew, it did not provide 'sufficient' food to feed the growing population in the secondary and tertiary sectors, nor did it meet the growing financial needs (including foreign exchange) of the emerging nation" (p. 112). Central to explaining the rapid expansion in agricultural output implied by the Ohkawa estimates is a hypothesized high rate of agricultural productivity increase, largely resulting from an adoption of new techniques and the increased use of improved fertilizer and seeds. Sinha's review of the evidence suggests that the rate of acceptance of new ideas was not as fast as believed (p. 116). It took twenty years after the discovery of high-yield rice variety in 1887 for it to be commonly accepted; saltwater sorting of paddy seed, discovered in 1882, was not widely used by the end of the century; governments passed laws to force acceptance of new procedures. Regarding fertilizer usage, Sinha notes that its financing by relatively poor farmers, who assumed all the risks, likely acted as a major constraint to large-scale adoption (p. 117). (This theme has also been developed by Oshima in "A Strategy for Asian Development," p. 298.) Furthermore, in appraising the usual evidence cited to support wide-scale fertilizer usage, Sinha argues that "it is not clear to what extent the magnitude of the increase suggested by the Shishido fertilizer-input index . . . represents an overall increase in fertilizer use rather than just a shift from domestically produced to commercially produced fertilizer" (p. 118). He concludes that "subsequent institutional reforms were not adequate to achieve a rapid increase in agricultural productivity, while the situation regarding the availability of agricultural inputs—similarly a major constraint on improvements—did not materially improve until towards the end of the century" (p. 119).

4. The land tax was computed on the basis of the value of gross agricultural output less taxes and intermediate inputs of seeds and fertilizers. Land tax evasions, taking the form of concealment, misclassification, and undermeasurement of arable land, together with underestimates of yields, were common. The most important factor in Nakamura's revisions are his benchmark rice yield estimates for 1878–82 of 1.6 *koku* per *tan*. As he underscores, the precise figure of 1.6 is not well supported (Nakamura, "The Nakamura vs. the LTES Estimates," p. 359). Indeed, he clearly notes that "much of the revision undertaken is based on assumptions guided by judgments built on historical evidence and understanding of agricultural techniques and practices" (idem, "Growth of Japanese Agriculture," p. 252). Key evidence takes several forms. (i) Average rice yields recorded in official documents for the Banroku period, three hundred

years before the Restoration, were 1.3; Ohkawa's estimates are 1.166, yet Thomas C. Smith (*The Agrarian Origins of Modern Japan,* chap. 7, p. 211) and others (Crawcour, "The Tokugawa Heritage") have documented an increase in agricultural productivity during the period. (Rosovsky, in "Rumbles in the Ricefields," p. 352, questions the veracity of economywide estimates of rice fields before 1873–74, the date when national production statistics commenced. He further argues that the wide variation in regional yields made aggregate calculations by government officials impossible [p. 354].) (ii) Nakamura finds little correlation between fertilizer indexes and yields during the period when major productivity increases were to have taken place (pp. 791–93). (iii) He proposes that the Ohkawa estimates are implausible given the experience of other countries. Japan was a peasant agricultural economy with limited land supply, yet "net product per worker growth ranked among the highest of any nation including nations where farming was highly commercialized and took place under virtually unlimited land supply conditions" (ibid.). Rosovsky ("Rumbles in the Ricefields," pp. 355–56), in contrast, challenges Nakamura's mid-seventy rice yield assumption which shows Japanese agriculture more productive than present-day Taiwan or Korea. (iv) Nakamura also cites the level of food imports and implied calorie levels to support the plausibility of his, and the implausibility of the Ohkawa, estimates ("Growth of Japanese Agriculture," pp. 791–93). Referring to the calories per person implied by the Ohkawa estimates (1,663 per person per day in 1874–77, 1,802 in 1878–82, 1,879 in 1883–87), he concludes that "these are consumption levels that could not have maintained the Japanese in that state of vigorous health and energy that carried him to sustained growth" (Nakamura, "The Nakamura vs. the LTES Estimates," p. 361). Oshima, in "Meiji Fiscal Policy," emphasizes that the implied calorie level per day of 1,400–1,600 using the official data are less than the current level of 2,000 per day for India. An alternative interpretation of the calorie debate is provided in Colin Clark in a review of *Agricultural Production and the Economic Development of of Japan, 1873–1922,* by James I. Nakamura. Rosovsky ("Rumbles in the Ricefields," pp. 355–56) counters that the *growth* of calorie intake implied by Nakamura's estimates suggests a zero income elasticity of demand for rice.

5. Oshima was an early critic of the Ohkawa output estimates for the secondary and tertiary sectors. In his review of Ohkawa's *The Growth Rate of the Japanese Economy since 1878,* he estimated national income for 1881 as 25 percent higher than Ohkawa's, due mainly to biases in secondary and tertiary production. In reviewing Ohkawa's book, Oshima questioned the output statistics on the basis of the low per capita incomes in the late 1930s and mid-1950s. He speculated that the lower than expected levels may have been due to growth being dissipated by military activities or that per capita

income at the end of the Tokugawa period may have been extremely low. The appearance of the Nakamura study strengthened Oshima's criticisms of the Ohkawa secondary and tertiary estimates. The tertiary estimates are tied directly to those of the agricultural sector. Furthermore, as Ohkawa himself notes, "our estimates . . . of net product in manufacturing . . . should be understood as being far weaker than that of primary industry" (Ohkawa et al., *The Growth Rate of the Japanese Economy since 1878,* p. 94).

6. These rates are computed from five-year moving averages over the period 1877–1915. The data are in 1934–36 prices in all cases. The labor force, population, and commodity output figures can be found in Appendix A, tables A.6, A.7, and A.8. The GNP figures are taken from K. Ohkawa, "National Product and Expenditure, 1885–1969," table A–2.

7. These figures are based on gross domestic product in constant prices. Hagen and Hawrylyshyn, "Analysis of World Income and Growth, 1955–1965," table 9, p. 47.

8. Appendix A contains a discussion of the quality of the Japanese historical capital stock estimates. It seems likely that the pre-1900 growth rates are underestimated.

9. Calculated from Appendix A, table A.1, col. (7), centered on 1910. See also Shionaya, "Patterns of Industrial Development," table 3–12, p. 92. The investment goods component includes construction materials. Shionaya's data yield a 72.3 index for 1907–16.

10. It could be argued that we have underestimated the extent of the relative decline in investment goods prices and thus the rise in the constant price investment share by failing to examine the capital goods sector explicitly. Shionaya's data confirm a sharper secular fall in producer durable prices than that for industrial goods as a whole.

11. Hayami and Ruttan, *Agricultural Development*, chaps. 6–10. Hayami and Ruttan do not explain the relative price decline in the prices of purchased inputs.

Chapter 7. Investment Spurts, Military Expenditures, and Meiji Fiscal Policy

1. Earlier applications of the long-swing framework to Japan can be found in Ohkawa and Rosovsky, "Economic Fluctuations in Prewar Japan," and Shinohara, *Growth and Cycles in the Japanese Economy.*

2. The (Asahi Shinbun) wholesale price index rises from an index (1886 = 100) of 284 in 1905 to 285 in 1911. In fact, the general price level *declines* from 1907 to 1911. The price inflation associated with World War I does not begin until 1912, seven years after the investment spurt is initiated. By 1916, the index stands at 538. Bank of Japan, *Hundred-Year Statistics of the Japanese Economy,* p. 76.

3. Landes, "Japan and Europe," pp. 13 and 503–4. Lockwood is

writing in 1954. A more recent reminder of the role of the Meiji military commitment can be found in the excellent paper by Oshima, "Meiji Fiscal Policy."

4. The above paragraph is summarized from Lockwood, *The Economic Development of Japan,* pp. 18–20.

5. The GNP figures are from Bank of Japan, *Hundred-Year Statistics of the Japanese Economy,* p. 32, which are, in turn, based on Professor Ohkawa's old estimates. These were the only GNP data available to us on a year-by-year basis. The revised GNP data would yield somewhat different average shares, but our interest here is in their relative movements over time. In any case, the share figures derived using Ohkawa's old estimates do not appear to be wide of the mark for a few sample years.

6. Oshima feels that military expenditures could have easily been cut by one-half by staying out of the Sino-Japanese and Russo-Japanese wars and still the Meiji government would have possessed ample defense for national independence ("Meiji Fiscal Policy," p. 380).

7. Attributed to T. S. Ashton by Lockwood, *The Economic Development of Japan,* p. 578. For a modern accounting of the impact of the Napoleonic wars on England see Hueckel, "The Napoleonic Wars and Their Impact on Factor Returns and Output Growth in England, 1793–1815."

Chapter 8. Demographic Change and Meiji Economic Development

1. Coale, "Population and Economic Development," pp. 54–55. A survey of various hypotheses of saving behavior in a model of growth can be found in Tsiang, "A Model of Economic Growth in Rostovian Stages."

2. Kuznets speculates that the negative saving impact of larger families is likely to be greater in less developed countries ("Population Change and Aggregate Output," pp. 331–32). This is consistent with the results of Leff's recent empirical study on the dependency rate ("Dependency Rates and Savings Rates," pp. 886–95). Gupta takes issue with both the Leff findings and the underlying theory. He notes that when income levels are very low, "there is no margin left for saving . . . it simply means that people are only sharing poverty" ("Dependency Rates and Savings Rates: Comment," p. 469). For a detailed analysis of family-size, saving rate interactions, consult Kelley, "Demographic Change and American Economic Development."

3. For a detailed review of these analytical considerations using a somewhat simpler dualistic framework, consult Kelley, Williamson, and Cheetham, "Biased Technological Progress."

4. Since our model uses labor force, and not population growth rates, we have assumed that the proportion of the labor force in the population remains constant over this period. We have thus tripled

the labor-force growth rate to implement the desired counterfactual: n is changed from .29 to .87 percent.

5. The impact of population pressure on agricultural development is documented in chapter 11, tables 11.1A and 11.1B.

6. It might be noted that the results of the present study are somewhat at variance with those found in a previous paper where we concluded that demographic factors may have been important in explaining the pace of Meiji development (see Kelley and Williamson, "Writing History Backwards," p. 774). The specific reason for the difference cannot be ascertained since the present analysis incorporates several substantial changes: different initial conditions and parameters, a revised model specification, and an altered set of Japanese data against which the model predictions are compared. Moreover, the analysis of population change in the previous study employed "structural elasticities," which focus on small variations in model parameters. The present counterfactual analysis examines large parameter changes. Any one, or more likely a combination, of these several factors could account for the difference in results.

CHAPTER 9. REAL WAGES, LABOR SLACK, AND LABOR SURPLUS

1. This issue is treated in greater detail in Kelley, Williamson, and Cheetham, *Dualistic Economic Development*, chaps. 2, 3, and 5.

2. Although these data are limited to Yamanashi Prefecture, Tussing argues persuasively for their representativeness. Furthermore, recall that silk-reeling "was the largest manufacturing activity in Japan from the beginning of the Meiji era to its end in terms of the number of establishments, the number of persons engaged, and the value of output" (Tussing, "The Labor Force in Meiji Economic Growth," pp. 208–9).

3. Watanabe and Egaitsu, "Gijutsu Shinpo to Keizai Seicho" [Technical Progress and Economic Growth]. The figures do not refer to a per annum rate, but the total percentage increase over the period.

4. Using data for the period 1914 to 1954 in the paper by Chenery, Shishido, and Watanabe ("The Patterns of Japanese Growth, 1914–1954"), Williamson found that the change in output composition was labor-using, not labor-saving ("Capital Accumulation, Labor Saving, and Labor Absorption: A New Look").

CHAPTER 10. THE PACE OF MEIJI INDUSTRIALIZATION AND THE ROLE OF DEMAND

1. These nonlinearities are documented in cross-sectional studies as well. See, for example, Chenery and Taylor, "Development Patterns."

2. Chenery and Taylor, "Development Patterns," p. 394. The income range considered is from $150–$250. This represents the case of large-country patterns where, of the Asian countries, the regressions include Burma, Thailand, Korea, the Philippines, and

Japan. The income range is roughly comparable to Japan's income per capita expansion from 1887 to 1915. See Kuznets, *Modern Economic Growth,* p. 402. The Kuznets data correspond to two income groupings, \$100–\$199 and \$200–\$349. The estimates for \$150–\$250 assume that Kuznets's figures apply to the mean of the income groupings and that the share changes linearly between these means.

3. The sample includes all countries in Kuznets's table for which data were available for the period before 1900. These countries are the United Kingdom, France, Germany, Denmark, Norway, Sweden, Italy, United States, and Australia. The periods and initial and concluding levels represent an unweighted average of the nine countries included in the sample.

4. It should be pointed out that our dualistic demand specification predicts variability over time in the economywide income elasticity of demand for food, $\eta_2(t)$. Increases in income itself (rises in $y(t)w(t)$) tend to make $\eta_{2j}(t)$ approach unity as successful growth takes place. On the other hand, chap. 3 argued at length for the relevance of a "demand dualism" specification. Thus, our empirical estimates in Appendix B have $\beta_{22} > \beta_{21}$: for identical income levels, the share of expenditures devoted to food is higher in rural areas. This specification is documented by Ohkawa ("Personnel Consumption in Dualistic Growth"), Kaneda ("Long-Term Changes in Food Consumption"), and Hayami and Ruttan (*Agricultural Development,* p. 219). The implication is that urbanization tends to diminish the aggregate income elasticity of food demand over time. When the rate of urbanization slows down, income effects may dominate. In short, our model predicts the following for Japan: an initial fall in $\eta_2(t)$ and a subsequent rise in later growth stages. Note that Kaneda's evidence ("Long-Term Changes in Food Consumption") confirms this result: while the pre-World War I $\eta_2(t)$ is debated, all participants seem to agree that $\eta_2(t)$ is low during the interwar period and much higher in the post-World War II years.

CHAPTER 11. AGRICULTURE AND MEIJI ECONOMIC DEVELOPMENT

1. Ohkawa and Rosovsky, "The Role of Agriculture," p. 44. While other nations have attained similar high rates on occasion, it is the sustained performance in the Japanese case which made the experience particularly unusual. See Ohkawa and Rosovsky, "A Century of Japanese Economic Growth"; Kelley, Williamson, and Cheetham, *Dualistic Economic Development,* p. 137.

2. Our analysis is at variance with that of Hayami and Yamada (p. 107) on only one small point: "The LTES . . . estimates . . . place Japan close to the level of Korea and Taiwan, implying that labor productivity in Meiji Japan would have been about the average of today's Asian countries." The comparison with contemporary Korea and Taiwan hardly seems relevant since both of those countries have been the recipients of "technology transfers" for forty years, most of which occurred under Japanese imperialism. The com-

parison with the rest of Asia as in table 11.2 seems more to the point. Labor productivity indices can be computed from table 11.2 by multiplying columns (1) and (2).

3. Nakamura, *Agricultural Production,* p. 137. Nakamura dates the first statement of the "stagnationist" view of Tokugawa Japan with Edgeworth's article appearing in 1895 ("Stationary State in Japan," pp. 480–81).

4. The term is attributed to Schultz, *Transforming Traditional Agriculture.*

5. The price series exhibit considerable secular variation. Even if the series were extended back to 1876, the rising trend in agricultural prices would still persist. The peak years in the industrial terms of trade were 1886 and 1907, yielding an index (1887 = 100) of 102 and 87, respectively. There is a clear secular decline in relative industrial goods prices between these peak years. Similarly, the trough years of 1879, 1896, and 1911 yield a declining industrial terms of trade index of 87, 82, and 78, respectively.

6. Ohkawa is not a member of the concensus. He agrees with our interpretation and notes that the relative price of "traditional" products tends to increase during this phase of development (Ohkawa, "Phases of Agricultural Development and Economic Growth," p. 27).

7. More explicitly, we have

$$V_L(t) = \frac{d(t)}{r(t)},$$

where $d(t)$ are current land rents per hectare, and $r(t)$ is the rate of return on efficiency capital.

8. As we pointed out in chapter 7, agriculture also underwent this impressive development during a period of burdensome commitment to international military aggression, much like England during her Industrial Revolution and Napoleonic Wars.

9. These rates are computed from Yamada and Hayami, "Agriculture," Appendix table C, p. 26.

10. In the tables which follow in this section, this counterfactual is denoted "Interwar TFPG in Agriculture." The "Actual" Meiji experience is the basic dualistic model constructed in chapter 3 and analyzed in subsequent chapters. The actual and counterfactual experiments differ *only* in that agricultural TFPG is set at 0.73 percent per annum in the counterfactual while the figure is 1.24 percent in the actual. This implies $\{\lambda_K = .0114, \lambda_L = .0194\}$ in the actual and $\{\lambda_K = .0133, \lambda_L = .0089\}$ in the counterfactual.

11. As in chapter 8, the counterfactual is identical to the actual simulation analyzed in the preceding chapters except for the labor force growth parameters. Population growth rates in contemporary Asia are approximately three times the rate which prevailed in Meiji Japan. Thus, while employment growth in commodity-producing sectors in Meiji Japan was 0.29 percent per annum ("actual"), the "counterfactual" experiment sets their rate at 0.87 percent per an-

num. The counterfactual is labeled "Contemporary Population Pressure."

12. In the tables which follow, this counterfactual is denoted "Elastic Land Supply." The "Actual" Meiji experience refers to the basic dualistic model analyzed in preceding chapters. The actual and counterfactual experiments differ *only* in that land stock growth is set at 2.2 percent per annum in the counterfactual while the "actual" employs the ovserved historical hectarage series. (The latter grows, as we have seen, by only 10 percent between 1880 and 1920.)

CHAPTER 12. TRADE AS AN ENGINE OF GROWTH

1. A similar model, without dualistic attributes, is analyzed by Corden, "The Effects of Trade on the Rate of Growth."

2. The figures are five-year moving averages centered on those dates. Hayami and Ruttan, *Agricultural Development,* table 10–1, p. 220.

3. The following analysis has been used for the American antebellum iron industry and for the American post-bellum Midwest grain sector. See Fogel and Engerman, "A Model for the Explanation of Industrial Expansion during the Nineteenth Century"; Williamson, *Late Nineteenth Century American Development,* chap. 9.

APPENDIX B. PARAMETERS AND INITIAL CONDITIONS

1. Bank of Japan, *Hundred-Year Statistics of the Japanese Economy,* pp. 356–59. The data for the year 1926 are the most historic budget data available for urban households where the sample size was significant.

2. The output and labor force series are found in Appendix A, tables A.6 and A.7.

Bibliography

Abramovitz, M. 1959. "Statement in United States Congress. Joint Economic Committee." *Employment, Growth and Price Levels.* Hearings, 86th Cong., 1st sess., pt. 2. Washington, D.C.: U.S. Government Printing Office.

———. 1961. "The Nature and Significance of Kuznets Cycles." *Economic Development and Cultural Change* 9 (April):225–48.

———. 1964. *Evidences of Long Swings in Aggregate Construction since the Civil War.* New York: National Bureau of Economic Research.

———. 1972. "Comment on Miyohei Shinohara's Paper." Mimeographed. Tokyo: The Japan Economic Research Center.

Abramovitz, M., and David, P. 1971. "Towards Historically Relevant Parables of Growth." Mimeographed. Stanford: Economic Growth Center.

Akino, M. Forthcoming. "Nogyo Seisan Kansu no Keisoku" [Estimation of the Agricultural Production Function]. *Nogyo Sogo Kenkyu.*

Akino, M., and Hayami, Y. 1972. "Sources of Agricultural Growth in Japan: 1880–1965." Mimeographed. Tokyo: The Japan Economic Research Center.

Amano, A. 1964. "Neoclassical Biased Technological Progress and a Neoclassical Theory of Economic Growth." *Quaterly Journal of Economics* 70 (February):129–38.

Baba, M., and Tatemoto, M. 1968. "Foreign Trade and Economic Growth in Japan: 1858–1937." In *Economic Growth: The Japanese Experience since the Meiji Era,* edited by L. Klein and K. Ohkawa. Homewood, Ill.: Richard D. Irwin.

Bank of Japan. 1966. *Hundred-Year Statistics of the Japanese Economy.* Tokyo: Bank of Japan.

Barnett, H. J., and Morse, C. 1963. *Scarcity and Growth: The Economics of Natural Resource Availability.* Baltimore: The Johns Hopkins Press.

Barten, A. 1964. "Consumer Demand Functions under Conditions of Almost Additive Preferences." *Econometrica* 32 (January): 1–38.

Bhagwati, J. 1958. "Immiserizing Growth: A Geometrical Note." *Review of Economic Studies* 25 (June):201–5.

Boserup, E. 1965. *The Conditions of Agricultural Growth: The Economics of Agrarian Change under Population Pressure.* Chicago: Aldine Press.

Bowen, W. G.; Davis, R. G.; and Kopf, D. H. 1960. "The Public Debt: A Burden on Future Generations?" *American Economic Review* 50 (September):701–6.

Bronfenbrenner, M. 1961. "Some Lessons of Japan's Economic Development, 1853–1938." *Pacific Affairs* 34 (Spring):7–28.

———. 1965. "Economic Miracles and Japan's Income Doubling Plan." In *The State and Economic Enterprise in Japan,* edited by W. W. Lockwood. Princeton, N.J.: Princeton University Press.

Brown, T. M. 1970. *Specification and Uses of Econometric Models.* New York: St. Martin's Press.

Burns, A. F. 1934. *Production Trends in the United States since 1870.* New York: National Bureau of Economic Research.

Caves, R. E. 1971. "Export-Led Growth and the New Economic History." In *Trade, Balance of Payments and Growth,* edited by J. N. Bhagwati. Amsterdam: North-Holland Publishing Co.

Cheetham, R. J.; Kelley, A. C.; and Williamson, J. G. 1972. "Demand, Structural Change and the Process of Growth." In *Nations and Households in Economic Growth,* edited by P. David and M. Reder. Stanford, Calif.: Stanford University Press.

Chenery, H. B. 1960. "Patterns of Industrial Growth." *American Economic Review* 50 (September):624–54.

Chenery, H. B.; Shishido, S.; and Watanabe, T. 1962. "The Patterns of Japanese Growth, 1914–1954." *Econometrica* 30 (January):98–138.

Chenery, H. B., and Strout, A. M. 1966. "Foreign Assistance and Economic Development." *American Economic Review* 56 (September):679–733.

Chenery, H. B., and Taylor, L. J. 1968. "Development Patterns: Among Countries and over Time." *Review of Economics and Statistics* 50 (November):391–416.

Chetty, V. K. 1969. "International Comparison of Production Functions in Manufacturing." Mimeographed. New York: National Bureau of Economic Research, August 1969.

Clague, C. K. 1969. "Capital-Labor Substitution in Manufacturing in Underdeveloped Countries." *Econometrica* 37 (July):528–37.

Clark, C. 1967. Review of *Agricultural Production and the Economic Development of Japan, 1873–1922,* by James I. Nakamura. *Journal of Agricultural Economics* 18 (January):428–30.

———. 1972. "Investment and Net Stock of Fixed Capital (Non-Residential) in Japan." Mimeographed. Tokyo: The Japan Economic Research Center.

Clark, C., and Haswell, M. R. 1964. *The Economics of Subsistence Agriculture.* New York: St. Martin's Press.

Coale, A. J. 1963. "Population and Economic Development." In *The Population Dilemma,* edited by Philip M. Hauser. Englewood Cliffs, N.J.: Prentice-Hall.

Conrad, A. H., and Meyer, J. R. 1964. *The Economics of Slavery and Other Studies in Econometric History.* Chicago: Aldine Press.

Corden, W. M. 1971. "The Effects of Trade on the Rate of Growth." In *Trade, Balance of Payments and Growth,* edited by J. N. Bhagwati. Amsterdam: North-Holland Publishing Co.

Crawcour, E. S. 1965. "The Tokugawa Heritage." In *The State and Economic Enterprise in Japan,* edited by W. W. Lockwood. Princeton, N.J.: Princeton University Press.

David, P. A. 1966. "The Mechanization of Reaping in the Ante-Bellum Midwest." In *Industrialization in Two Systems: Essays in Honor of Alexander Gerschenkron,* edited by H. Rosovsky. New York: Wiley.

———. 1967. "The Growth of Real Product in the United States before 1840: New Evidence, Controlled Conjectures." *Journal of Economic History* 27 (June):151–97.

Diamond, P. 1965. "National Debt in a Neoclassical Growth Model." *American Economic Review* 55 (December):1126–51.

Dixit, A. 1969. "Theories of the Dual Economy: A Survey." Mimeographed. Berkeley: University of California.

———. 1970. "Growth Patterns in a Dual Economy." *Oxford Economic Papers* 3 (July):229–34.

Domar, E. D. 1957. "A Soviet Model of Growth." In *Essays in the Theory of Economic Growth.* New York: Oxford Economic Press.

Eckaus, R. S. 1955. "The Factor Proportions Problem in Underdeveloped Areas." *American Economic Review* 55 (September): 539–65.

Economic Planning Agency. 1965. "Long-Term Model II." In *Econometric Models for Medium-Term Economic Plan 1964–*

1968: A Report by the Committee on Econometric Methods. Tokyo: Ōkurashō Insatsukyoku.

Edgeworth, F. Y. 1895. "Stationary State in Japan." *Economic Journal* 5 (September):480–81.

Emi, K. 1972*a*. "Government Expenditure." Mimeographed. Tokyo: The Japan Economic Research Center.

———. 1972*b*. "Long-Term Movements of Gross Domestic Fixed Capital Formation in Japan, 1869–1940." Mimeographed. Tokyo: The Japan Economic Research Center.

Ezaki, M., and Jorgenson, D. W. 1972. "Measurement of Macroeconomic Performance in Japan, 1951–1968." Mimeographed. Tokyo: The Japan Economic Research Center.

Fei, J. C. H., and Ranis, G. 1961. "A Theory of Economic Development." *American Economic Review* 51 (September): 533–65.

———. 1963. "Innovation, Capital Accumulation, and Economic Development." *American Economic Review* 53 (June):283–313.

———. 1964. *Development of the Labor Surplus Economy: Theory and Policy.* Homewood, Ill.: Richard D. Irwin.

———. 1966. "Agrarianism, Dualism, and Economic Development." In *The Theory and Design of Economic Development,* edited by I. Adelman and E. Thorbecke. Baltimore: Johns Hopkins Press.

Ferguson, C. E., and Moroney, J. R. 1969. "The Sources of Change in Labor's Relative Share: A Neoclassical Analysis." *Southern Economic Journal* 35 (April):308–22.

Fishlow, A. 1965. *American Railroads and the Transformation of the Ante-Bellum Economy.* Cambridge, Mass.: Harvard University Press.

Fogel, R. W. 1964. *Railroads and American Economic Growth: Essays in Econometric History.* Baltimore: Johns Hopkins Press.

———. 1967. "The Specification Problem in Economic History." *Journal of Economic History* 27 (September):283–308.

Fogel, R. W., and Engerman, S. L. 1969. "A Model for the Explanation of Industrial Expansion during the Nineteenth Century: With an Application to the American Iron Industry." *Journal of Political Economy* 77 (May/June):306–28.

Fujino, S. 1966. "Business Cycles in Japan, 1868–1962." *Hitotsubashi Journal of Economics* 7 (June):56–79.

———. 1968. "Construction Cycles and Their Monetary-Financial Characteristics." In *Economic Growth: The Japanese Experi-*

ence since the Meiji Era, edited by L. Klein and K. Ohkawa. New Haven, Conn.: Yale University Press.

Geary, R. C. 1950–51. "A Note on a Constant-Utility Index of the Cost of Living." *Review of Economic Studies* 18:65–66.

Gerschenkron, A. 1952. "Economic Backwardness in Historical Perspective." In *The Progress of Underdeveloped Areas,* edited by B. Hoselitz. Chicago: University of Chicago Press.

Goldberger, A. S. 1967. "Functional Form and Utility: A Review of Consumer Demand Theory." SFM 6703, Social Systems Research Institute. Mimeographed. Madison, Wis.: University of Wisconsin, November 1967.

Green, J. 1970. "The Effect of the Iron Tariff in the United States, 1847–1859." Mimeographed. Rochester, N.Y.: University of Rochester, April 1970.

Gupta, K. 1971. "Dependency Rates and Savings Rates: Comment." *American Economic Review* 61 (June):469–71.

Hagen, E. E., and Hawrylyshyn, O. 1969. "Analysis of World Income and Growth, 1955–1965." *Economic Development and Cultural Change* 18 (October).

Hansen, B. 1969. "Employment and Wages in Rural Egypt." *American Economic Review* 59 (June):298–313.

Harris, D. J. 1972. "Economic Growth with Limited Import Capacity." *Economic Development and Cultural Change* 20 (April):524–28.

Hayami, Y. 1971. "Elements of Induced Innovation: An Historical Perspective for the Green Revolution." *Explorations in Ecomic History* 8 (Summer):445–72.

———. 1972. "Rice Policy in Japan's Economic Development." *American Journal of Agricultural Economics* 54 (February): 19–31.

Hayami, Y., and Ruttan, V. 1970*a*. "Factor Prices and Technical Change in Agricultural Development: The United States and Japan, 1880–1960." *Journal of Political Economy* 74 (November):1115–41.

———. 1970*b*. "Agricultural Productivity Differences among Countries." *American Economic Review* 60 (December):895–911.

———. 1971. *Agricultural Development: An International Perspective.* Baltimore: Johns Hopkins Press.

Hayami, Y., and Yamada, S. 1968. "Technological Progress in Agriculture." In *Economic Growth: The Japanese Experience since the Meiji Era,* edited by L. Klein and K. Ohkawa. Homewood, Ill.: Richard D. Irwin.

———. 1970. "Agricultural Productivity at the Beginning of Industrialization." In *Agriculture and Economic Growth: Japan's Experience,* edited by K. Ohkawa, B. F. Johnston, and H. Kaneda. Princeton, N.J.: Princeton University Press.

Houthakker, H. S. 1957. "An International Comparison of Household Expenditure Patterns, Commemorating the Centenary of Engel's Law." *Econometrica* 25 (October):532–51.

———. 1960. "The Influence of Prices and Income on Household Expenditures." *Bulletin de L'Institute International de Statistique* 37:9–22.

Hueckel, G. 1972. "The Napoleonic Wars and Their Impact on Factor Returns and Output Growth in England, 1793–1815." Ph.D dissertation, University of Wisconsin.

Ishikawa, S. 1963. "Nohon no keiken wa tekiyō kanō ka" [Is the Japanese Experience Applicable?] *Keizai Kenkyū* 14 (April): 114–22.

Johnston, B. F. 1951. "Agricultural Productivity and Economic Development in Japan." *Journal of Political Economy* 59 (December):498–513.

———. 1970. "The Japanese 'Model' of Agricultural Development: Its Relevance to Developing Nations." In *Agriculture and Economic Growth: Japan's Experience,* edited by K. Ohkawa, B. F. Johnston, and H. Kaneda. Princeton, N.J.: Princeton University Press.

Jorgenson, D. W. 1961. "The Development of a Dual Economy." *Economic Journal* 71 (June):309–34.

———. 1966. "Testing Alternative Theories of the Development of a Dual Economy." In *The Theory and Design of Economic Development,* edited by I. Adelman and E. Thorbecke. Baltimore: Johns Hopkins Press.

———. 1967. "Surplus Agricultural Labor and the Development of a Dual Economy." *Oxford Economic Papers* 19 (November): 288–312.

Kaneda, H. 1970. "Long-Term Changes in Food Consumption Patterns in Japan, 1878–1964." In *Agriculture and Economic Growth: Japan's Experience,* edited by K. Ohkawa, B. F. Johnston, and H. Kaneda. Princeton, N.J.: Princeton University Press.

Kelley, A. C. 1969. "Demand Patterns, Demographic Change, and Economic Growth." *Quarterly Journal of Economics* 83 (February):110–26.

———. 1973. "Demographic Change and American Economic Development: Past, Present and Future." *Proceedings of the*

Commission on Population Growth and the American Future. Washington, D.C.: U.S. Government Printing Office.

Kelley, A. C., and Williamson, J. G. 1971. "Writing History Backwards: Meiji Japan Revisited." *Journal of Economic History* 31 (December):729–76.

———. 1972. "Simple Parables of Japanese Economic Progress: Report on Early Findings." Mimeographed. Madison, Wis.: University of Wisconsin.

———. 1973. "Modelling Economic Development and General Equilibrium Histories." *American Economic Review* 63 (May): 450–58.

Kelley, A. C.; Williamson, J. G.; and Cheetham, R. J. 1972*a*. "Biased Technological Progress and Labor Force Growth in a Dualistic Economy." *Quarterly Journal of Economics* 86 (August):426–47.

———. 1972*b*. *Dualistic Economic Development: Theory and History.* Chicago and London: University of Chicago Press.

Kindleberger, C. P. 1962. *Foreign Trade and the National Economy.* New Haven, Conn.: Yale University Press.

Klein, L. R., and Shinkai, Y. 1963. "An Econometric Model of Japan, 1930–59." *International Economic Review* 4 (January): 1–28.

Kuznets, S. 1930. *Secular Movements in Production and Prices: Their Nature and Their Bearing upon Cyclical Fluctuations.* Boston: Houghton Mifflin.

———. 1959. *Six Lectures on Economic Growth.* Glencoe, Ill.: Free Press.

———. 1960. "Population Change and Aggregate Output." In *Demographic and Economic Change in Developed Countries,* edited by A. J. Coale. Princeton, N.J.: Princeton University Press.

———. 1966. *Modern Economic Growth: Rate, Structure and Spread.* New Haven, Conn.: Yale University Press.

———. 1968. "Trends in the Level and Structure of Consumption." In *Economic Growth: The Japanese Experience since the Meiji Era,* edited by L. Klein and K. Ohkawa. Homewood, Ill.: Richard D. Irwin.

Landes, D. S. 1965. "Japan and Europe: Contrasts in Industrialization." In *The State and Economic Enterprise in Japan,* edited by W. W. Lockwood. Princeton, N.J.: Princeton University Press.

Leamer, E., and Stern, R. M. 1970. *Quantitative International Economics.* Boston: Allyn & Bacon.

Leff, N. 1969. "Dependency Rates and Savings Rates." *American Economic Review* 69 (December):886–95.

Leibenstein, H. 1957. *Economic Backwardness and Economic Growth.* New York: Wiley.

Levine, S. 1965. "Labor Markets and Collective Bargaining in Japan." In *The State and Economic Enterprise in Japan,* edited by W. W. Lockwood. Princeton, N.J.: Princeton University Press.

Lewis, W. A. 1954. "Economic Development with Unlimited Supplies of Labour." *Manchester School of Economics and Social Studies* 20 (May):139–92.

———. 1958. "Unlimited Labour: Further Notes." *Manchester School of Economics and Social Studies* 26:1–32.

Lockwood, W. W., ed. 1954. *The Economic Development of Japan: Growth and Structural Change, 1868–1938.* Princeton, N.J.: Princeton University Press.

McCloskey, D. N. 1970. "Did Victorian Britain Fail?" *Economic History Review* 23 (December):457–58.

McKinnon, R. 1964. "Foreign Exchange Constraints in Economic Development and Efficient Aid Allocation." *Economic Journal* 74 (June):388–409.

Mahalanobis, P. C. 1952. "Some Observations of the Process of Growth of National Income." *Sankhya* 12:307–12.

Maizels, A. 1968. *Exports and Economic Growth of Developing Countries.* Cambridge: Cambridge University Press.

Marglin, S. 1966. "Comment." In *The Theory and Design of Economic Development,* edited by I. Adelman and E. Thorbecke. Baltimore: Johns Hopkins Press.

Minami, R. 1968. "The Turning Point in the Japanese Economy." *Quarterly Journal of Economics* 82 (August):380–402.

———. 1970*a*. "Further Considerations on the Turning Point in the Japanese Economy (II)." *Hitotsubashi Journal of Economics* 12 (June):66–89.

———. 1970*b*. "The Supply of Farm Labor and the 'Turning Point' in the Japanese Economy." In *Agriculture and Economic Development: Japan's Experience,* edited by K. Ohkawa, B. F. Johnston, and H. Kaneda. Princeton, N.J.: Princeton University Press.

Minami, R., and Ono, A. 1972. "Economic Growth with Dual Structure: An Econometric Model of the Prewar Japanese Economy." Mimeographed. Tokyo: The Japan Economic Research Center.

Modigliani, F. 1961. "Long-Run Implications of Alternative Fiscal

Policies and the Burden of the National Debt." *Economic Journal* 61 (December):730–55.

Moulton, H. 1931. *Japan: An Economic and Financial Appraisal.* Washington, D.C.: Brookings Institution.

Nakamura, J. I. 1965. "Growth of Japanese Agriculture, 1875–1920." In *The State and Economic Enterprise in Japan,* edited by W. W. Lockwood. Princeton, N.J.: Princeton University Press.

———. 1966. *Agricultural Production and the Economic Development of Japan, 1873–1922.* Princeton, N.J.: Princeton University Press.

———. 1968. "The Nakamura vs. the LTES Estimates of the Growth Rate of Agricultural Production." *Keizai Kenkyu* 19 (October):358–61.

Nelson, R. R. 1956. "A Theory of the Low-Level Equilibrium Trap in Underdeveloped Economies." *American Economic Review* 46 (December):894–908.

Nerlove, M. 1967. "Recent Empirical Studies of the CES and Related Production Functions." In *The Theory and Empirical Analysis of Production,* edited by M. Brown. New York: National Bureau of Economic Research.

Noda, T. 1972. "Commodity Prices and Wages." Mimeographed. Tokyo: The Japan Economic Research Center.

Nurkse, R. 1959. *Patterns of Trade and Development.* New York: Oxford University Press.

Odaka, K., and Ishiwata, S. 1972. "Effective Demand and Cyclical Growth of the Japanese Economy, 1906–1938." Mimeographed. Tokyo: The Japan Economic Research Center.

Ogura, T. 1963. *Agricultural Development in Modern Japan.* Tokyo: Kinokuniya Bookstore Co.

Ohkawa, K. 1968. "Changes in National Income Distribution by Factor Share in Japan." In *The Distribution of National Income,* edited by J. Marchal and B. Ducros. New York: St. Martin's Press.

———. 1970. "Phases of Agricultural Development and Economic Growth." In *Agriculture and Economic Growth: Japan's Experience,* edited by K. Ohkawa, B. F. Johnston, and H. Kaneda. Princeton, N.J.: Princeton University Press.

———. 1972*a*. "Comments on Productivity Gaps and Dualism in Japanese Development." Mimeographed. Tokyo: The Japan Economic Research Center.

———. 1972*b*. "National Product and Expenditure, 1885–1969." Mimeographed. Tokyo: The Japan Economic Research Center.

———. 1972*c*. "Personal Consumption in Dualistic Growth." Mimeographed. Tokyo: The Japan Economic Research Center.
———. 1972*d*. "Intersectoral Differences in Product per Worker." Mimeographed. Tokyo: The Japan Economic Research Center.
Ohkawa, K., and Rosovsky, H. 1960. "The Role of Agriculture in Modern Japanese Economic Development." *Economic Development and Cultural Change* 9, no. 2 (October):43–67.
———. 1961. "The Indigenous Components in the Modern Japanese Economy." *Economic Development and Cultural Change* 9 (April):476–501.
———. 1962. "Economic Fluctuations in Prewar Japan: A Preliminary Analysis of Cycles and Long Swings." *Hitotsubashi Journal of Economics* 3 (October):10–33.
———. 1965. "A Century of Japanese Economic Growth." In *The State and Economic Enterprise in Japan,* edited by W. W. Lockwood. Princeton, N.J.: Princeton University Press.
———. 1968. "Postwar Japanese Growth in Historical Perspective: A Second Look." In *Economic Growth: The Japanese Experience since the Meiji Era,* edited by L. Klein and K. Ohkawa. Homewood, Ill.: Richard D. Irwin.
Ohkawa, K.; Shinohara, M.; and Umemura, M. 1966–72. *Estimates of Long Term Economic Statistics of Japan since 1868,* vols. 3–12. Tokyo: Tokyo Keizai Shinpo Sha.
Ohkawa, K. (in association with Shinohara, M.; Umemura, M.; Ito, M.; and Noda, T.). 1957. *The Growth Rate of the Japanese Economy since 1878.* Tokyo: Kiholuniya Bookstore Co.
Orcutt, G. H. 1950. "Measurement of Price Elasticities in International Trade." *Review of Economics and Statistics* 32 (May): 177–32.
Oshima, H. T. 1953. "Survey of Various Long-Term Estimates of Japanese National Income." *Keizai Kenkyu* 4 (July):243–51.
———. 1958. Review of *The Growth of the Japanese Economy since 1878,* by Kazushi Ohkawa and associates. *American Economic Review* 48 (September):685–87.
———. 1962. "A Strategy for Asian Development." *Economic Development and Cultural Change* 11 (April):294–316.
———. 1965. "Meiji Fiscal Policy and Agricultural Progress." In *The State and Economic Enterprise in Japan,* edited by W. W. Lockwood. Princeton, N.J.: Princeton University Press.
———. 1970. "Review Article: Accelerated Growth: Japan's Experience." *Economic Development and Cultural Change* 19 (October):111–27.
Parks, R. 1969. "Systems of Demand Equations: An Empirical

Comparison of Alternative Functional Forms." *Econometrica* 37 (October):629–50.

Passell, P., and Schmundt, M. 1971. "Pre-Civil War Land Policy and the Growth of Manufacturing." *Explorations in Economic History* 8 (Fall):35–48.

Patrick, H. T. 1961. "Lessons for Underdeveloped Countries from the Japanese Experience of Economic Development." *Indian Economic Journal* 9 (October):156–59.

Pope, C. 1972. "The Impact of the Ante-Bellum Tariff on Income Distribution." *Explorations in Economic History* 9 (Summer): 375–422.

Raj, K. N., and Sen, A. K. 1961. "Alternative Patterns of Growth under Conditions of Stagnant Export Earnings." *Oxford Economic Papers* 13 (February):43–52.

Ranis, G. 1970. "The Financing of Japanese Economic Development." In *Agriculture and Economic Development: Japan's Experience,* edited by K. Ohkawa, B. F. Johnston, and H. Kaneda. Princeton, N.J.: Princeton University Press.

Rosovsky, H. 1961. *Capital Formation in Japan, 1868–1940.* Glencoe, Ill.: Free Press.

———. 1966. "Japan's Transition to Modern Economic Growth, 1868–1885." In *Industrialization in Two Systems: Essays in Honor of Alexander Gerschenkron,* edited by H. Rosovsky. New York: Wiley.

———. 1968. "Rumbles in the Ricefields: Professor Nakamura vs. the Official Statistics." *Journal of Asian Studies* 27 (February):347–60.

Rostow, W. W. 1960. *The Stages of Economic Growth: A Non-Communist Manifesto.* Cambridge: At the University Press.

———. 1966. "The Take-Off into Self-Sustained Growth." *Economic Journal* 66 (March):25–48.

Sawada, S. 1960. "Nōgyō Seisansei Kōjō ni Okeru Gijutsu to Keiei [Technique and Management in the Structure of Agricultural Productivity]. *Nōgyō Keizai Kenkyū* 37 (January).

———.1965. "Innovation in Japanese Agriculture, 1880–1935." In *The State and Economic Enterprise in Japan,* edited by W. W. Lockwood. Princeton, N.J.: Princeton University Press.

———.1970. "Technological Change in Japanese Agriculture: A Long-Term Analysis." In *Agriculture and Economic Growth: Japan's Experience,* edited by K. Ohkawa, B. F. Johnston, and H. Kaneda. Princeton, N.J.: Princeton University Press.

Schultz, T. W. 1964. *Transforming Traditional Agriculture.* New Haven, Conn.: Yale University Press.

Sen, A. K. 1966. "Peasants and Dualism with or without Surplus Labor." *Journal of Political Economy* 74 (October): 425–50.

Shinohara, M. 1962. *Growth and Cycles in the Japanese Economy*. Tokyo: Kiholuniya Bookstore Co.

———. 1967. *Estimates of Long-Term Economic Statistics of Japan since 1868: Personal Consumption Expenditures*. Tokyo: Tokyo Keizai Shinpo Sha.

———. 1972*a*. "Kuznets and Juglar Cycles during the Industrialization of 1878–1940." Mimeographed. Tokyo: The Japan Economic Research Center.

———. 1972*b*. "Personal Consumption Expenditures." Mimeographed. Tokyo: The Japan Economic Research Center.

Shionoya, Y. 1968. "Patterns of Industrial Development." In *Economic Growth: The Japanese Experience since the Meiji Era*, edited by L. Klein and K.Ohkawa. Homewood, Ill.: Richard D. Irwin.

Shionoya, Y., and Yamazawa, I. 1972. "Industrial Growth and Foreign Trade in Pre-War Japan." Mimeographed. Tokyo: The Japan Economic Research Center.

Sicat, G. 1968. "Economic Incentives, Industrialization, and Employment in the Developing Economies." IEDR, Discussion Paper no. 68–30. Mimeographed. Quezon City: University of the Philippines, 29 September 1968.

Sinha, R. P. 1969. "Unresolved Issues in Japan's Early Economic Development." *Scottish Journal of Political Economy* 16 (June): 109–51.

Smith, A. 1937. *An Inquiry into the Nature and Causes of the Wealth of Nations*. New York: Random House.

Smith, T. C. 1955. *Political Change and Industrial Development in Japan: Government Enterprise, 1868–1880*. Stanford, Calif.: Stanford University Press.

———. 1959. *The Agrarian Origins of Modern Japan*. Stanford, Calif.: Stanford University Press.

Solow, R. M. 1956. "A Contribution to the Theory of Economic Growth." *Quarterly Journal of Economics* 70 (February): 65–94.

Spengler, J. J. 1951. "The Population Obstacle to Economic Betterment." *American Economic Review* 41 (May):343–54.

Stigler, G. J. 1951. "The Division of Labor Is Limited by the Extent of the Market." *Journal of Political Economy* 59 (June): 185–93.

Stone, R. 1964. "Linear Expenditure Systems and Demand Analysis: An Application to the Pattern of British Demand." *Economic Journal* 64 (September):511–27.

———. 1966. *Mathematics in the Social Sciences and Other Essays.* London: Chapman & Hall.

———, ed. 1962. *A Programme for Growth.* Vol. 1, *A Computable Model of Economic Growth.* London: Chapman & Hall.

———., ed. 1965. *A Programme for Growth.* Vol. 5, *The Model in Its Environment: A Progress Report.* London: Chapman & Hall.

Swan, T. W. 1956. "Economic Growth and Capital Accumulation." *Economic Record* 32 (November):334–61.

Taira, K. 1970. *Economic Development and the Labor Market in Japan.* New York: Columbia University Press.

———. 1971. "Education and Literacy in Meiji Japan." *Explorations in Economic History* 8 (Summer):371–94.

Tang, A. M. 1963. "Research and Education in Japanese Agricultural Development, 1880–1938." *The Economic Studies Quarterly* 13 (February):21–41; 13 (May):91–99.

Temin, P. 1964. *Iron and Steel in Nineteenth-Century America: An Economic Inquiry.* Cambridge, Mass.: MIT Press.

———. 1971. "General-Equilibrium Models in Economic History." *Journal of Economic History* 31 (March):58–75.

Theil, H. 1965. "The Information Approach to Demand Analysis." *Econometrica* 33 (January):67–87.

———. 1967. *Economics and Information Theory.* Chicago: Rand McNally & Co.

Tsiang, S. C. 1964. "A Model of Economic Growth in Rostovian Stages." *Econometrica* 32 (October):619–48.

Tussing, A. R. 1970. "The Labor Force in Meiji Economic Growth: A Quantitative Study of Yamanashi Prefecture." In *Agriculture and Economic Growth: Japan's Experience,* edited by K. Ohkawa, B. F. Johnston, and H. Kaneda. Princeton, N.J.: Princeton University Press.

Ueno, H., and Kinoshita, S. 1968. "A Simulation Experiment for Growth with a Long-Term Model of Japan." *International Economic Review* 9 (February):114–48.

Umemura, M. 1961. *Chingin, Koyō, Nōgyō* [*Wages, Employment, and Agriculture*]. Tokyo: Taimeidō Press.

———. 1970. "Agriculture and Labor Supply in the Meiji Era." In *Agriculture and Economic Growth: Japan's Experience,* edited by K. Ohkawa, B. F. Johnston, and H. Kaneda. Princeton N.J.: Princeton University Press.

Uzawa, H. 1961. "On a Two-Sector Model of Economic Growth, I." *Review of Economic Studies* 29 (October):40–47.

———. 1963. "On a Two-Sector Model of Economic Growth, II." *Review of Economic Studies* 30 (June):105–18.

Watanabe, T. 1968. "Industrialization, Technological Progress, and Dual Structure." In *Economic Growth: The Japanese Experience since the Meiji Era,* edited by L. Klein and K. Ohkawa. Homewood, Ill.: Richard D. Irwin.

Watanabe, T., and Egaitsu, F. 1970. "Gijutsu Shinpo to Keizai Seicho" [Technical Progress and Economic Growth]. In *Keizai Seicho to Shigen Haibun* [Economic Growth and Resource Allocation], edited by M. Kaji. Tokyo: Kiholuniya Bookstore Co.

Wellisz, S. 1968. "Dual Economies, Disguised Unemployment, and the Unlimited Supply of Labour." *Economica* 35 (February): 22–51.

Williamson, J. G. 1965. "Regional Inequality and the Process of National Development." *Economic Development and Cultural Change* 13, no. 4, pt. 2 (suppl.) (July):1–84.

———. 1968. "Personal Savings in Developing Nations: An Intertemporal Cross-Section from Asia." *Economic Record* 44 (June):194–210.

———. 1969. "Capital Accumulation, Labor Saving, and Labor Absorption: A New Look at Some Contemporary Asian Evidence." EDIE 6932, Social Systems Research Institute. Mimeographed. Madison, Wis.: University of Wisconsin, February 1969.

———. 1971*a*. "Capital Accumulation, Labor Saving, and Labor Absorption Once More." *Quarterly Journal of Economics* 85 (February):40–65.

———. 1971*b*. "Relative Price Changes, Adjustment Dynamics, and Productivity Growth: The Case of Philippine Manufacturing." *Economic Development and Cultural Change* 19 (July): 507–26.

———. 1972. "The Railroads and Midwestern Development: A General Equilibrium History." *EH 72–7, Graduate Program in Economic History*. Mimeographed. Madison, Wis.: University of Wisconsin.

———. 1973. "Late Nineteenth Century American Retardation: A Neoclassical Analysis." *Journal of Economic History* 33 (September):581–607.

———. Forthcoming. *Late Nineteenth Century Development: A General History*. Cambridge: Cambridge University Press.

World Bank. 1972. *Population Planning*. Washington, D.C.: World Bank.

Yamada, S., and Hayami, Y. 1972. "Agriculture." Mimeographed. Tokyo: The Japan Economic Research Center.

Yoshihara, K. 1969*a*. "Demand Functions: An Application to the Japanese Expenditure Pattern." *Econometrica* 37 (April): 257–74.

———. 1969*b*. "Long-Term Models of the Japanese Economy." *The Economic Studies Quarterly* 20 (December):41–64.

———. 1972. "Productivity Change in the Manufacturing Sector, 1906–65." Mimeographed. Tokyo: The Japan Economic Research Center.

Yuize, Y. 1964. "Nōgyō ni Okeru Kyoshiteki Seisan Kansu no Keisoku" [Micro Production Function Estimation in Agriculture] *Nōgyō Sōgō Kenkyū* 28 (October):1–53.

Index